Coursework in English

Barbara Comiskey

Causeway Press

Design and artwork by Susan and Andrew Allen

Published by
Causeway Press Ltd
PO Box 13
Ormskirk
Lancs L39 5HP

© Barbara Comiskey 1988

First published 1988

British Library Cataloguing in Publication Data

Comiskey, Barbara
Coursework in English.
1. English language—Grammar—1950-
I. Title
428   PE1112

ISBN 0-946183-36-8

Printed and bound by
The Alden Press, Oxford

Contents

Index of activities/skills

Index of quoted material

Introduction

Coursework in English has been written for students of GCSE English. It has also been written *with* them — students' work and comments are included in the book.

As a student, you will be encouraged to talk in groups, to do your own research, to analyse, to use your imagination and to produce work designed for particular audiences. To assist you the book takes a step by step approach leading to the development of skills in writing, reading, speaking and listening. A range of activities based on both literary and non-literary sources provides practice for coursework and examinations.

There are eight units in the book. Each leads to a range of assignments which provide individual coursework folders for a one of two year course. There are many opportunities to assess skills in speaking and listening. The book is equally valuable as prepartion for the written examination.

Barbara Comiskey

Unit 1 Stories from Experience

Aim: to write a story based on life.

On the way: to help you to achieve your aim, here are some of the things to do in the unit:

- giving titles to stories from everyday life
- listening to stories others have to tell
- tracing the progress of stories from speech to writing
- practising the opening to a piece of writing
- reviewing your opening

- working with a partner to develop your writing
- commenting on other students' writing
- considering stories by students of different ages.

By the end: of the unit you will have a story for your coursework folder *and* know more about the steps writers take in turning an experience from life into a piece of writing.

Assignment: writing

choice of story from experience, for your folder.

1

Personal Experience: A Memorable Event

Many stories start life as events which happen to ordinary people. We sometimes tell others about memorable events. Here is an example to read.

> It was one of those odd incidents and it happened years ago. We were on the promenade – a bright summer's day – high spring tide battering, banging against the prom.
> I said to the rest of the gang, "Dare anyone hang over the water, hanging onto the railings with his hands?" and of course no one else was daft enough to do this. Well, I swung over the railings and lowered myself down, hanging on by my hands. The water was slapping against the prom. It was quite a rough sea. Then it dawned on me – I couldn't pull myself up. My hands were slipping on the salt on the railings and I was gradually losing my grip. I shouted in panic but they all laughed. They thought I was just joking. Then the eldest of the gang, always a sensible lad, grabbed me by the wrist, and they did pull me up afterwards.

1. Task

This story is based on a memory. Give the story a title and make a note of your title.

2. Thinking back

Remember that your aim at the start of this unit was to write from experience. Giving a title helps you to focus on what is important to **you** in a memory.

Three students did the same as you and gave titles to the memorable event at the start of this unit. Comparing their titles with your own will help you to see different ways in which a memory could be developed into a written story, for others to enjoy.

Read their titles, and their reasons for choosing them, before doing the activity which follows.

3. Students' work

Titles chosen:

Being Thirteen

Reasons
I think age is important and that as well as to a boy, it could happen to a girl of that age.
ANNE

The Daring Challenge

Reasons
The dare stays in my mind. I would make it into an adventure story, so I picked the word **challenge**. The end could be different, unhappy.
STEPHEN

Promenade Capers OR Daft Lads

Reasons
Both titles are for a comic story, as I would bring out the comedy. If I set it a long time ago, I'd call it *Promenade Capers*, but if I set it now, I'd call it *Daft Lads*. I would start the story in a different way because I would want to know more about the characters and what made them do mad things.
PAUL

4. Activity

● Compare your title with that of another person in your class.
● Tell each other the reasons why you chose your titles.
● In view of the titles each of you chose, how might your stories differ?
● Briefly comment on the titles given by Anne, Stephen and Paul. Which title do you like best? Why?

5. To discuss

Why are titles important, why do they matter? What do they do for a story?

6. Titles and choice

Titles influence choice. Imagine standing outside a cinema looking at the titles of films showing tonight. Think of looking through the *TV Times* and *Radio Times* at the programmes on offer or browsing through the fiction section of your school or local library. To some extent titles will influence your choice of film, T.V. programme and book.

Some titles give straightforward information like *News at Ten*. Others suggest danger, excitement or fun. Some aim to catch your eye by being original. Think of a title of a film, television programme, song or record, magazine or book. What does the title you thought of aim to do?

7. Activity

Look at the four titles of films 'showing tonight'.
Judging from the titles, which film would you choose to see?
Briefly say why.
After you have completed this activity you may like to turn to the back of this book for a brief description of each film.

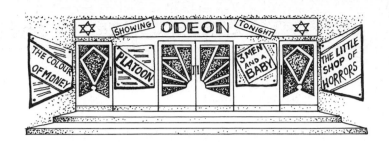

Changing a Story

Why change a story?
- Writing differs from telling. You cannot be there to indicate things to the reader by tone of voice or gesture.
- You can make the story your own and improve it in your own way.
- You can bring out the things you feel are important and interesting in a story. These might change as you grow older.

Here is an example of how to change a story using the memory at the beginning of this unit. A teacher was told about this event. She chose to write it down, as if it had happened to her, in the form of a poem. She began with her recollection of the story (on the left), made comments on it (in the middle), then produced a final version (on the right).

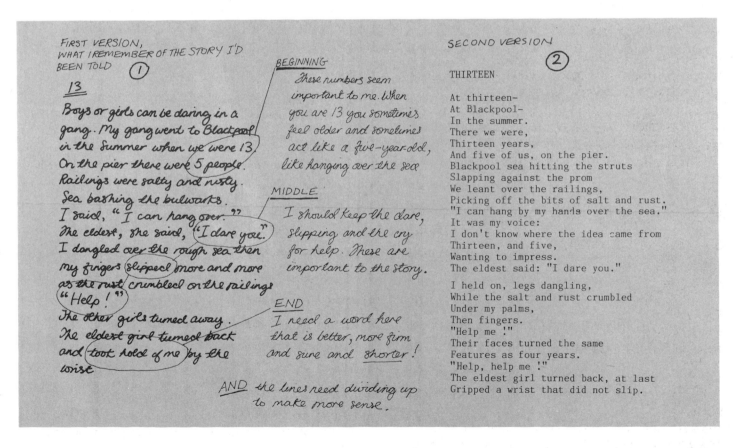

Activity

Read the two versions the teacher wrote.

1. Pick out two or more things she kept the same in the handwritten and the typed versions.

2. Pick out two or more things that were changed.

3. Now look back at the memory about the dare at the start of this unit – what has the teacher altered to make the story seem as if it happened to her?

4. What do you think of the teacher's poem compared to the story at the start of the unit?

5. Do you think the teacher chose a suitable title for her version? Give reasons for your answer.

Drafting

Look at the way the teacher has developed her poem from the first version to the final version. This is an example of **drafting**. It means doing several versions with changes and improvements. Drafting is a technique most writers need to develop — even teachers. It is a skill you will need from now on.

Some first steps to this skill are shown in the drafting of the poem *Thirteen*.

- In your rough version, pick out the important things and possible changes by using circles, underlining, or a different coloured pen.
- Leave plenty of space in the margin for notes, ideas and changes.
- Stories have a beginning, a middle and an end — these stages should be noted as you draft a story.

Listening: Exchanging Stories/Collecting Stories

Activity

1. Think of a memorable event which happened to a real person. It need not be so dramatic as the example you have read in this unit.

The event could be about
— you, when you were a small child
— you, in recent years
— someone you know.

2. Spend a few minutes — not too long — telling the anecdote to a partner in class. Now listen to your partner's story. (An **anecdote** is a story from life without many changes.)

You have a lot of experience to draw on.

3. Collect stories from people you know, by asking them to tell you a memorable thing that happened to them.

You could ask people in school and out of school.

Option:
Report back to the class by telling your favourite anecdote from your collection.

4. Not forgetting your aim

Starting to write is often the hardest stage.

Writers can feel that they have nothing to write about.

You have now collected lots of anecdotes, so you have plenty of material to draw on to get you over this first stage.

A student shared your aim of writing from a memorable event. She narrowed down her collection of favourites to two and could not choose between them. Give her some advice – read the two anecdotes and say which one you would advise her to pick, explaining why. You could suggest titles and ways she might develop the anecdote into a longer written story.

Examples of anecdotes from a student's collection

1

My gran was in the war and she lived in the house where we live now. There's an air-raid shelter at the bottom of the garden – it was meant for everyone.

My gran told me one night – there was an air-raid and the warning sirens were going and everyone was running for this shelter. My gran had just hurried inside with my mum and my uncle – they were just toddlers then – and all the neighbours were sitting down when my gran went "Oh" and put her hand over her mouth. She ran out of the shelter and down the path, with all these 'planes going overhead. She had just had a new pair of false teeth and she was determined – very determined – not to leave those teeth behind.

2

When I was about four or five I used to annoy my mother because I always wanted my own way and was very strong-willed. One day I saw my friend across the road with a watering can, so I ran in and said to my mum, "I want our watering can."

"You'll have to wait," she said. She was busy but I kept on and on at her about playing with our watering can. My mum got more and more annoyed because this was typical of me, and she said, "I'm going to lock that watering can away so you can just forget about it." That made me want the can more! I didn't forget though, and as soon as my dad came home that evening, I said, "Dad, dad, she won't let me play with our watering can!" My mum was getting really cross, but she started laughing. "I've just realised", she said, "we don't own a watering can."

The Next Steps: Shaping a Story

Now that you have a small collection of anecdotes, you can choose the best to concentrate on and mould into a final shape – like making a model from clay. You might need to add sections here, take away a bit there, to make the finished piece satisfying as a whole.

To shape your anecdote, do this:
– Choose one and, leaving **wide** margins on both sides of your page, write down a short version from memory.
– Use the following questions to add notes in the margins of the story you have written down. You are now **drafting** an anecdote.

Shaping a story.

5

Questions

1. **Who?** Is the story happening to you or to another person?
TO YOU: **I** went to the pier ...
SOMEONE ELSE: **She/he** went to the pier ...

2. **When?** Is the story set in the past or the present time? A story set in the future is another possibility to choose from.

3. **Where?** Where will the story take place?

4. **What?** What is the title?
What does the title suggest about the things you think are important in the story?

5. **Beginning**
Look at your opening few lines. Does anything need to be added? Is everything clear for the reader? You could 'rewind' to include earlier events. OR you could 'fast forward' to a later point and start there.

6. **Middle**
Where is the middle of your story?
Do you need to add anything? What else would you like to know about: the characters, the time, the place? Where is the high point of the story? Are you saving it for the end?

7. **End**
How will you round off your story?

When you have answered these questions you will have a framework for your story – you will have drafted it.

Students' work

Here is a short example of the effects such re-shaping can have. Two students talk about the anecdote which opens this unit.
What are the good and bad effects of getting straight into the adventure?

STEPHEN: I would start *The Daring Challenge* with the part where the eldest boy says 'I dare you'. I would get straight into the adventure.

PAUL: It would have a dramatic start. I might get lost if I were reading it though. What were the people doing there? You'd have to find a way of letting readers know about the setting and characters. Erm ... They could be talking.

STEPHEN: They could have a conversation and mention where they were and what they were doing.

Stories by Students of Different Ages

Before continuing your story writing, it is useful to read stories written by other people.

- You can see which of the writers' ideas work well.
- You can use some of these ideas in your own writing.
- You can avoid some of the pitfalls of writing, e.g. something is not made clear.
- You can put yourself in the position of the reader.
- Your reactions to the stories which follow can help you to:
  – plan your essay
  – improve your essay
  – keep the reader in mind when writing
  – comment on a friend's essay.

Over the next few pages are four essays by students:
The Den is by a writer aged fifteen.
An Unpleasant Meeting is by a writer aged eleven.
A Bus Ride with a Cow is by a writer aged eight.
The Empty Room is by a writer aged sixteen.

Work by younger writers is included because:
– you may want to write your story for younger readers
– you have more writing experience than younger writers and can therefore give expert advice.

The Den is a worked example with notes on planning and comments on the finished product. You can use the notes as a framework for your own comments:
– on the other three essays
– on friends' essays.

THE DEN

Last weekend I was sent round to my Grandad's to help him clear his garden. He gave me a plastic bin bag, a rake and a mallet and asked me to start with the pile of wood and rubbish in the far corner. It looked like nothing more than wet planks, but it had been our den.

We built the den in the summer holidays when we were six - myself, Sheila and Christine, that is. The walls were made of well-used planks which we leant against the fence and draped with a moth-eaten carpet, leaving a gap by way of a door. Inside we put a 'Fanta' crate for a table and three old cushions with half their stuffing missing. When I think back, it seems that we spent all summer there plotting our next stunts, practising songs that we were going to sing for the rest of the children in the street (we were all convinced we were going to be pop singers) and looking after our treasures. It was also our place for avoiding the terror of the street, a boxer dog called Kim. I don't think Kim ever bit us, but she growled at us a few times and we were terrified.

Once or twice when it went dark before our bedtime we had 'midnight' feasts in the den of pop and biscuits from my gran. We were always leaving crisps packets around so perhaps that's what attracted Kim. Sheila heard something in the garden next door. We all listened. When I heard the snuffling and snorting on the other side of the wooden fence I new it had to be Kim. The squashed face of the Boxer meant it couldn't breathe properly. I didn't feel much like singing now. We all kept quiet. I couldn't see much in the dusk. We were all thinking about the dogs wet mouth and nose so near to us, trying to breath like someone with a bad cold.

It started to rain hard. Soon I couldn't hear the dog anymore, just the rain pelting on the wood while we were perfectly dry. The dog could never get in from the other side of the fence. Sheila and Christine were smiling and we all felt safe and clever in the den.

The thoughts of their faces are interrupted by the sound of my Grandad's voice. "Haven't you started yet?" he yells. "I need that space for planting."

I step back from the den, raise the mallet and bring it crashing down on my childhood memories.

Notes on planning and shaping

When the student told this story, she began with the visit to her grandfather's **and** breaking up the planks. In planning the essay, she decided to leave the destruction of the den until the end to make a framework for the childhood incident. More description of the den and of the dog was included, and feelings were made more explicit in the written version, where you cannot rely on gesture or facial expression to tell someone how you felt. The essay was written in thirty minutes of a lesson and a free choice of personal short story was given.

Comments

The title is a good one because it brings together the recent past and the distant past – the den links both.

The description of the children waiting for the dog to find them is interesting, as is the reflection on childhood. The new events are believable. There seems to be more description than narrative (story) however.
Most things are clear, apart from the use of the present tense at the end.

Spellings to correct

practising (when used as a verb)
biscuits
their (when used: thoughts of **their** faces)
interrupted

Punctuation to correct

apostrophe – the dog's wet mouth

More than half of the few errors were careless or made through rushing. Most could have been put right by reading through the completed essay.

Activity

Read *An Unpleasant Meeting* by an eleven-year-old. What advice would you give him? Use the questions below as a guide to help you decide on what advice to give.

Questions
1. What did you find in the writing that was interesting or enjoyable?
2. Was there anything missing?
3. Was the title a good one? Suggest another.
4. Were the beginning and ending suitable. Can you suggest others?
5. Do you think the piece is too long or too short?
6. Can anything be missed out?
7. Are there any spelling mistakes? List the correct version(s).
8. Check the punctuation. Write out the correct versions.

Compare your comments with those of a partner. Where they differ you can get a new view and add to your comments.

An Unpleasant Meeting
The title of the essay was fixed. It was written over 3 forty-five minute lessons using a word processor by a student of eleven.

I was stood in the Market car park waiting for my parents. We had been shopping and we had split up. I wanted to go to the Model Shop for some Airfix colours. My dad said we'll all meet up at the car.

There were lots of cars parked. Our car is an Escort. Its alright but sometimes it won't start and my dad has to work on it. Sometimes we have to push it which is alright if its facing downhill. I hope it doesn't give any trouble today.

Across from where I was standing there was a new Mercedes and an XR3. I went across to look at them. They were ace. You could see that the Merc went up to 180 miles per hour on the speedometer and it was an automatic. I wouldn't mind having an XR3 though. It was dark red.

The car park had a very low roof. You could jump up and touch it. There was a lot of litter about, cans and newspapers, and a strong smell of petrol fumes that make me feel sick when I am in the car.

I don't like waiting on my own, it gets boring. My dad bought me Warlord so I read that and ate some Minstrels. They said they wouldn't be long and they'd get there before me but they hadn't.

There was nobody about. I was the only one in the car park.

Suddenly a lad came up the ramp and saw me. He looked like a fifth former but he didn't go to our school. He was wearing jeans and a jeans jacket. He was tall and thin with short back and sides and he wore Dockys. He came up to me and looked at me. Then he snatched my comic.

"What your doing here? Have you been nicking?" he said.

"I'm waiting for my mum and dad." I replied.

He got hold of my arm.

"What's your name?" he said.

His fingers were digging in my muscle and it hurt. I couldn't get free and I though he was going to nut me.

"You're hurting. Leave me alone." I said.

A car drove up the ramp and passed us. As it did I pulled my arm away and ran to the Exit door. The lad ran after me but a man came through the door and he had to let me go. I walked with the man and he couldn't do anything about it.

The man got into his car. What would happen when he drove away. The lad would get me. Suddenly my parents and my sister came through the Exit door and the lad had to go. Was I relieved. My mum said

"Have you been waiting long? You look as if you've seen a ghost." "I was nearly mugged." I told her.

We got in the car and drove down the ramp. It started alright this time. My heart was still beating and my arm hurt but I was safe. When we drove out of the car park I looked behind and the lad was still looking at me with his fist.

Practising and Reviewing your Opening

Remember that you must interest your readers. An opening is especially important – if you don't like the start of a T.V. programme you might well switch off. The same applies to a story.

Activity

- Write out the first two paragraphs of a personal short story which you have chosen. (Have a dictionary by you if you can. There is also a section at the back of this book to help you with basic writing skills.)

- Read out your work to a partner, who should use questions 1 to 6 on page 8 to comment.

- Listen to your partner's work and comment in the same way.

- Read the work of your partner, who should read yours. Use questions 7 and 8, circling any mistakes and listing the correct versions. Show on the writing where you would make any alterations.

- Write out your own work with any changes you now want to make. You should bear in mind your strengths and weaknesses when choosing and writing your assignment.

As your skills develop, this process should get quicker.

Option

Read the opening paragraph of *The Den* and *An Unpleasant Meeting*. Did they make you want to read on? If so why? If not, why not?

Developing your Writing: Filling in the Shape

1. Opening a story

Your opening should persuade readers to continue. You want to keep their interest until the end of the story. How you fill in the shape in the middle and end of your essay is important.

Think about watching a film or television programme. What the camera can show in pictures, you must do with description when you fill in the details of your writing. You have one big advantage over the camera – being able to picture clearly in your mind's eye the things you want to describe any time you wish to do so. Talking about experiences, choosing one, and giving titles as you have done in this unit, should help to focus these mental pictures.

Filling in the story

2. Why fill in the details?

Suppose a writer put: 'The man at the door wore something on his head.'

The writer doesn't help the reader to picture the man or his headgear.

The reader is
left to do all
the work – is this

or this

or this

or this

what the writer intends?

The reader needs to know what the man is wearing on his head to avoid confusion.

3. The next steps

● Have clearly in your mind the thing, person or feeling you want to describe – focus on it.
● What makes it special or individual? It might be its smell, taste, sound or touch, as well as the way it looks.
● Observation can help you with the details of description – if you want to describe, say, a favourite jacket, look at it, study it, to refresh your memory. If you want to include some talk at a bus stop in your writing, listen to some on your way home and pick up hints from real life!
● Comparisons can help to make description real and vivid for readers.

Two sorts of comparisons are:

Similes

Inventing a simile shows imagination in describing something by saying what it is **like**.

Examples of similes
1. He eats *like a hog.*

2. The old man's tanned skin looked *like well-used leather.*
3. You look *like a million dollars* – all green and crinkly.

Metaphors

Metaphors are also imaginative comparisons of two things. Metaphors go a stage further and say one thing **is** another.

Examples of metaphors

1. He *is a hog.*
2. The child *was a ray of sunshine* in his parents' lives.
3. The boxer, *a raging bull,* terrified his opponent in the ring.

Activity

Some of the following metaphors and similes could solve the confusion for readers by describing the man and his headgear more precisely and vividly.
Match each picture with the metaphor or simile you think appropriate.

a) His dark, clouded expression gave a warning of bad news.
(metaphor … *clouded*)

The helmet he wore was hard as a bullet.
(simile … *as a bullet*)

b) He came to tell me that I had won the competition for the best egg recipe, and his headgear was as slippery as a greasy breakfast plate.
(simile … *slippery as a greasy breakfast plate*)

His smile was false, like a salesman's when he's selling shoddy goods.
(simile … *like a salesman's when he's selling shoddy goods*)

c) The duck-billed peak on his cap made it hard to take him seriously, despite his thoughtful expression.
(metaphor … *duck-billed*)

His cap looked like a strap-on diving board to me – perhaps the birds were going to take a plunge?
(simile … *like a strap-on diving board*)

4. To fill in more details

You could also add:

Description

Of what? Of which person? Of yourself?
What will this add?
Can you describe a place to build up the right atmosphere?

Comparisons – metaphors and similes – can also make the description more vivid for the reader.

Thoughts and feelings

What emotions did you feel? About which events or people? Can you show why people acted as they did, that is, their motives?

Thinking back

Reflection on events. Did they change you? Do you see things differently now? How did others in the story see events?

A moral

Do you think there is anything to be learned from the story?

Conversation

Between which of your characters? For what reasons? What will it add to the story?

Assignment: Writing A Story from Experience

Here are some suggestions which you could use for your own story from experience. You could choose from them or invent your own.

1.   Write a story from experience which would interest readers of your age. Base the story on events when you were a child OR events which happened to you recently. Give a title to the story.
2.   Write a story from the experience of someone you know, for readers of your own age. Give a title to the story.
3.   Based on something which happened to you, write a story which could be read by first year pupils in your school. Invent a suitable title.
4.   Write a personal short story which ends with the words: 'I never saw that person again.'
5.   Write a personal short story which includes the words "I dare you", which should be spoken by a character in the story.

6.   Write a personal short story which contains this sentence: 'I surprised myself by my actions.'
7.   Write a short story based on real life which could be included in a collection with the general title: *Life in Wartime.*
8.   Imagine that you are a parent with children of your own age. Write a story for your children to read, based on events when you were a teenager.
9.   Think of your own idea for writing a story from life.

Thinking back

Perhaps you have the story, its shape and detail in your mind just ready to put on paper. Lucky you! Many writers find they need to make a plan, change, improve and check as the writing develops, as you have seen other students do in this unit. You have read and commented on their work. Try to put yourself in the shoes of a reader of your story – do any of your comments on others' writing apply to yours? Thinking about the reader can help to improve your writing for your coursework folder.

Reality and Imagination

So far we have looked at stories based on experience. However, it is possible to create a story based on both experience and imagination, stories which blend reality with imagined events. In fact, most short stories and novels are like this.

Here are two essays by students – *A Bus Ride with a Cow* and *The Empty Room* – which blend reality and imagination. Read them with the following questions in mind. When you have read the essays, answer the questions and add any comments of your own.

Questions

1.   Which parts of the writing did you find realistic and which imaginative?

2.   Do you think that the writer has got the right balance between reality and imagination? Explain why.

3. For each essay, decide whether you think it is:
- Science Fiction
- Mystery
- Crime
- Comedy
- Another category. If so, which?

Each type of short story or novel which has 'rules' and content which is to some extent fixed is called a **genre**.

For example:
We generally expect love stories to contain some romance and horror stories to contain something frightening.

Aim

To add awareness of imagination to your skills as a writer and learn about balancing imagination and reality.

On the way

- You can use your answers to pick out different types or genres of imaginative story when you read and when you watch films and television.

- You might want to write by the 'rules' of a particular genre yourself, e.g. you might want to write a story based on the 'rules' of science fiction.

Use your imagination.

A Bus Ride with a Cow

The teacher told this class that their stories should be based on a journey. The children acted out some journeys, discussed their journeys in groups and then wrote stories. The writer was aged eight.

One day I went to see my nan who lives in the city which is two bus rides away.

I was half way to my nan's on the second bus when onto the bus walked a cow it walked to the back and sat down next to me then the conductor came up the bus calling "Tickets, tickets please" I asked the conductor if they had a fare for cows "No" he replied "I think this is the first cow we've had on any of our buses" any way he can go on for nothing. This will be history I'll have to write this in my book"

"Today 11/3/86 a cow walked on to the bus we did'nt have a fare for cow's so I gave it a free ride

The bus stopped and it was time for me to get of, I took the cow with me As we were walking down the street to my nan's people were looking at us.

We got to my nan's and I left the cow in the garden. I went in the house and I told my nan about the bus ride with a cow she did'nt before "Look out of the window and see what eating your daisy" "My word your wright there is a cow, and it is eating my daisy's" "Ah" I cried "I've just thought of a name for the cow. Doisy, Yes Doisy the cow".

The Empty Room

The Empty Room was given as a title. The essay was written in a fifty minute lesson. The writer was aged sixteen.

The door to the bedroom gave way to my pressure with little opposition. It ground slowly to a halt on rusted hinges, allowing the musty air of years gone by to rush out past my face. The room was spacious, with fading blue wall-paper peeling away from the walls. The carpet had been eaten away to a thin skeleton of nylon revealing the bare, warped boards.

I entered with great trepidation. On the walls were framed photographs of smiling children and of a baby in a pram in the green countryside. The window on the far wall was covered with the delicate lacing of dusty cobwebs. The surrounding wood of the window was partially covered in flaked white paint which was riddled with holes infected many years before with woodworm. The view from the window was of Battersea Power Station which lay idle and no longer belched forth its yellow and grey fumes into the sky.

On the adjacent wall there stood various other pieces of furniture — an old chair, hardly able to support itself, let alone a person, a table in a similar state, and then a cot. I noticed some newspapers in the cot, their delicate paper printed with faded ink. I carefully removed the top newspaper, which fell into little pieces. They floated on the air, highlighted by passing through a ray of dying orange sunlight. The second newspaper had the headline 'War Imminent' in large red type. There was a poor photograph of distressed people in black suits. Underneath it lay a newspaper which conformed to the shape of the object beneath it. This time the headline ran, 'Government Devises Flimsy Defence Plan'. Underneath that was an article on how to survive in a nuclear attack, which appeared to be the work of a strange looking bespectacled woman.

On removing the final newspaper, the form of a flimsy skeleton of an infant focussed upon my eyes. The empty sockets stared deep into my eyes, crying and screaming in the silence. I dropped the newspaper, turned and made my way swiftly to the door and away from the stifling atmosphere of death. I closed the door behind me with some force and I heard the sound of breaking glass. Taking one last glance into the room, I saw the fallen picture frame with a cloud of dust rising above it, in the fearful shape of a mushroom.

Would you believe it?

In front of the television, you might watch Superman fly off a tall building and Dracula turn into a bat without much surprise. If a character in *Eastenders* or *Coronation Street* suddenly took off into the air, though, how would you react? Your expectations would be different.

A programme based, however loosely, on real life has to keep the rules of real life, even if the events never really happened.

What if Soap Opera writers decided to pin viewers to the screen by having seven murders, eight births, an aeroplane crash and nine or ten explosions, topped off with a tidal wave which destroys the buildings and all the people in them, in the fifteen minutes before the advertisements? It is not easy to see where the story could go in the **next** fifteen minutes once the advertisements are over.

Activity

This activity includes an article on *Dallas*, a popular television series, and shows some of the problems in making a story believable. Reading it and answering the questions can also show that most writers, like you, have similar problems to face.

Resurrection—or is it?—at Southfork

From Alex Brummer in Washington

DINNER parties were cancelled, restaurants closed their doors, and there was a run on blank video tapes last night, as Americans prepared themselves for the answer to the greatest mystery since the identification of Mister W. H. in Shakespeare's sonnets.

The speculation has gone on since that fateful day last summer when a mirage, or was it the real thing, appeared jovial, muscular and starkers in the shower-room at Pamela Ewing's wedding night love nest. It was unmistakably Bobby Ewing, alias Patrick Duffy (left).

But how could it be? The man died before the eyes of 300 million Dallas fans in 98 countries some 31 one-hour episodes before.

The producer, Leonard Katzman, sees nothing strange in Bobby's reincarnation. "In a soap opera, anyone who dies on camera has a 50-50 chance of coming back alive." This is especially so when the ratings and big bucks are involved.

The real shock was that Dallas, which for eight years ruled majestically as America and the world's greatest soap and most profitable television show, had slipped.

The slick competition from the pastel shades and rollicking beat of Miami Vice, the glitz of Joan Collins, and the craziness of the Cosby family had knocked Dallas off its perch. In the 1985-86 television year, Dallas sank, almost without trace to eighth place in the ratings.

That was before the Dallas producers with the skill of Agatha Christie at her worst, began to cook up the theories of Bobby's return. First there was the twin brother scam. "You can forget that idea," Mr Katzman says.

Nor was Bobby kidnapped by his brother, the irrepressible Larry Hagman. "JR would lie, cheat and steal," explains Mr Katzman, "but he would never hurt his mama by letting her think Bobby was dead if he wasn't."

Dick Francis, and other literary sleuths, could not miss Mr Katzman's clue. Despite spending some $25,000 filming three special sequences to confuse visitors to the Dallas set over the outcome, the producer had effectively confirmed that Bobby never died. For the last 31 episodes he has clearly been recovering from near death at a secret location. Or was the last year just one long dream?

Questions

1. Is there anything in the proposed story which you would find difficult to believe?
2. What problems do the script writers face in trying to re-introduce Bobby Ewing (actor Patrick Duffy) into the plot of *Dallas?*

3. The producers finally decided that Bobby's wife had 'dreamed' all 31 episodes since his 'death'. How far do you think this solution works?

Option

To discuss

– Do you enjoy stories and programmes about real life more than out-and-out fantasy?
About the same?
Less?
Try to explain why and give examples.

– Have your preferences changed as you got older? Give examples where you can. How far do you think it is true that younger readers and writers prefer fantasy?

– Both fantasy and realistic fiction are also popular with adults. Do you think there are different reasons for their popularity? What might these reasons be?

What does this mean for your writing?

Like television script writers, if you decide to blend imagination with reality, you need to get the balance right. Your aim in this unit is to write a story based on experience. Shaping that experience with your imagination and adding details are ways of making the story interesting, especially for an audience of readers who may not know you in person.

Here are three points to keep in mind for your own story.

● Ask yourself: *Would I believe it?*
● Too many outrageous incidents can make it difficult for readers to believe any of the story.
● It often helps to build up to a really dramatic event and to balance it with quieter sections of writing.

Unit 2 Short Stories in Publication

Aims: to see what makes stories tick in books, magazines, films and on television and to help others to enjoy them; to put yourself in an editor's shoes for your assignment.

On the way: the following activities will help you to achieve these aims:

- arranging pictures into different plots
- considering covers for 'types' or genres of short story
- gaining some insight into the tasks of an editor of a collection of short stories
- completing plots, by yourself, and in a group
- reading short stories and editing collections of them
- making a time graph for a television, film or radio story
- filling in a chart on your reading
- considering the work of other students in draft form (that is, their first ideas)
- becoming an editor for your assignment
- thinking again about your work.

By the end: you will have a different type of writing for your coursework folder. It will show that you can stand back from a story you have read.
(Your syllabus — that is, the list of items which your course must include — will mention *wide reading* of *whole works* of literature.)

Assignments: reading and writing
(for your coursework folder)
making a collection of short stories you have enjoyed; helping others to understand and enjoy them by reviewing or introducing the stories.

Speaking and listening
reading aloud and talking about stories in groups.

Option
recording your own *Book Review* programme, as if for radio or television.

'Publication': What does it Mean?

This section will help you to understand what goes into a publication to create the finished product. When reading a book or magazine, or watching a film on television, it is easy to think that what we see just appeared out of thin air. This is fine when we want to relax and enjoy what we see. However, there are things we can miss if we take this view.

How does this affect your work?

Here are some reasons for being aware that stories do not just appear out of thin air.

- Professional writers work long and hard to produce a short story, novel, television or radio script or even a school textbook. They write and re-write, change things and worry about their choice of words and phrases. Remember this when reading their work. It may help you see things you might otherwise miss.

- Remember it also when you do your own writing. Like a professional writer you must work hard and take care with your choice of words and phrases. When you are having problems, don't forget that even famous novelists have similar problems.

- Professional writers are helped, encouraged, criticised and shouted at by their editors. They often miss deadlines – the time when the book should have been completed. If you think about it, your teacher is rather like an editor. As such she or he can really help you with your writing.

- Seeing how a published work is put together is fascinating. It is also useful for you. Once you see how the professionals do it you can apply some of the lessons to your own writing.

Activity

Opposite is a brief outline of how this book – *Coursework in English* – was produced. To identify some stages of publishing, match these tasks with people in the drawing – who does what?

1.

Tasks: Planning and writing the words on the page and re-writing if needed.	**Tasks:** Picking out the best from the writing and suggesting improvements.
Tasks: Drawing cartoons and illustrations to go with the words and choosing or taking photographs.	**Tasks:** Setting the written book into printed words.

2.   Turn to page ii of this book and find the name of the artists and the name of the printing firm.

Using the activity

In reading

● Like this book, a published story takes time to produce. There are stages of planning, writing, editing and production. It can be useful to take a story apart to see what makes it work in order to appreciate the whole thing better.

● When you look at a collection of short stories, see whether the editor is a different person from the writer(s). Ask yourself how the editor's aims may differ from the writers'.

In your own writing

● You can be your own editor by breaking down the production of a piece of writing into stages, or by talking it through with others in the early stages.

In viewing

● When watching films or television, pick out the name of someone other than the author/writer from the credits which usually follow the programme. Ask yourself what this person has contributed to the story.

Pictures which Tell a Story

One way of understanding how stories are built up is through a **story-board** of pictures.

Pictures arranged to tell a story are familiar in cartoon-strips and comics. In film and television, drawings are used to map out the order of a story, in the form of a story-board.

Activity

These sketches (A – F) could be the basis of a story-board for a television or film drama.
Arrange the sketches in the order you would like, by making a list of their letters, for:
1. A romantic comedy with a happy ending.
2. A murder mystery with an unhappy ending.
For both versions, you should decide what object the girl in sketch F will take from her handbag.

Choices

Then

3a) A **caption** puts into words the events of the picture, as briefly as possible.
Provide captions for each picture for either the 'comedy' or the 'mystery' version of the sequence.

b) Give a title to each version and provide several lines of dialogue for each picture for both the 'comedy' and 'mystery' versions.

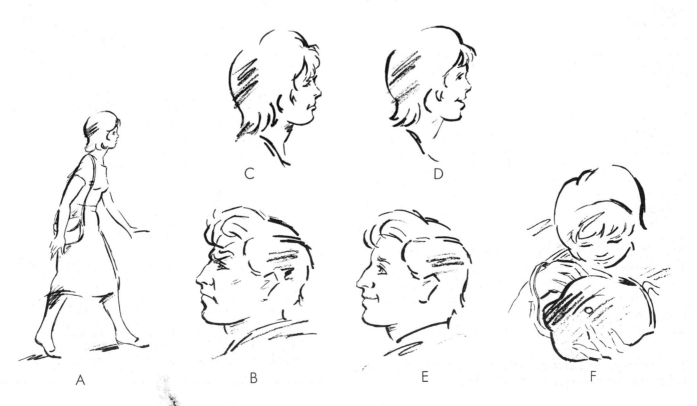

A   B   C   D   E   F

Using the activity

Now that you have made a story-board, you can use the technique in a number of ways.

- Plan your own stories in sketch form to help you to organise them.

- Turn a published story into a story-board of sketches to focus on what is important in it.

or

- By adding dialogue to the sketches, you can turn them into a radio play, script for acting, or video.

- Make a story-board of rough sketches when watching television, film or video to help you to remember it and discuss it afterwards.

The next steps

Perhaps you have an objection: that other people put the pictures in exactly the same order as you did. What is the point of the activity if the results are the same?

The sameness **is** one important point. We all expect the mystery stories to be alike in many ways. The things mystery stories share makes them a **type**. You will find out more about different types of story in the rest of this unit.

Covers for Short Stories

One way of understanding stories in more detail is by being aware of their type – the name in literature for a type of story, book, film, etc. is a **genre**.

Activity

1. Look at four covers opposite.
What would you expect from the stories found inside?
You could make your notes in the form of a spider plan, as below.

In Science Fiction I would expect:

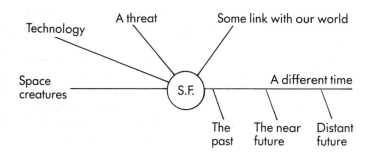

Discuss with a partner whether you think there are any differences **within** a genre you enjoy, such as realistic science fiction and science fiction based on fantasy.

2. You can't judge a book by looking at the cover – but many people do. Publishers of paperbacks have found that printing the title in metallic ink sells more books. Each genre has its own style of cover. For example, horror stories are likely to have similar covers.

a) Why is this?
b) Do you think it is a good idea?
c) Choose one genre, invent a title for a book and design a suitable cover. Give reasons for your choice of cover.

How does this help?

- You now have a way of seeing how one story differs from another by asking whether they belong to different genres such as romance, science fiction, horror, crime and comedy.

- You have more options open to you in your writing – you might decide to write a story of one particular type.
- You might like to design a cover for your own piece of writing.

Completing Stories

Completing stories can help you to play an editor's role and to consider stories in detail in an enjoyable way.

Activity

Part of the work of an editor is to decide on the layout of each page. This can involve **cutting and pasting,** sectioning off the story and re-arranging the sections into the new page layout.

For the two short stories that follow, imagine that the last paragraph of each has been lost by the editor.

1. Reading

Read one of the stories on your own and write a suitable last paragraph.

2. Group work

Read aloud the other story in a group.

Appoint one person in the group to note down in rough any ideas for the ending as they occur.

Appoint another person in the group to write out the final version. Try to justify your ending by referring to the rest of the story.

Uses

Remember that one aim in starting the unit was to see what makes stories work – completing plots helps you to focus on this in detail by seeing how one thing leads to another in a story.

(The published endings of these stories can be found at the back of the book. You can compare them with your versions when you have finished.)

The Specimen

Ray Mason

Stuart, weary from the lengthy interplanetary journey, finally pushed the engine cut-out button and leaned back in his couch, rubbing his eyes with gloved hands. He had seen the planet surface through his telescreen; he had seen it through his viewport. He had seen it, the lush green meadows and the tall forest, casting its deliciously cool shadows onto the grass. He felt so tired now, tired with the ultimate content of having found such a beautiful place after a year and a half of inky, solitary blackness and weird indescribable planets. And for a while, with a smile on his haggard face, he slept.

He awoke, hours later, refreshed, happy and, yes – he told himself – human! He stood, stretched deliciously, feeling the muscles stretching, the slightly cramped and displaced bones sliding back into place. He swore to himself with sheer ecstasy, washed himself, shaved thoroughly and changed into his fresh light military tunic. And briskly, knowing the atmosphere outside was perfectly breathable, he strode through the airlock and out, gloriously out into the bright mid-afternoon sunshine, his exposed face and hands tingling with the first feel of true sunlight after the ultra-violet and infra-red lamps of the spacecraft.

And his nose smelt afresh the green, rich scent of spring, the tang of a vague pine-like smell on the gentle, cooling breeze; his ears heard anew the rustle of long grass in the wind and the whispering chatter of trees whispering among themselves. And his eyes wept sweet tears of relief as they saw the scenery that he had left behind.

'Thank you, Lord, oh thank you!' he breathed, and walked, lost awhile in his own private thoughts, tender thoughts, of girls and friends and kinsfolk, the clear salty tears running down his newly-smoothed cheeks. He brushed them away, fist clenched, with the back of his sleeve, with a happy-sad smile of inner content on his face.

Presently, brought by the scurrying, hurrying breeze, came the sound of a brook or stream, the silver tone of its headlong flight to the sea drawing Stuart on as clear cool waters drew him when he was a small boy. And soon he found it, running through a small cleft in a rock, falling two or three feet before rushing across country, tree-lined, through the meadow and forests, somewhere on its laughing journey meeting up with a river, ever larger until it met the sea. But Stuart was content watching the small fraction before him, gurgling silver, clear and then gold in the bright sunlight, stemming from the pool created beneath the rock.

And he bent down on the grassy, flowered bank of the pool, sipping a little water, and sat there staring into the clear pool, watching the tiny fishes darting erratically between the fronds and brightly coloured weeds, and the occasional glimpse of the large, dark form of a fish deep in the pool, swimming lazily in the silt and murky depths.

Stuart was sitting quietly, gathering his thoughts together, basking in, and becoming accustomed to, the natural splendour of his newly found planet when a rustling on the bank beside him broke his train of thought. For an instant he froze in sheer terror, not knowing if he was being threatened by an alien being or not. He turned hot and cold, all his elation falling from him like the drops of sweat upon his brow. Slowly, very carefully he looked round to see a strange sight: a small, cone-shaped machine hovered just above the ground. It was a good metre in length, made of bright shiny metal, with the outline of a hatch at its pointed end and a large aperture at the wide end. One or two antennae bristled at its point, quivering as though in scent of something. It hummed faintly and electrically for a second, and then quite suddenly a lens popped up from the top and focused a beam of light on the water. In this beam, where it struck the water, appeared an image of a strange insect. Within seconds, one of the small fish darted towards this projected tasty morsel and made to swallow it whole. And then, terribly quickly and without

any sound, a long, hair-thin needle darted from the very nose of the machine, impaling the fish perfectly through the head. Stuart watched wide-eyed as the wriggling victim was drawn toward the silver cone and popped into the small flap at the front. From the machine came an assortment of poppings and clickings, followed by a swift typewriter noise, and from the rear and larger end of the machine dropped a box.

Stuart cautiously crept behind the machine, and with a strange and terrible fascination, turned the box over, revealing its true purpose.

The box was made of a clear perspex-like material on five sides, the back being faced with a black surface. Against this black surface, set inside the plastic cube, was the fish, perfectly dissected and labelled in a strange language, finished off with a computer punch-tape attached to it.

Stuart knelt amazed and amused; to him this strange specimen hunter represented a kind of black comedy.

Because of this, and perhaps because so much tension had been relieved by discovering this planet, he began to laugh gently to himself.

'Does it amuse you so, Earthman?'

Stuart dropped the box and snapped to his feet. The honey-sweet voice from behind him took him completely by surprise. Standing beneath a tree, by the stream, was

?

The Conjurer's Revenge

Stephen Leacock

'Now, ladies and gentlemen,' said the conjurer, 'having shown you that the cloth is absolutely empty, I will proceed to take from it a bowl of goldfish. Presto!'

All around the hall people were saying, 'Oh, how wonderful! How does he do it?'

But the Quick Man on the front seat said in a big whisper to the people near him, 'He – had – it – up – his – sleeve.'

Then the people nodded brightly at the Quick Man and said, 'Oh, of course,' and everybody whispered round the hall, 'He – had – it – up – his – sleeve.'

'My next trick,' said the conjurer, 'is the famous Hindustani rings. You will notice that the rings are apparently separate; at a blow they all join (clang, clang, clang) – Presto!'

There was a general buzz of stupefaction till the Quick Man was heard to whisper, 'He – must – have – had – another – lot – up – his – sleeve.'

Again everybody nodded and whispered, 'The – rings – were – up – his – sleeve.'

The brow of the conjurer was clouded with a gathering frown.

'I will now,' he continued, 'show you a most amusing trick by which I am enabled to take any number of eggs from a hat. Will some gentleman kindly lend me his hat? Ah, thank you – Presto!'

He extracted seventeen eggs, and for thirty-five seconds the audience began to think that he was wonderful. Then the Quick Man whispered along the front bench, 'He – has – a – hen – up – his – sleeve,' and all the people whispered it on. 'He – has – a – lot – of – hens – up – his – sleeve.'

The egg trick was ruined.

It went on like that all through. It transpired from the whispers of the Quick Man that the conjurer must have concealed up his sleeve, in addition to the rings, hens, and fish, several packs of cards, a loaf of bread, a doll's cradle, a live guinea-pig, a fifty-cent piece, and a rocking-chair.

The reputation of the conjurer was rapidly sinking below

zero. At the close of the evening he rallied for a final effort.

'Ladies and gentlemen,' he said, 'I will present to you, in conclusion, the famous Japanese trick recently invented by the natives of Tipperary. Will you, sir,' he continued, turning to the Quick Man, 'will you kindly hand me your gold watch?'

It was passed to him.

'Have I your permission to put it into this mortar and pound it to pieces?' he asked savagely.

The Quick Man nodded and smiled.

The conjurer threw the watch into the mortar and grasped a sledge hammer from the table. There was a sound of violent smashing, 'He's – slipped – it – up – his – sleeve,' whispered the Quick Man.

'Now sir,' continued the conjurer, 'will you allow me to take your handkerchief and punch holes in it? Thank you. You see, ladies and gentlemen, there is no deception; the holes are visible to the eye.'

The face of the Quick Man beamed. This time the real mystery of the thing fascinated him.

'And now, sir, will you kindly pass me your silk hat and allow me to dance on it? Thank you.'

The conjurer made a few rapid passes with his feet and exhibited the hat crushed beyond recognition.

'And will you now, sir, take off your celluloid collar and permit me to burn it in the candle? Thank you, sir. And will you allow me to smash your spectacles for you with my hammer? Thank you.'

By this time the features of the Quick Man were assuming a puzzled expression. 'This thing beats me,' he whispered, 'I don't see through it a bit.'

There was a great hush upon the audience. Then the conjurer drew himself up to his full height and, with a withering look at the Quick Man, he concluded:

'Ladies and gentlemen, you will observe that I have, with this gentleman's permission, broken

?

Making a Time Graph

What was the last television programme that had you on the edge of your seat? Were some sections more gripping than others? Whether in print, on radio or on screen, many stories have high points. Tension, interest and involvement seem to build up and build up to the point where the members of the audience are on the edge of their seats, then reduce before the climb to the next high point. The following activity helps you to look at this aspect of stories.

Activity: viewing and listening

Choose a story which everyone in your group has access to, on radio, on film or on television.
Find out from the newspaper, teletext, *Radio Times* or *TV Times* how long the story will be. Mark off the bottom of a sheet of paper in minutes, like the example below, for the

number of minutes in the story you have chosen.
As the story is broadcast, put a dot every minute or so to show the level of **tension, interest and involvement**. Join up the dots and you have a time graph.

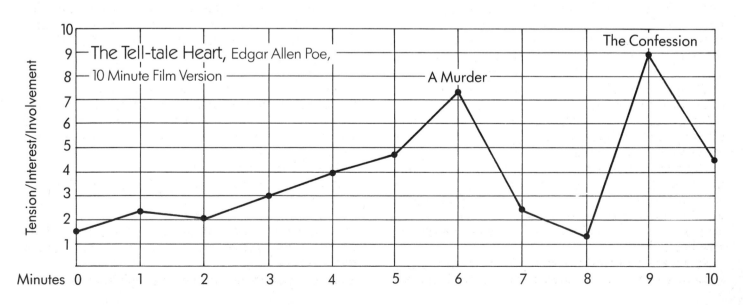

Students' work

The time graph was devised by a class of Fourth Year GCSE students when they watched a ten-minute film version of Edgar Allen Poe's short story, *The Tell-Tale Heart.* When individual graphs were compared, most members of the class found that they had marked the start as low key, building up to a high point about two-thirds of the way through when a murder was committed. They noted the peak or climax of the story near the end, when the murderer confessed with dramatic screams.

Uses

● Radio, television and film can emphasise a high point or climax by music and sound effects. See if you can notice any devices like this in your viewing and listening.

● A time graph can be used for a printed story by putting the number of paragraphs instead of 'minutes' along the bottom of the graph. If you were making the story into a film or radio version, what sound effects would you use and where would you use them? Write them in on the graph.

● You could comment on the high points or emotional tension and involvement in the short stories dealt with in your assignments.

Building on your skill

A time graph allows you to see the way a story builds up. By using a time graph to examine stories by famous writers you can learn some of the skills of writing – how to create excitement, how to build up tension, how to develop interest. You can then apply these skills to your own writing.

Activity

1. Read *The Tell-Tale Heart.*

2. Draw a time graph for the story. Divide the bottom line of the graph into the number of paragraphs in the story. Put a dot for every paragraph to show the level of tension, excitement and interest.

3. Compare your graph with the time graph for the film of *The Tell-Tale Heart.*
What are the similarities and differences?

4. Did you find this activity (numbers 1 – 3) useful? Did it help you to understand how the story was put together, what made it work? Give reasons for your answers.

Option: to discuss

Think of examples of films or books which **begin** with the most exciting events. What are the advantages and disadvantages of doing this?

THE TELL-TALE HEART
Edgar Allan Poe

TRUE! – nervous – very, very dreadfully nervous I had been and am; but why *will* you say that I am mad? The disease had sharpened my senses – not destroyed – not dulled them. Above all was the sense of hearing acute. I heard all things in the heaven and in the earth. I heard many things in hell. How, then, am I mad? Hearken! and observe how healthily – how calmly I can tell you the whole story.

It is impossible to say how first the idea entered my brain; but once conceived, it haunted me day and night. Object there was none. Passion there was none. I loved the old man. He had never wronged me. He had never given me insult. For his gold I had no desire. I think it was his eye! yes, it was this! One of his eyes resembled that of a vulture – a pale blue eye, with a film over it. Whenever it fell upon me, my blood ran cold; and so by degrees – very gradually – I made up my mind to take the life of the old man, and thus rid myself of the eye for ever.

Now this is the point. You fancy me mad. Madmen know nothing. But you should have seen *me.* You should have seen how wisely I proceeded – with what caution – with what foresight – with what dissimulation. I went to work! I was never kinder to the old man than during the whole week before I killed him. And every night, about midnight, I turned the latch of his door and opened it – oh, so gently! And then, when I had made an opening sufficient for my head, I put in a dark lantern, all closed, closed, so that no light shone out, and then I thrust in my head. Oh, you would have laughed to see how cunningly I thrust it in! I moved it slowly – very, very slowly, so that I might not disturb the old man's sleep. It took me an hour to place my whole head within the opening so far that I could see him as he lay upon his bed. Ha! – would a madman have been so wise as this? And then, when my head was well in the room, I undid the lantern cautiously – oh, so cautiously – cautiously (for the hinges creaked) – I undid it just so much that a single thin ray fell upon the vulture eye. And this I did for seven long nights – every night just at midnight – but I found the eye always closed; and so it was impossible to do the work; for it was not the old man who vexed me, but his Evil Eye. And every morning, when the day broke, I went boldly into the chamber, and spoke courageously to him, calling him by name in a hearty tone, and inquiring how he had passed the night. So you see he would have been a very profound old man, indeed, to suspect that every night, just at twelve, I looked in upon him while he slept.

Upon the eighth night I was more than usually cautious in opening the door. A watch's minute hand moves more quickly than did mine. Never before that night had I *felt* the extent of my own powers – of my sagacity. I could scarcely contain my feelings of triumph. To think that there I was, opening the door, little by little, and he not even to dream of my secret deeds or thoughts. I fairly chuckled at the idea; and perhaps he heard me; for he moved on the bed suddenly, as if startled. Now you may think that I drew back – but no. His room was as black as pitch with the thick darkness (for the shutters were close fastened, through fear of robbers), and so I knew that he could not see the opening of the door, and I kept pushing it on steadily, steadily.

I had my head in, and was about to open the lantern, when my thumb slipped upon the tin fastening, and the old man sprang up in the bed, crying out – "Who's there?"

I kept quite still and said nothing. For a whole hour I did not move a muscle, and in the meantime I did not hear him lie down. He was still sitting up in the bed listening; – just as I have done, night after night, hearkening to the death watches in the wall.

Presently I heard a slight groan, and I knew it was the groan of mortal terror. It was not a groan of pain or of grief – oh, no! – it was the low stifled sound that arises from the bottom of the soul when overcharged with awe. I knew the sound well. Many a night, just at midnight, when all the world slept, it has welled up from my own bosom, deepening, with its dreadful echo, the terrors that distracted me. I say I knew it well. I knew what the old man felt, and pitied him, although I chuckled at heart. I knew that he had been lying awake ever since the first slight noise, when he had turned in the bed. His fears had been ever since growing upon him. He had been trying to fancy them causeless, but could not. He had been saying to himself – "It is nothing but the wind in the chimney – it is only a mouse crossing the floor," or "it is merely a cricket which has made a single chirp." Yes, he had been trying to comfort himself with these suppositions; but he had found all in vain. *All in vain;* because Death, in approaching him, had stalked with his black shadow before him, and enveloped the victim. And it was the mournful influence of the unperceived shadow that caused him to feel – although he neither saw nor heard – to *feel* the presence of my head within the room.

When I had waited a long time, very patiently, without hearing him lie down, I resolved to open a little – a very, very little crevice in the lantern. So I opened it – you cannot imagine how stealthily, stealthily – until, at length, a single dim ray, like the thread of the spider, shot from out the crevice and fell upon the vulture eye.

It was open – wide, wide open – and I grew furious as I gazed upon it. I saw it with perfect distinctness – all a dull blue, with a hideous veil over it that chilled the very marrow in my bones; but I could see nothing else of the old man's face or person: for I had directed the ray as if by instinct, precisely upon the damned spot.

And now have I not told you that what you mistake for madness is but over-acuteness of the senses? – now, I say, there came to my ears a low, dull, quick sound, such as a watch makes when enveloped in cotton. I knew that sound well, too. It was the beating of the old man's heart. It increased my fury, as the beating of a drum stimulates the soldier into courage.

But even yet I refrained and kept still. I scarcely breathed. I held the lantern motionless. I tried how steadily I could maintain the ray upon the eye. Meantime the hellish tattoo of the heart increased. It grew quicker and quicker, and louder and louder every instant. The old man's terror *must* have been extreme! It grew louder, I say, louder every moment! – do you mark me well: I have told you that I am nervous: so I am. And now at the dead hour of the night, amid the dreadful silence of that old house, so strange a noise as this excited me to uncontrollable terror. Yet, for some minutes longer I refrained and stood still. But the beating grew louder, louder! I thought the heart must burst. And now a new anxiety seized me – the sound would be heard by a neighbour! The old man's hour had come! With a loud yell, I threw open the lantern and leaped into the room. He shrieked once – once only. In an instant I dragged him to the floor, and pulled the heavy bed over him. I then smiled gaily, to find the deed so far done. But, for many minutes, the heart beat on with a muffled sound. This, however, did not vex me; it would not be heard through the wall. At length it ceased. The old man was dead. I removed the bed and examined the corpse. Yes, he was stone, stone dead. I placed my hand upon the heart and held it there many minutes. There was no pulsation. He was stone dead. His eye would trouble me no more.

If still you think me mad, you will think so no longer when I describe the wise precautions I took for the concealment of the body. The night waned, and I worked hastily, but in silence. First of all I dismembered the corpse. I cut off the head and the arms and the legs.

I then took up three planks from the flooring of the chamber, and deposited all between the scantlings. I then replaced the boards so cleverly, so cunningly, that no human eye – not even *his* – could have detected any thing wrong. There was nothing to wash out – no stain of any kind – no blood-spot whatever. I had been too wary for that. A tub had caught all – ha! ha!

When I had made an end of these labours, it was four o'clock – still dark as midnight. As the bell sounded the hour, there came a knocking at the street door. I went down to open it with a light heart, – for what had I *now* to fear? There entered three men, who introduced themselves, with perfect suavity, as officers of the police. A shriek had been heard by a neighbour during the night; suspicion of foul play had been aroused;

information had been lodged at the police office, and they (the officers) had been deputed to search the premises.

I smiled, – for *what* had I to fear? I bade the gentlemen welcome. The shriek, I said, was my own in a dream. The old man, I mentioned, was absent in the country. I took my visitors all over the house. I bade them search – search *well*. I led them, at length, to *his* chamber. I showed them his treasures, secure, undisturbed. In the enthusiasm of my confidence, I brought chairs into the room, and desired them *here* to rest from their fatigues, while I myself, in the wild audacity of my perfect triumph, placed my own seat upon the very spot beneath which reposed the corpse of the victim.

The officers were satisfied. My *manner* had convinced them. I was singularly at ease. They sat, and while I answered cheerily, they chatted familiar things. But, ere long, I felt myself getting pale and wished them gone. My head ached, and I fancied a ringing in my ears: but still they sat and still chatted. The ringing became more distinct: – it continued and became more distinct: I talked more freely to get rid of the feeling: but it continued and gained definitiveness – until, at length, I found that the noise was not within my ears.

Harry Clarke's illustration to *The Tell-Tale Heart;* 'But, for many minutes, the heart beat on with a muffled sound.'

No doubt I now grew *very* pale; – but I talked more fluently, and with a heightened voice. Yet the sound increased – and what could I do? It was *a low dull, quick sound – much such a sound as a watch makes when enveloped in cotton.* I gasped for breath – and yet the officers heard it not. I talked more quickly – more vehemently; but the noise steadily increased. I arose

and argued about trifles, in a high key and with violent gesticulations, but the noise steadily increased. Why *would* they not be gone? I paced the floor to and fro with heavy strides, as if excited to fury by the observation of the men – but the noise steadily increased. Oh God! what *could* I do? I foamed – I raved – I swore! I swung the chair upon which I had been sitting, and grated it upon the boards, but the noise arose over all and continually increased. It grew louder – louder – *louder!* And still the men chatted pleasantly, and smiled. Was it possible they heard not? Almighty God! – no, no! They heard! – they suspected! – they *knew!* – they were making a mockery of my horror! – this I thought, and this I think. But any thing was better than this agony! Any thing was more tolerable than this derision. I could bear those hypocritical smiles no longer! I felt that I must scream or die! – and now – again! – hark! louder! louder! louder! *louder!*–

"Villains!" I shrieked, "dissemble no more! I admit the deed! – tear up the planks! – here, here! – it is the beating of his hideous heart!"

Thinking back

You are aiming for an assignment that shows your understanding of stories and helps others to enjoy them.

When you read or watch a story for the first time, you might think, **'That's pretty good'** or even, **'That's great!'** This is a very good starting point for your aim.

The next step

To produce your assignment on short stories, though, you will need to **re-read** the stories you have chosen. You will need to put into words the things you like about each story and perhaps test your early ideas on other people when planning your assignment.

How can you go back to the story without too much boredom?

What to do: here are some ways of working on a story which can help. They can often give rise to ideas that you didn't have at first. You could use these techniques on one of the three short stories in this unit.

1.   With a partner: question swopping

Read the same short story – you could do this at home before you meet. Jot down any questions that occur to you about the story as you read it. Questions can be on anything you like from major matters like,

Why did the hero die?

to details like,

What does that word mean?

Now exchange questions with your partner – answer as many as you can and talk through your questions and answers together.

2. Choosing a cover

On page 20 are possible covers for collections of short stories.

In which collection would you include *The Specimen?*
Where would you assign *The Conjurer's Revenge?*
Judging from the covers, in which collection would you put the story, *The Tell-Tale Heart?*

What are the reasons for your decisions?

Design a cover for the short story you have read. You will probably find that this adds to your understanding of the story.

3. Attaching labels

Labels can be useful where stories are longer than a few pages – they help you to get a grip on a lengthier story and to see how one thing leads to another.

How to use the labels

Copy the labels below onto a sheet of paper. Cut them out and use them for a short story in this unit, or another from your reading. This will help you to decide how a short story is built up and what the different sections within it achieve.

For example, some short stories open with description of the setting, so you would place the label SETTING by the opening paragraph.

Editors and writers sometimes use these techniques. They are faced with the same problems as you. They need to re-read, check references and put ideas into words.

Reviewing a Story

Many of you will have read the short film reviews in *Radio Times* and *TV Times*. They give brief descriptions of the plot together with the reviewer's opinions about the good and bad points of the film. Some of you may have read book reviews in newspapers. The 'quality' Sunday newspapers such as *The Observer* and *The Sunday Times* contain a range of book reviews. When writing an assignment on a short story, you are acting as a reviewer. You describe the plot, the characterisation, the style, you praise, criticise and so on.

Activity 1 – reviewing

Put yourself in the position of a reader of a review. Spend a few minutes listing the things you would like to see in a review of a work of fiction.

This list was compiled by a class of Fourth Years, near the start of their GCSE course. The list is in the order that the points were mentioned. Change the order so that it would be more helpful to you as a reader.

What would you omit from the list? What would you add?

Author(s),

Where and how to get the book.

The title and how it relates to the story – is it straightforward, a mystery? Does the title have a double meaning?

Who has read the story? Is it best for a particular type of audience? Has it been made into a film or television version? Could it be?

What type of story is it? E.g. everyday life, science fiction.

Who tells the story? Is there a hero or heroine? Anything interesting about the characters – which character has our sympathy?

Whether the author has any message for the readers. How he gets his message across. Anything interesting in the style, way it is written?

Something about the plot, but without giving away too much of the story. If the review was meant to be read <u>before</u> the story, this would spoil the story for the reader.

Where the story is set, especially if it's in the past or an unfamiliar place. Also a glossary – some notes on unfamiliar words, expressions, place names.

Links with other stories read or films seen.

Activity 2 – research

Find a review of a work of fiction and see if you can identify any of the points on your list, e.g. does it mention the type of story – science fiction, romance, etc.

Some sources

Newspapers

Teletext

Magazines

Booklets and posters in libraries

Book reviews on radio and television

Group work – writing

Pick one of the stories you have read – it could be one in this unit – and write a short review. Exchange your review with others in the group to read.

Group work – charting

Now that you have read a number of short stories you need a way of comparing them and keeping a record of your reading. A chart is a useful way to do this. Take a large sheet of paper or a double page of an exercise book and make out a chart as shown. Fill in a section of the chart with the rest of the group for each of the stories you have read. The chart could be used for reference when you are preparing your next assignment.

Short Story Chart

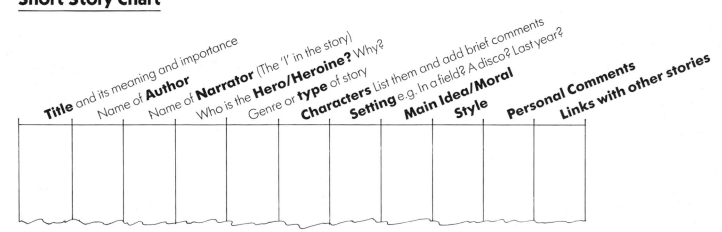

Using the chart

You now have a record at a glance of the stories you have read, some notes about them from your group work, and a way of comparing the stories in, say, their settings or their main ideas. Use it for reference.

The chart can help in **deciding on an assignment title**. Look down column (4), for example, on 'type' or 'genre' of the story. Can you find two stories which you decided were the same type? If so, you might like to base your assignment on the similarities and differences between them.

Thinking again about your own work

Earlier in this unit, you were asked to write a short review. Think of this as practice and use it to help you plan the next piece of work for your folder by using these questions.

Questions

In your 'practice' review:

● How good was the choice of story to review? (Sometimes, students glance at the opening, commit themselves to a story, **then** find that it is not really the right one for them. Others choose a story because it looks very brief, rather than because of the interesting things they have to say about it.)

● Was the end of your review as interesting and thoughtful as the opening section? (Some students start off well, knowing that the opening of any piece of writing has to make the reader want to continue – but lose stamina so that the quality of the writing tails off. The end of a piece of work is the impression you leave with your readers.)

● Did you read, talk about and make notes on the story before writing the review?

● Try to put yourself in the position of a reader of your review. Check whether the comments were in a helpful order and that the expression was clear. Was everything readable?

● Which are the strengths to build on for your next piece of coursework?

● Which are the points to work on before you complete the next piece?

A review can form part of your coursework.

Remember that GCSE English courses include evidence of **wide reading** of **literature** as well as **language work**.

Reading Short Stories: Assignments

Choices: reading and writing

Here are some suggestions for reading and writing. Choose from these titles or invent your own.

1.   You have been asked to contribute to a booklet of reviews of short stories available for use:
– in your class
or
– in the school library
or
– in the local public library.

Choose a number of stories which you have enjoyed and write a section of this booklet. Try to help the readers understand and enjoy the stories – you might like to provide illustrations, graphs or charts, as well as written comments.

2.   Choose a number of stories which you have enjoyed and review them for a specific newspaper or magazine which you have read. Name the newspaper or magazine you have chosen and write with its typical reader in mind.

3.   There are now a number of fiction prizes for short story writers. Imagine that you have been asked to judge a number of stories for a teenage fiction prize. Write your reply to the panel of judges on each story, deciding which one you think should win and stating why.

4.   Most of the stories which you have read could form part of collections or anthologies. Select several stories which you think could form part of the same anthology and write the introduction to the book. Give the anthology a title – you may also like to design a cover.

5.   In this unit, you have been asked to complete the ending to two stories before looking at the published ending. If some of the stories you have read seem to lend themselves to this treatment, design a 'completion' assignment on one or more of them. Explain why you would omit a particular section of a story for completion by other students. You should provide all the materials needed for a class to do the activity you have designed.

Speaking and listening

1.   Read aloud a section of a story of your choice to a group in your class. Your aim is to help them to see if they would like to read that story, so you should be ready to discuss it and answer their questions.

Option

1.   Make a short book review programme on a choice of short stories. The programme could be for an adult audience such as listeners to *Radio 4,* or for listeners of your own age for a local radio station. It may be possible for you to do this in a group, so that introductions, link passages, quotations or dramatised readings from the stories could be read in different voices.

2.   You could record the programme on tape, as if for radio,
or
perform it for others, as if for television.

Thinking back

One aim at the start of Unit 2 was to help others enjoy and understand stories, so try not to forget your readers as you plan and write your assignment.

You have been asked to make a choice of short stories. Have you chosen stories which you enjoyed? You will find your task easier if you have – it is hard to find enough to say about a story which you dislike. If, in the back of your mind, is the thought, **'This story is boring rubbish,'** then you might need to pick another. It is difficult to help others enjoy a story if you dislike it yourself.

Unit 3 Persuading

Aims: to understand some of the ways used to persuade others in speech and writing,
to be able to use these methods of persuasion in your assignments.

On the way: these activities will help you achieve these aims:
- considering two famous speeches
- listing ways of persuading others
- trying out some persuasion yourself – with a partner
  – in a role in a small group
  – in a Public Meeting with the class
- considering ways of persuading in pictures, speech and writing

- observing television advertisements
- researching a topic and reading 'actively'
- commenting on other students' work
- researching for a piece of persuasive writing
- reviewing your work.

By the end: you will have completed two assignments on persuasion, one in speech and one in writing. In addition, you will be able to judge some of the ways that others try to persuade you.

Assignments: Speaking – a role play.

Writing – a piece of persuasive writing for your coursework folder.

Graffiti as persuasion

Considering Speeches

Speeches are often intended to persuade. The aim of this section is to look at examples of how speeches do this.

Martin Luther King, a leader of the Civil Rights Movement in the U.S.A., addressed huge crowds to promote racial equality between black and white Americans.

Here is an extract from his speech in Washington D.C. in 1963, in which he spoke of his vision of equality for black people.

Activity

1. Read the opening to the speech, then choose from the words below and fill in the gaps.

2. Read it aloud when you have placed all the words and phrases. This helps you to see:
– how a speech is built up
– the effects of repetition in making a point.

I have a dream that one day on the red hills of Georgia the sons of former slaves and the sons of former slave-owners will be able to sit down together at the table of brotherhood. I have a dream that one day even the state of Mississippi, a state sweltering with the heat of oppression, will be transformed into an oasis of freedom and justice.

_____ that one day every valley shall be exalted, every hill and mountain made _____ . This is the faith that I go back to the South with. With this _____ we will be able to hew out the mountains of despair the stone of _____ ._____ we will be able to work together, to pray _____ , to struggle together, to go to jail together, to stand up for freedom _____ , knowing we will _____ one day.

Questions

1. Now that you have read this speech several times, look away from the page and write down the three or four words and phrases which stay in your mind.

2. Find two things in the speech which would make it easy for listeners to follow and remember.

Martin Luther King delivering his 'I have a dream' speech, Washington D.C., 1963

Follow up to 'filling in the gaps'

1. Here is the Martin Luther King extract without gaps, as it was spoken in Washington D.C. Compare this with your version, then read the comments in the boxes.

2. the boxes explain the techniques used to
– make the speech easy to follow

– make the speech memorable and appealing
– get the basic points across to a large audience.

3. When you have read the comments in the boxes make a list of at least three persuasive techniques explained there.

Martin Luther King speech

I have a dream that one day on the red hills of Georgia the sons of former slaves and the sons of former slave-owners will be able to sit down together at the table of brotherhood.

I have a dream that one day even the state of Mississippi, a state sweltering with the heat of oppression, will be transformed into an oasis of freedom and justice.

I have a dream that one day every valley shall be exalted, every hill and mountain made low. This is the faith that I go back to the South with. With this faith we will be able to hew out of the mountains of despair the stone of hope. With this faith we will be able to work together, to pray together, to struggle together, to go to jail together, to stand up for freedom together, knowing we will be free one day.

Simple and direct words are used. *I* is personal. The personal touch helps to make the speech convincing.

I have a dream is repeated. Hearing the words and rhythms repeated gives shape for listeners. They cannot go back over parts they missed as readers can. Repetition means the shape sticks in their minds so that the whole speech can be recalled.

There is a pattern here too. *Low* and *valley* go together, *hill* and *exalted* (made high) go together. There is contrast as well as similarity. *Hill* is opposite to *valley* and *high* is opposite to *low*.

We will be free sounds certain. This helps to convince hearers that this dream will become reality.

The word *we* is chosen now instead of *I*. Martin Luther King is inviting the audience to share his dream of equality.

Together is repeated. Hearers expect the word to be said in the same place in every phrase. The repetition makes the idea of working together stay in the minds of the hearers.

We could show the shape of this speech as:

I have a dream …
I have a dream …
I have a dream …
… that we will be free.

If the speech has a clear and simple shape or structure it will help to make it easy to follow, memorable and persuasive.

Making Speeches Memorable

Professional speech-makers are aware of the need for shape and pattern. If someone mentioned *bacon,* you might well add the word *eggs*. The two automatically form a pair, by association, like *fish and chips*. Language experts say such pairs help us to think and speak clearly and quickly. Pairs can be linked by opposition as well as similarity; they may be opposites like *top and bottom* or similar like *gold and silver.*

1. Activity

Without stopping to think, complete these:

1. Up and …
2. Left and …
3. War and …
4. Work and …

2. Comment

Patterns of three linked things are also common. You might have overheard small children chanting 'Ip, dip, dip' or 'Ready, steady, GO!' Traditional stories such as 'Goldilocks and the Three Bears' and 'The Three Little Pigs', use patterns of three. Visiting princes or princesses in children's stories often arrive in trios.

The art of persuasive speaking is called *rhetoric*. Though rhetoric is no longer the major subject of university studies, as it was for hundreds of years, it is still part of the advertising world, the law courts and the speeches of politicians. Listen for patterns of emphasis and repetition in courtroom dramas on television, in speeches from the House of Commons and the House of Lords on television and radio.

3. Activity

Here is the opening to a speech made near the start of the Second World War, by Winston Churchill in Parliament. Words and ideas are grouped in patterns of twos, threes and fours. Pick out as many of these patterns as you can.

I have nothing to offer but blood, toil, tears and sweat. You ask: what is our policy? I will say, it is to wage war, by sea, land and air, with all our might and with all the strength that God can give us; to wage war against a monstrous tyranny, never surpassed in the dark, lamentable catalogue of human crime. That is our policy. You ask: what is our aim? I can answer in one word: victory – victory at all costs, victory in spite of all terror, victory, however long and hard the road may be; for without victory there is no survival.

4. Comment

Churchill's aim was to declare the new Government's policy in a stirring way which would gain the support of his fellow M.P.'s.

5. Questions

Which words seem to be chosen to stir emotions? Pick out these words. Which emotions do you think the speaker was trying to stir?

6. Option: library research

Your local public library has records and cassette tapes of famous speeches from real life and from fictional characters in plays. You could ask for recordings of Martin Luther King or Winston Churchill, or ask your librarian to help you find other famous speeches. It is usual, though, for public libraries to make a small charge for borrowing records and tapes – books are free to borrowers.

Uses

Now that you have completed this section of the unit:

- You have learned how repetition and simple patterns help to get a speaker's point across and make it memorable.
- You can apply what you have learned when listening to speeches on television or radio.
- You can use these patterns to organise your own persuasive speaking.

Winston Churchill addressing the Conservative Party Conference in 1952.

Advertising – Persuasion in Words and Pictures

The aim of this unit is to see how people try to persuade others. Looking at advertisements will help you to realise this aim. The purpose of advertisements is to persuade.

Activity

1. Short activity – observation.
Look at the *Flabfighter* advertisement below.

Convincing others depends on both the material in the advertisement and the way it is put together, on content as well as organisation. Why might this advertisement fail to persuade readers to buy *Flabfighter?* What is wrong with the organisation of the pictures? How would you put it right?

21 days free trial from

FLABFIGHTER
You will be astounded how a few minutes a day can change your shape.

A   B   C

Are you out of shape, overweight and flabby?
Do you want to transform your figure?
Exercise with **Flabfighter** and see the difference.

2. A more detailed task
Now assess the effectiveness of the *Cambridge Diet* (on page 36) and *Oxfam* advertisements, using the checklist below. Use each item on the checklist (where appropriate) to provide a comment on the advertisements.

Checklist
Effect of:
- eyecatching pictures
- the people chosen for the pictures
- use of different lettering or printing (e.g. bold black type)
- the catch phrase or phrases
- use of personal appeals (e.g. *You'll be surprised, Please accept my gift*)
- the organisation into paragraphs or sections
- use of emotional words
- appealing to your worries or wishes
- appealing to your better nature or conscience

3. Using your own advertisement
Choose an advertisement, which includes a picture, from a newspaper or magazine. Assess its effectiveness using the above checklist.

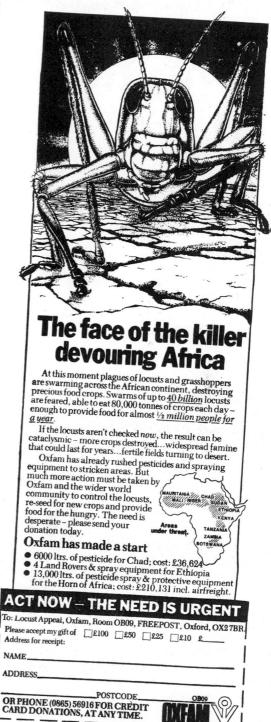

The face of the killer devouring Africa

At this moment plagues of locusts and grasshoppers are swarming across the African continent, destroying precious food crops. Swarms of up to 40 *billion* locusts are feared, able to eat 80,000 tonnes of crops each day – enough to provide food for almost ½ *million people for a year*.

If the locusts aren't checked *now*, the result can be cataclysmic – more crops destroyed...widespread famine that could last for years...fertile fields turning to desert.

Oxfam has already rushed pesticides and spraying equipment to stricken areas. But much more action must be taken by Oxfam and the wider world community to control the locusts, re-seed for new crops and provide food for the hungry. The need is desperate – please send your donation today.

Oxfam has made a start
- 6000 ltrs. of pesticide for Chad; cost: £36,624
- 4 Land Rovers & spray equipment for Ethiopia
- 13,000 ltrs. of pesticide spray & protective equipment for the Horn of Africa; cost: £210,131 incl. airfreight.

ACT NOW – THE NEED IS URGENT

To: Locust Appeal, Oxfam, Room OB09, FREEPOST, Oxford, OX2 7BR.
Please accept my gift of ☐£100 ☐£50 ☐£25 ☐£10 £____
Address for receipt:

NAME_____

ADDRESS_____

_____POSTCODE_____ OB09
OR PHONE (0865) 56916 FOR CREDIT CARD DONATIONS, AT ANY TIME. **OXFAM**

"Doctors spent fourteen years developing this diet.

It changed my life in as many days."

MRS. SUSAN WALSH OF TOOTING EXPLAINS HOW THE CAMBRIDGE DIET HAS CHANGED HER LIFE.

"I'd never been pleased with my weight and always felt I could do with losing a couple of stone or so. But the worst point came after the birth of my second child when I reached 12 stone 2lbs. That's when I really started getting depressed.

Unfortunately, diets never seemed to work for me however hard I tried, but at that time one of my friends had just reached her target weight on the Cambridge Diet.

'If she can do it, then so can I', I said to myself - and I was right. Within a month on the Diet I'd lost well over a stone. From then on, even though I am 5'9" tall, I knew I could reach my 'dream' weight of around 9½ stone and two months later I had.*

It's completely changed my life!"

go out is a pleasure and no longer a chore. It's given me a totally new outlook on life."
MRS. C. HOOTON, CHELMSFORD.

FEWER CALORIES, YET MORE NUTRITION.

The Cambridge Diet is a low calorie diet which contains all the vitamins, nutrients and trace elements you need for a dieting period in just 330 Calories a day.

It is one of the most nutritionally dense foods known to man and is the only low calorie diet to have been granted patents worldwide.

the worst point came after the birth of my second child when I reached 12 stone 2 pounds. That's when I really started getting depressed.

I knew I could reach my 'dream' weight of around 9½ stone and two months later I had. It's completely changed my life!

Read what other users have to say:
"I lost 18lbs in 4 weeks and I'm now back to the measurements I had when I was married - and that's over 20 years ago."*
MRS. B. BROCKWELL, WINDSOR.

"I started to lose weight literally in the first few days and within 5 weeks I'd lost 1st 10lbs without any difficulty."*
MRS. J. FREEMAN, NORTHANTS.

"I now enjoy buying clothes. Dressing up to

DEVELOPED BY DOCTORS AND CLINICALLY TESTED.

The Cambridge Diet was developed and tested by doctors over a period of fourteen years - a longer test than any other diet in history.

The man who pioneered it is Dr. Alan Howard MA, PhD, nutritional research lecturer and Chairman of the Food Education Society.

EASY TO STICK TO. SIMPLE TO PREPARE.

When you start the Cambridge Diet, you won't believe how easy it is to stick to. There's no need for the usual calorie counting, or measuring out of tiny portions of food. That's already done for you. All you have to do each meal time is mix up your chosen meal.

ALL YOUR FAVOURITE FLAVOURS FOR NO MORE THAN 60p A SERVING.

There are currently eleven delicious soups and drinks available. Like Chicken, Beef and Minestrone soups for instance, as well as Chocolate, Strawberry and Peach flavour drinks.

Then there are 160 Calorie chocolate-coated Meal Bars which can replace one liquid meal per day, adding only 50 extra Calories to your daily intake.

Don't think the Cambridge Diet can't work for you, because it can, just as it has for millions of others. You'll be surprised just how quickly you could reach your target weight with this effective, yet safe, diet.

Don't waste any more time. Send off the Freepost coupon today for full details.

It could change your life.

THE CAMBRIDGE DIET HAS HAD THE LONGEST CLINICAL TRIALS OF ANY DIET IN HISTORY. AT THE 3RD INTERNATIONAL CONFERENCE ON OBESITY IN ITALY IN 1980, 21 DOCTORS AND MEDICAL RESEARCHERS FROM NINE COUNTRIES PRESENTED NINE SCIENTIFIC PAPERS ON CLINICAL TESTS OF THE CAMBRIDGE DIET. ALL INDICATED IT TO BE SAFE AND EFFECTIVE.

*THE CAMBRIDGE DIET SHOULD NOT BE TAKEN AS A SOLE SOURCE OF NUTRITION FOR A CONTINUOUS PERIOD EXCEEDING FOUR WEEKS. DIRECTIONS FOR USAGE BEYOND THIS PERIOD ARE GIVEN IN THE INSTRUCTION BOOKLET. THE TESTIMONIALS USED IN THIS ADVERTISEMENT HAVE FOLLOWED THIS PROCEDURE AS PART OF A CALORIE-CONTROLLED DIET.

the Cambridge Diet

TO: CAMBRIDGE NUTRITION LIMITED, DEPT. WEK 8P FREEPOST, 69-75 THORPE ROAD, NORWICH, NR1 1BR.
Please send me, by return, further information about the Cambridge Diet (no stamp required) and ask my local Cambridge Counsellor to contact me.

NAME MR/MRS/MISS

ADDRESS

POST CODE (To help avoid delays)   TELEPHONE

36

Television and advertising

Printed advertisements rely on pictures and the printed word to persuade. Television advertisements can make the pictures move, the words speak and add music and sound effects. The lessons you learned in the above activity can also be applied to television advertisements. The following activity will help you assess the effects of moving pictures and sound.

Activity

1. Choose a television advertisement which is repeated several times during a week *or* arrange for one to be video recorded if you can.
2. Turn down the sound and watch the pictures in the advertisement.

- How do they get the message across?
- What sticks in your mind?
- How effective are the pictures?

3. Turn your back on the television the second time the advertisement is on.
- How well does the sound get the message across?
- What sticks in your mind?
- How effective is the sound?

4. The third time you view the advertisement, watch and listen. You are now in a position to assess the contribution of the pictures and sound to the total effect of the advertisement.

- Is one more effective than the other in getting the message across? If so, why?
- Do sound and pictures work together equally? If so, how?
- What is the most memorable thing about the advertisement. Why is it memorable?
- Does the advertisement make you want the product or service? Why or why not?
  (If not, it may be that you have no need for the product or service e.g. you may be female and the ad is for aftershave. In such a case describe the people to whom the ad applies. Do you feel the ad will make them want the product or service? Why or why not?)

Advertising : group work

Often we learn best by *doing*. Here is an exercise in which you are asked to conduct an advertising campaign. It is now your job to persuade.

The after school club

Situation: your school can open for two hours every evening for young people to use gym and games facilities and for adult aerobics and cookery classes. A small entrance fee of 20p will be charged.

Aim: you must decide how to advertise the facility to people in school and in your local community.

Here is the agenda for your meeting

(an agenda is a list of things to discuss and act on)

1. WHO will see the advertisement?
2. WHAT METHOD(S) will be used and why?
3. HOW MUCH will it cost?
4. HOW will the success of the advertising campaign be judged?

Budget: you have a grant of £300 to carry out your advertising campaign.

Other ways: you may have better ideas than those suggested here for attracting people to the after school club. You may use your own ideas but you should estimate the costs and work within your budget.

Some advertising costs

Hand drawn posters
cost of paper = 10p per sheet

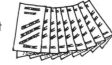

Leaflets = 30p per leaflet

Local newspaper
ad = 50p per word

Large poster
professionally
printed = £2 each

T shirt and slogan = £5 each

1 minute of local radio
advertising = £250

30 seconds of television
advertising = £600

OTHER WAYS?

37

Ways of Convincing Others: Collecting Ideas

Activity

What would you do to achieve the following?
Make brief notes in in a numbered list.

1. Persuade a close friend to lend you 10p.

2. Persuade members of your class to give 10p each to Oxfam.

3. Sell a new design of school sweatshirt to as many students as possible in your school.

4. Help a class of primary school children to be more careful on the roads.

5. Encourage drivers to leave their cars at home at Christmas as part of a national campaign against drinking and driving.

6. Persuade young people to drink more, on behalf of a brewery.

7. Encourage young people to drink less as part of a national health campaign.

8. Persuade people you know who smoke to give up their habit.

9. In assembly, persuade third and fourth years to join a new book club for which you are responsible.

10. Do the same in the school magazine.

11. Convince a small group of your classmates to share your opinion on something about which you feel strongly.

12. As a journalist, persuade readers, of any newspaper you choose, to support a Government decision on education.

13. As a journalist on a rival newspaper, persuade readers to oppose the same Government decision.

With a partner

Compare your lists and arrange them in columns under these headings. For example, if you think that you would use posters to help primary children to be safer on the roads, write **posters** in the column headed VISUAL/PICTURES. Where you have used a different approach from your partner, discuss why you did so.

NUMBER	VISUAL/PICTURES	SPOKEN	WRITTEN
1			
2			
3			

Option

With the class

● Assemble a class list like your own in columns.
● Look for the similarities and differences in approach e.g. you may find that most people have decided to use a visual presentation for primary school children.

● Find reasons for the similarities and differences in methods of persuasion used by members of the class.

Assignment: Speaking: a Role Play

Now here is your chance to try out some persuading in a group. You will need to form a committee of four members and appoint a chairperson.

Cash and Choice

THE CASH

An ex-pupil has given £30,000 (thirty thousand pounds) to the school on condition that the pupils make a decision on how it's spent.

THE CHOICE

There have been endless meetings. Finally, a long list has been made. Now it's decision time. The decision will be made by a small committee of four people.

THE COMMITTEE

The following parts are *optional*.
1. A 6th former – to say how the upper school would feel about the choice.
2. Middle school pupil – to say how the middle school would feel.
3. Lower school pupil – to say how the lower school would feel.
4. Chair – to stop everyone yelling at each other, and keep everyone thinking about making the *final* choice.

HOW TO START

- Read the list very carefully and make up your mind what *you* want.
- Make a list of your choices – make sure they add up to £30,000.
- The Chair should then make a list of the ones that everyone already agrees on.
- Take turns to argue why you have chosen the ones you have.
- If you can't agree at all, the Chair decision is final!

THE LIST

Here is the list that the school has made. It contains everything that people want. If they were all bought, the cost would be £130,000. The school has only £30,000. So a lot have to go. Which will they be?

1. A MINIBUS for small school outings	8,000
2. TWENTY GUITARS and a guitar teacher	10,000
3. A SCHOOL TELEVISION STUDIO so pupils can make their own programmes	10,000
4. A NURSERY so pre-school children could join the school and be looked after by pupils	11,000
5. A COUNTRYSIDE CENTRE near London that all the pupils could visit and learn about life in the countryside, to be shared with one other school nearby	20,000
6. NEW CHAIRS for the classrooms	8,000
7. A TUCK SHOP that sold snacks & dinners	7,500
8. BUYING THE SPACE to have games nearer the school so there would be no more coach journeys to games	15,000
9. THIRTY BENCHES for the playground	1,500
10. DAY TRIPS for every pupil in the school in the summer	2,000
11. A COMPUTER ROOM containing a computer network	10,000
12. TWO COMMON ROOMS for the middle and lower school	13,000
13. DRIVING LESSONS and equipment for the middle school	12,000
14. LOCKABLE CLOAKROOMS, one for each year	2,000
	£130,000

Originally devised by Judith Hemming.

Option

THE PUBLIC MEETING

1. Decide on a speaker for each group.

2. Help your group's speaker to plan a speech. You do not need to write out a speech in full. A plan and notes should be enough.

3. Decide on the best order for the points your group would like to make in the speech.

4. Be ready to answer questions after your speech.

5. As a class, hold a Public Meeting at which all speakers justify the group decisions on spending.

6. Take a vote, in secret, on slips of paper OR in public, by a show of hands. You could appoint your teacher as vote counter.

7. Which group won the vote? Why were they successful in persuading people to vote for them?

Persuasive Writing

Persuasive writing attempts to convince you that something is true. It puts over a point of view and tries to persuade you that this view is correct.

In this section you are asked to examine two different articles about **graffiti** – writing on a wall. In the first activity the paragraphs which make up an article have been jumbled. You are asked to put them into the correct order.

How does this help?

- Whatever view you want to put across, convincing others in writing needs good organisation. Putting the writing of others into order helps you to concentrate on getting organised, whether this is for your coursework folder or as part of an examination.
- You can see how an argument develops over paragraphs, how one thing leads to another.
- You are starting to learn ways of **understanding** persuasive writing as well as producing it yourself.

Some GCSE English syllabuses (a syllabus is a description of what your course must include) have jumbled paragraphs for you to re-organise as part of the examination. In English syllabuses, the task of putting jumbled paragraphs into order is often called a **sequencing exercise.**

Activity (1)

Put the paragraphs of this short article into order by copying these boxes

1st	2nd	3rd	4th	5th	6th

and putting the letter of a paragraph into each.

E No doubt there will be those who baulk at the severity of the sentence quoting lack of facilities, deprived childhood and all the other excuses which will be wheeled out in the youth's defence. Piffle.

F The writing on the wall

B Deprived they may be, but not every child feels the need to scrawl their illiterate thoughts on the walls and bridges of our society.

A Then, just then, we might start to deter these teenage hooligans who destroy other people's property with their pestilence.

D A three month custodial sentence seems fair, but how about providing the young lout with a bucket and brush for another three months and let him remove his vile outpourings.

C THANKS to the efforts of the Police, south Manchester citizens can rejoice in the knowledge that something is being done about the graffiti craze sweeping the area.

The New York subway

Activity (2) reading and commenting

a) In the middle column below is the original order of the article. At either side of the article are comments on the clues that help find the order. These clues relate to **language** and styles of **printing** which apply to many articles, whatever their subject or content.

Read the comments.

b) Using a short newspaper article of your own choice, find as many clues to the order as you can and explain them with comments at the side like the example below.

Example

COMMENTS	THE WRITING ON THE WALL	COMMENTS
Capital letters so this is the start of an article.	THANKS to the efforts of the Police, south Manchester citizens can rejoice in the knowledge that something is being done about the graffiti craze sweeping the area.	Of the five paragraphs to choose from, this has the clearest connection with the headline. This paragraph announces the general issue.
The repeated words connect these two paragraphs.	No doubt there will be those who baulk at the severity of the sentence quoting lack of facilities, deprived childhood and all the other excuses which will be wheeled out in the youth's defence. Piffle.	Middle paragraphs can be hard to place. In this example, the small word **but** is an important clue. **But** often shows the middle of a line of argument where the writer changes direction. In previous paragraphs possible excuses for writing on walls are given. Now the writer dismisses these excuses and argues for harsh punishment for graffiti writers.
	Deprived they may be, but not every child feels the need to scrawl their illiterate thoughts on the walls and bridges of our society. A three month custodial sentence seems fair, but how about providing the young lout with a bucket and brush for another three months and let him remove his vile outpourings.	
Sounds as if a conclusion will follow. This is probably the end.	Then, just then, we might start to deter these teenage hooligans who destroy other people's property with their pestilence.	

Thinking back and building up your skills

Earlier in this unit, you were asked to consider persuasion and emotional appeals in speeches and in advertising. Now you can apply what you have learned by answering the following questions on 'The Writing on the Wall.'

1. Pick out any words which seem to show anger in the writer.

2. Pick out any words which seem to exaggerate.

3. Why do you think that the writer would want to make an emotional appeal?

4. Do you find the writing effective in persuading you or not? Why or why not?

5. What do you think is the writer's view of teenagers?

Activity (3) headlining

This second article on graffiti is taken from *The Guardian* newspaper. The argument and the way it is organised are quite complex. This activity will help you see how a complex argument is built up.

Remember that **understanding** the writing of others is a part of your English course. This activity is an example of ACTIVE READING, that is, doing things when you read to help you make sense of that reading.

Headlining is one active reading technique and involves dividing the writing into sections and giving a headline to each one. (Some active reading techniques are summarised on page 45).

Students' work

The article below has been sectioned off into numbered paragraphs. On the right-hand side of page 43 are some headlines which a small group of fifth formers gave to the paragraphs. Match the headlines to the paragraphs.

Option

You could think of more concise sub-headlines than those given and re-write the general headline at the start of the article (called the **banner headline**).

When the writing on Belshazzar's wall is a credit to Kilroy

Richard Boston

1. NOWADAYS you can't open a newspaper without reading that research has shown that some sort of food or other is good or (more often) bad for you. It is generally assumed that this scientific, experimental, statistical approach to dietary matters is something new. Not so, as can be seen from the Book of Daniel, which starts by telling of how Nebuchadnezzar took a number of the children of Israel with the idea of giving them the best education that money could buy. In particular, he gave orders that they should not have the usual school dinners, but the same meat to eat and wine to drink as he himself had.

2. Doubtless his motives were of the highest but he reckoned without Daniel, who was one of the children of Israel, playing the part of d'Artagnan to the Three Musketeers of Shadrach, Mishach and Abednigo of fiery furnace fame.

3. Like many children, Daniel was fussy about his food, and he didn't fancy the king's meat and drink. Accordingly he did an Oliver Twist in reverse. He chatted up the chief eunuch who was in charge of the catering arrangements, and suggested that some of the children should be given the king's meat and wine, while he and his friends should be given pulse to eat and water to drink. The results were dramatic. "And at the end of ten days their countenances appeared fairer and fatter than all the children which did eat the portion of the king's food."

4. In a later experiment, conducted in a den of lions, Daniel proved equally successfully that, just as he didn't eat animals, they didn't eat him. Meanwhile a change had come over the diet of Nebuchadnezzar, who had taken to eating grass. Furthermore his hair had become like eagle's feathers and his nails like birds' claws. He sounds a bit like Howard Hughes in his later years.

5. Nebuchadnezzar's son was Belshazzar who didn't eat grass but probably smoked it and gave the most splendid parties. He may well have invented mass catering, for at his famous feast there were a thousand guests. There they all were, the king, his lords, his princes, his wives and concubines, drinking wine and making merry when a mysterious hand appeared and wrote the words Mene Mene Tekel Upharsin on the wall. As far as I know this is the earliest recorded example of graffiti, and was probably the most famous –

until it was toppled by Kilroy Was Here in the Second World War.

6. The writing on Belshazzar's wall had much the same effect on the party as did the equally unexpected arrival of Banquo's ghost just as the Macbeths and their friends were sitting down to supper. While everyone was surprised by the writing on the wall, none was more so than the king of the Chaldeans himself. "Then the King's countenance was changed, and his thoughts troubled him, so that the joints of his loins were loosed, and his knees smote one against another."

7. Graffiti do have that effect on some people. A few ill-written words in a bus shelter, telephone kiosk or public lavatory will have them frothing at the mouth, writing letters to the papers deploring the decline in the

moral fibre of the nation, and generally hopping up and down while their countenances change, their thoughts trouble them, the joints of their loins are loosed, and their knees smite one against another.

8. What is strange is that they are not worried by the fact that the bus shelter offers no protection from the elements, that British Telecom has passed a just sentence on the telephone kiosk, and that there is no toilet paper in the public lavatories. No, it's the graffiti that gets up their noses.

9. Obviously graffiti, with sexist and racist slogans and images are offensive (and are intended to be). So are these words and images when printed or spoken, but this doesn't mean that print and speech should be prohibited. Indeed, in many parts of the world freedom of speech is so restricted that graffiti are the only remaining means of expressing political opposition. I bet that Hadrian's wall hadn't been up for long before it had "Romans Go Home" written all over it.

10. The walls of Paris were much enlivened in May 1968 with such slogans as "let imagination seize power", "forbidding is forbidden" and "I am a Marxist of the Groucho tendency" and what a debt of gratitude British Rail's Western Region passengers owe to whoever wrote in huge letters on an otherwise undistinguished wall near Paddington Station the words "Far Away is Close at Hand in, Images of Elsewhere". Unfortunately, most of that wall has now been knocked down, but for something like 15 years it gave train passengers something to think about. More recently, on the other side of the track there have

appeared words that might well be the work of the same author, they say, "Arise, the Ungood Proles from your TVs. You Are Watching Big Brother."

11. Of course, it is annoying when people carve their initials on some ancient monument, but that great travel writer Robert Byron made an interesting point about this when he said that "one may laugh – one may deplore them – yet there is often something touching about the names that are to be found on ancient monuments. It is a primitive rather than a vulgar instinct that impels the cutting of them, they imply not self-advertisement but a deep-felt appreciation of the spot itself and an honest pride in having visited it." Another point is that the ones which offend are those that were done last week. If they date from three or four centuries ago they actually seem to add something as Ivy does to an old tree.

12. In fact, most graffiti do not appear on beautiful objects but on ugly ones. Graffiti artists have an unerring eye for really ugly architecture and town planning, and their contributions can only be improvement. In France they get some really interesting effects with stencils and spray guns and the idea is slowly catching on here. In London some of the drabbest areas have been greatly improved by the unofficial wall artists, but much remains to be done on all that post war featureless concrete. A good place to start would be the Arts complex of the South Bank, but almost any post war shopping precinct would do.

13. Not that I am in any way suggesting that this kind of thing should be encouraged or permitted. Far from it. Encouragement would be its death sentence. Graffiti would fall straight into the hands of architects, designers and art galleries. No, graffiti should be treated with complete disapproval. Indeed, they should be cracked down on. That way they will remain unrespectable and retain their irresponsible vitality. That is the writing on the wall.

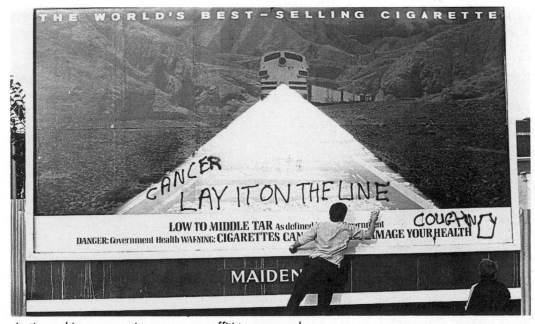

Anti-smoking campaigners use graffiti to persuade.

43

Activity (4) comparing notes

Here is part of the article on pages 42-43, with the **active reading** notes from the group who worked on it.

Read their notes, then pick a **different** section of the article and make your own notes on it. Choose three paragraphs, summarise what they say and make up your own headline for each paragraph.

KING'S KNEES KNOCKING AT WARNING ON WALL

(The past) Effect on King – he is troubled – worried guilty.

The writing is a warning.

6. The writing on Belshazzar's wall had much the same effect on the party as the equally unexpected arrival of Banquo's ghost just as the Macbeths and their friends were sitting down to supper. While everyone was surprised by the writing on the wall, none was more so than the king of the Chaldeans himself. "Then the King's countenance was changed, and his thoughts troubled him, so that the joints of his loins were loosed, and his knees smote one against another."

FEAR AND ANGER AT TODAY'S GRAFFITI

The article has looked at the past – now it moves to the present.

Strong feelings about graffiti in both past and present.

7. Graffiti do have that effect on some people. A few ill-written words in a bus shelter,.telephone kiosk or public lavatory will have them frothing at the mouth, writing letters to the papers deploring the decline in the moral fibre of the nation, and generally hopping up and down while their countenances change, their thoughts trouble them, the joints of their loins are loosed, and their knees smite one against another.

8. What is strange is that they are not worried by the fact that the bus shelter offers no protection from the elements, that British Telecom has passed a just sentence on the telephone kiosk, and that there is no toilet paper in the public lavatories. No, it's the graffiti that gets up their noses.

PUBLIC VANDALISM UNNOTICED

'strange' – writer thinks it odd, people more angry about graffiti. Examples of *public* places that *don't work*, but people don't get angry.

Active reading – a summary of what to do

1. Divide the piece of writing into stages. The stages often coincide with paragraphs.
2. Circle the most important words in each section.
3. Make connecting lines between the words if they are spread out.
4. Write the words at the side, with brief comments and short summaries.
5. Print a headline above your extracted words.

Your list of of headlines shows that you have already begun to understand the piece of writing by re-phrasing and summarising it.

Belfast, 1971 – the politics of graffiti.

Factual Persuasion

On pages 46-49 is a report on smoking from *Which?* magazine.

The report is an example of the use of factual information to convince readers. It shows how facts can be used to build a case – here, the case against smoking.

● The way the information is set out helps you to be more familiar with simple graphs, tables and illustrations – GCSE courses include understanding of information presented in this way.

● In preparing your assignments on persuasion, you will probably want to look at some factual information on the topic you have chosen. Working on the *Which?* report, you will learn ways of handling information efficiently.

Activity – searching for information

1. a)   In the table headed *Support for more no-smoking areas,* find the percentage of people who were in favour of more smoke-free areas in cinemas.

You probably looked at the section on cinemas, and glanced at the key to see what the shaded areas meant.

The table does not tell you exactly how many people in the survey prefer more smoke-free areas when they watch a film. To estimate the number, you would have to look at the section 'Our smoking surveys' at the bottom of column three on page 46, then do some calculations.

b)   Look through the report and find the proportion of 15 and 16 year olds who smoke regularly.

You probably looked at the section headed *Young smokers* and glanced through for key words, phrases or numbers like 15 and 16.

> This type of reading is known as **scanning** or **scan reading** – searching for particular pieces of information.

The first sentence of each paragraph often announces the main topic for the rest of that paragraph and so provides the first and most natural place to glance when searching for the information you want.

c)   Scan the section *Tips on how to give it up* for two ways in which a Doctor can help smokers to give up.

2.

> A second type of reading is known as **skimming** or **skim reading**. Here you aim for a general impression of the whole piece of writing rather than searching for just one or two pieces of information.

Thinking back

Earlier in this unit you were asked to consider the effectiveness of examples of persuasion. You have now worked on a piece of factual persuasion.

Skimming can be used when you think that the whole piece of writing might have information which is relevant to your needs. Glance at the chapter headings, using the first sentence of each paragraph where there is a long stretch of writing without headings or subheadings. For each paragraph pick out a key word. Jot down these words on a piece of paper. If the book or article is your own property, you could underline key words in pencil. You have now made a start in summarising the information.

3.   Use the **skimming** techniques noted above to write a short summary of the main points made in the *Which?* report.

4.   Graphics – diagrams and pictures – can present facts and opinions in a clear and interesting way. They can summarise a large amount of information and present it in a nutshell.
a)   Look at the graph entitled *Smoking on the decline.* Briefly summarise what it shows. Do you think it is an effective way of presenting this information? Why or why not?
b)   Look at the picture of the ashtray at the end of the report. How does it help to reinforce the message of the article?

How effective do you find it? Do you think it would persuade smokers to give up? How important do you think the use of facts is in getting the message across? Give reasons for your answers.

What you have learned

After completing the activity on the *Which?* report you will have learned how:

● facts can be used to persuade
● graphics can present facts and opinions
● to scan for a particular piece of information
● skim read a longer piece of writing.

Scanning and skimming are useful tools. They can be used when you are gathering information for your own assignments.

No smoking

On average, out of every four people who regularly smoke cigarettes, one will be killed by it. Two of the others may have their health impaired. Most smokers regret ever starting

The health risks affect cigarette smokers themselves. But smoking-related issues affect all of us. There's the question of how to persuade children not to take up smoking (at least one in four 16-year-olds smokes regularly). The effect of smoke on non-smokers has recently attracted research interest. And wider questions involve the whole community – including the cost to the country of illness related to smoking.

In this report, when we talk about smoking we mean cigarette smoking; unless you inhale (which many ex-cigarette smokers do), smoking cigars or a pipe *may* be less damaging to your health.

The dangers

We've recently tackled several challenging health topics in *Which?*, and where controversy still rages among the experts we've taken great care to present both sides – to help you make up your own mind. But there is an overwhelming consensus among medical experts about the dangers of smoking. It is the single biggest preventable cause of illness and death. It can – and often does – kill. The risk is higher the more heavily you smoke and, particularly, the younger you start.

Around one in eight regular smokers die from tobacco-related **coronary heart disease**. What small risk there is of a fatal heart attack in your 30s or early 40s is increased by many times if you smoke; but it is among those in their 40s and 50s that the risk difference between smokers and non-smokers is most marked. In effect, smoking makes you run the same risk of a fatal heart attack as much older non-smokers.

Smoking increases the risk of narrowing of the arteries, leading particularly to rupture of the aorta (the great artery leading from the heart), and to a lesser extent to fatal strokes. If someone has narrowing of the leg arteries, this makes walking painful and they may in extreme cases face leg amputation; on the other hand, if they stop smoking, their condition usually improves. For women on the contraceptive pill, especially those over 35 the otherwise very small extra risk of heart disease or strokes is much increased by smoking.

Chronic bronchitis (except in smokers) has now been virtually eliminated by cleaner air and improved treatment. But it and emphysema (another lung disease which makes breathing distressingly difficult) still damage nearly one in five cigarette smokers. These diseases eventually kill about one in 15 regular smokers.

The great majority of **lung cancer** deaths are related to long-term smoking: the disease claims around one in ten regular smokers – more than one in eight if they smoke over 25 a day. The younger someone starts smoking, the greater the eventual risk. Smokers also face more risk of cancers of the mouth, throat, bladder, kidney and pancreas – so smoking is associated with about one in three of *all* cancer deaths.

In general, smokers' health tends to be poorer than other people's, since smoking may lower the body's ability to fight infection. Smokers lose more days off work, and spend more time ill in bed. They are more likely to suffer from illnesses such as flu. They run more risk of stomach and duodenal ulcers, and get more diseases of their gums and mouth. Finally, when they need an operation, recovery may be more prolonged and troublesome than normal.

Women who smoke reach their menopause earlier – on average, by one or two years – than those who don't.

Taking all the risks together, being a regular smoker cuts your life expectancy by about five years. And this average figure includes people who give up soon after starting. If you start smoking young, and never give up, your life expectancy is cut by as much as ten or fifteen years.

A cigarette smoker aged between 35 and 60 is twice as likely to die *in the coming year* as a non-smoker of the same age. A middle-aged heavy smoker is about as likely to die during the next year as a non-smoker ten years older.

So, if you smoke, the health arguments for giving up are overwhelming. As soon as you stop, health, and the likelihood of a long life, start improving. The first gain is in heart function and blood circulation –

Smoking, pregnancy and the baby

Women trying to conceive, and finding it difficult, find it roughly twice as difficult if they smoke around 20 a day. Smoking also makes men less fertile – although how much in practice this lowers the chance of fathering a child has not yet been measured. Smoking has also been implicated in impotence in men.

Women who smoke during pregnancy are more likely to have premature babies, and they have smaller babies (around 200g or 7oz lighter). The slight risk that the baby will be stillborn or will die shortly after birth is also increased. Though some studies have suggested an increased risk of miscarriage, this has not been confirmed by others.

measurably improved just 24 hours after giving up. After a few weeks, lung function also starts improving measurably, and your body's ability to fight infection is returning to normal.

The benefits increase as the months and years pass. Of course, it's best to give up before symptoms show; if you wait until they do, some permanent damage may already have been done.

Breathing other people's smoke

Babies whose parents smoke run an extra risk of developing bronchitis or pneumonia, and smokers' children are much more prone to coughs, particularly when young but even into their teens. They are also more likely to wheeze. These effects are most marked if the mother smokes. Asthmatic children suffer more if their parents smoke.

The effect on adults of breathing air containing other people's cigarette smoke has now become a subject of great public interest, and of continuing research. There is still a lively controversy about how many people are at risk from this, and about how serious the risk is. But a picture is beginning to emerge.

First, people who already suffer from heart or lung disease may have their condition aggravated by very smoky air. Second, smoke from other people's cigarettes contains powerful carcinogens (cancer-inducing chemicals). These are particularly highly concentrated in the smoke from the cigarette's tip – unfiltered by the cigarette itself and by the smoker's lungs, though the smoke is greatly diluted in the surrounding air. Some studies of the health of non-smokers who live with smokers suggest that exposure to smoky air involves a small increase in the risk of lung cancer.

Secondhand smoke may be less of a health risk at work than at home, though it depends how well ventilated the workplace is. Exposure to other people's smoke in cinemas, restaurants and so forth may be irritating but is brief in comparison with living or working alongside a smoker.

Overall, the cancer risk to adults from secondhand smoke is probably very small. Measurement of smoke by-products in the bodies of child and adult non-smokers confirms that living with a heavy smoker may be like smoking the

---

Our smoking surveys
In 1984 we interviewed a representative national sample of 1,254 smoking and non-smoking adults about their attitudes to smoking in general. We arranged 813 further interviews towards the end of 1985.

please

occasional cigarette yourself (say, one or two a week). Few people are likely to be in the riskiest circumstance – continuous exposure to heavy smoke over many years. But the risk is still there, and non-smokers do have some health grounds for objecting to smoke in the air around them – quite apart from the discomfort or irritation it can cause.

And secondhand smoke is certainly irritating. Our surveys showed that around two-thirds of non-smokers are sometimes irritated by other people's smoke (one in four smokers are, too). Around half have at one time or another wanted to ask other people not to smoke – and about three out of ten people have done so.

Most non-smokers usually sit in no-smoking areas if they get the chance. And most would like more of them, as the Diagram shows. You can also see that many smokers would like more no-smoking areas, too. In fact, there was considerable support from many smokers and non-smokers for a total ban in all the places we asked about except pubs.

We also asked whether restaurants should **by law** have no-smoking areas, as they must in some states in the US. More than half the smokers agreed with the three-quarters of non-smokers who said they should.

More than half the people questioned also think that, by law, employers should now have to provide smoke-free areas for people to work in.

These figures are mainly from our 1985 survey; in almost every case, more people wanted extra no-smoking areas than in our earlier, 1984, survey.

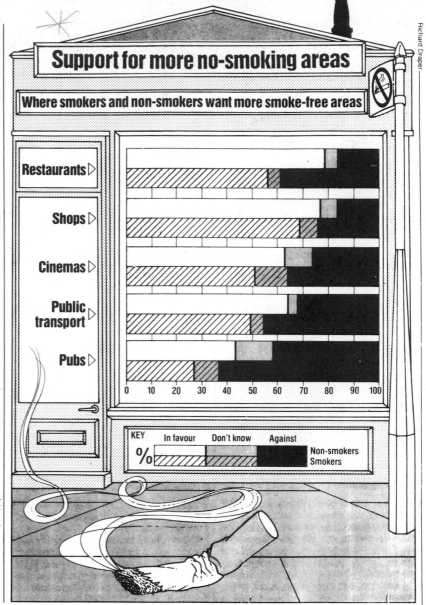

Paying for smoking

Smokers know their habit is expensive – for a typical smoker in his or her 20s, the lifelong cost of cigarettes will be around £20,000 (at today's prices). But it's virtually impossible to add up the cost of smoking to the country as a whole. For example:

● **Lost production** The cost in terms of working days lost of illness associated with smoking has been estimated at around £3,500 million a year. But this loss may well be creating jobs for people who would otherwise remain unemployed. And it's very difficult indeed to estimate what the effects on the economy would be if cigarettes ceased to exist. Cigarette sales earn the tobacco industry around £1,600 million a year: much of this money might be spent on other things if people no longer bought cigarettes, but some of it might go on imports, and some of it might simply be put into people's savings accounts.

● **National Health Service** People suffering from illnesses associated with smoking tie up over 4,000 hospital beds all the time, at a cost of £111 million a year. But, if everyone stopped smoking, there would eventually be more old people – and caring for them would probably impose extra costs on the NHS.

● **Social security** Payments to people suffering from smoking-related illnesses or disability – and to their dependants – cost around £600 million a year. But because so many people would live longer if smoking stopped, nearly £800 million a year might then be added to the old age pensions bill.

● **The taxman** The Government collects nearly £5,000 million a year in taxes on cigarettes. If there were no smoking, alternative sources of revenue would have to be found. But much of what people now spend on cigarettes would be spent on other things, which in turn provide tax revenue. It's hard to work out what tax changes might be needed.

● **Other costs** One additional cost arises through the **Common Agricultural Policy** where British consumers pay around £150 million a year in taxes to subsidise tobacco-growing in southern Europe. A second arises through **fires**. Those started by smoking or smokers' materials cause an estimated £100 million a year of damage, and account for four out of every ten people killed by fires. The disaster at the Bradford City football stadium is an example of a fire where careless smoking has been blamed.

It would be hard to argue from all this that smoking places a financial burden on the rest of society. But the savings made by the National Health Service and social security budgets which arise when smokers die early are hardly arguments in favour of smoking. And in all these calculations, the one factor on which it isn't possible to put a price is the most important of all – the suffering and death associated with smoking.

The trend against smoking

The Chart shows how the number of smokers has been falling since the early 1970s: now, just over a third of men smoke, just under a third of women. Our own surveys show:

● **Many smokers succeed in giving up . . .** Roughly a third of the people who had ever smoked regularly told us they had now given up.

● **Other smokers try to quit but fail . . .** Of those who've gone on smoking, about one in three have tried to give up but failed in the last two years. (This suggests that some of the people who told us they no longer smoked will take it up again.) Nearly half the rest have at least tried to cut down.

● **Many smokers want to quit . . .** Our surveys show that altogether three-quarters of adult smokers want to give up or cut down. People who smoke most also wish most they could give it up. Nearly two-thirds of the non-smokers who live with smokers have asked them to give up or cut down.

● **Most smokers wish they'd never started . . .** The most striking of our findings is that only one in 50 smokers told us that they were glad they'd started. Three-quarters said they wished they'd never started. In general, this feeling becomes stronger, the older the age group: two-thirds of those aged 16 to 24 said they wished they'd never started, but among 45 to 54 year olds, this proportion rose to nine out of ten.

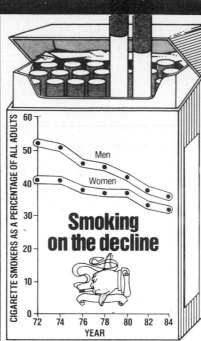

Smoking on the decline

CIGARETTE SMOKERS AS A PERCENTAGE OF ALL ADULTS

Men

Women

YEAR

Source: General Household Surveys. OPCS

Young smokers
Though fewer adults in general smoke now than in the past, this isn't so true of young adults. Other surveys have shown that it's adolescents and young people – particularly the less well educated, and those from poorer families – who are most likely to start smoking. And the eventual health risks are greatest for those who start smoking youngest.

If anything, the proportion of teenagers who smoke has recently been increasing slightly. About one in five children at secondary school now smoke. By the time they are 15 or 16, at least one in four have become regular smokers. After just a year of smoking children get more coughs and get out of breath more easily with moderate exercise.

Persuading children to resist pressures to start smoking can be difficult – particularly if parents smoke. At least, if you do smoke yourself, it's important to make it clear to your children that you hope they won't – and why you hope so: children whose parents condemn smoking run less risk of starting to smoke themselves. For schools there are now several excellent teaching packages which can help children resist pressures to start smoking.

But it's important to remember that sound logic about the long-term health risks and even about more immediate bad effects may not carry much weight with youngsters. Talk of lung cancer and heart attacks may seem far more remote to them than the common image which smoking has for older children – that it's fun, gives confidence, calms the nerves, and helps to keep girls slim.

Tips on how to give up

The best way of giving up depends on you. What you need most of all is a **conscious decision** that you're really going to give up, and to persevere with it. Work out in advance why you are giving up: be sure of your reasons, and stick to your plans.

Some ways to strengthen your determination include:

● **set a stop day** and stick to it; it may strengthen your will if you tell other people – National No-Smoking Day, 12 March 1986, is a good time

● **illness**, such as flu or a bad cold, is a good moment to stop

● **set a savings target** for the money you're not spending on cigarettes – a holiday, a clothes-buying spree, a video recorder, say; or sponsor a charity

● **think of the advantages** – you'll have a good chance of living longer, you'll probably feel better, and you'll be free of an expensive habit. Each time you're tempted, remember the average smoker dies five years younger. Some people find it useful to write the points which mean most to them on a card, and keep it with them

● **take more exercise**, jogging say, even just climbing stairs quickly or walking up escalators – at first it'll rub in how much smoking has harmed your lungs, and as time passes it'll emphasise your increasing fitness; if you are really unfit to start with, check with your doctor

before you launch into any real exertions

● **deep breathing** lessens the craving in some people

● **learn how to relax** – the commonest reason given by smokers for failing to give up is stress, worry or nerves; there are specific relaxation techniques which you can learn from books, tapes and courses

● **keep busy** – when your fingers fidget for a fag, have something else for them to do (even a pencil to fiddle with can be a big help for some); line up lots of things to do instead of smoking (one in eight smokers who tried to give up say they failed because they got bored)

● **change your eating habits** if you're used to a cigarette after eating, and have a positive plan for what to do in those after-eating minutes

● **avoid smoking situations** – work out if there are places or situations in which you smoke more, or even foods and drinks that you associate with smoking, and try to avoid them

● **don't accept cigarettes from friends** – even just one at a party might start you off again

● **avoid things which prompt smoking** – put away ashtrays and matches, try not to read magazines filled with smoking advertisements, and keep to no-smoking areas

● **pray** if you're religious

● **don't switch to a drink or a spicy**

snack for stimulation – they may make you want to smoke even more; in the early days after giving up many people find fruit juice seems to help.

Be ready for side-effects. Some people do get bored, depressed, irritable and so forth for a while after they stop smoking. And many people tend to put on weight when they stop smoking. Try to avoid monster meals and resist the temptation to nibble when you might otherwise have smoked. Remember that giving up smoking is the number one health priority – lick that first. Any weight problem generally disappears in a few months, anyway.

If you smoke most when you're worried, tense or upset, your vital task is to work out in advance how you'll cope with worries, tension and depression.

Don't be lulled into a false sense of security when you've given up. Remember that 'just the one' cigarette could – by starting you smoking again – undo all your good work.

Getting help
Stop smoking clinics give active support. Clinics and courses are not widespread. The best source of information about them is your local Health Education Unit (administered within your District Health Authority, whose number you'll find in the phone book) or Community Health Council.

What the community can do

On the national level, much effort has already gone into campaigns to discourage smoking. The Government has financed posters and advertising. Several TV programmes about smoking have had an impact. The Health Education Council campaigns hard against smoking. Many schools, with support from the Council, run don't-smoke programmes.

Independent organisations – such as ASH (Action on Smoking and Health, a pressure-group founded by the Royal College of Physicians and partly funded by the Government) and the doctors' organisation, the British Medical Association – have run their own vigorous campaigns. And, between 1962 and 1983, the Royal College of Physicians published four influential reports on smoking and health. As a result, some important progress has been made:
● TV cigarette advertising has been banned for the last 20 years
● the way cigarettes are presented in advertisements is subject to a voluntary code of practice, and cigarette packets carry a health warning on the side
● shopkeepers are liable to penalties if they sell cigarettes to children under 16, and cigarette machines are much less accessible to children than they were
● there is a growing number of no-smoking areas, particularly in public transport.

ASH has recently drawn up a checklist to help people trying to get no-smoking areas established. Called *Non-Smoking Provision in Public Places*, it's available free from ASH, 5-11 Mortimer St, London W1N 7RH. Please send a self-addressed A4 envelope.

But the campaigners point out that, each day, another 1,000 or so people (mainly young people) take up smoking regularly for the first time.

The British Medical Association argues that the main problem is the set of influences which lead people to think that cigarette smoking is a normal part of life. So they and other campaigners have pressed the Government hard for:
● a complete ban on cigarette advertising
● a ban on tobacco-industry sponsorship of sports, arts and other events
● a ban on the use of cigarette names and brand images on other products such as toys, clothes and holidays
● much tighter restrictions on smoking in public places.

Following up these recommendations would need a great deal of political courage. Quite apart from opposition from the tobacco industry itself, there is the question of the direct effect on sports, arts and the media.

Cigarette advertising supports magazines and newspapers to the extent

At its last World Congress, the International Organization of Consumers Unions – representing consumer organisations throughout the world, including Consumers' Association – launched a major campaign to halt tobacco advertising and sponsorship.

of around £56 million a year – a small part of their total income, but by no means negligible.

Tobacco companies provide around £8 million for sports sponsorship, and around £5 million for cultural events.

These sums of money are very small in relation to what is spent on cigarettes – and on taxes raised from them. But no-one can pretend that replacing this source of funds would be easy.

Even so, it's questionable whether the financial issue of support for sports and so forth should even be considered in the same balance as the pain and loss of life caused by smoking. We found in our most recent survey that only about one in four people think it right that cigarette firms should sponsor sports. About one in three think it wrong; most of the rest have no view.

We think that, in considering the call for a ban on cigarette promotion and for wider curbs on smoking in public places, the Government should recognise the over-riding importance of the health issue.

Otherwise, try your doctor or public library.

Doctors can be a great support. Let him or her know you're planning to give up, and ask for suggestions to keep you on the straight and narrow.

Nicotine chewing gum – the best known is Nicorette, available on prescription only, but not normally available on the NHS – is a real help to some of the smokers who have become dependent on nicotine, especially if used as part of a stop-smoking course by a clinic or by a GP. But it doesn't work well on its own – it won't replace your own commitment to giving up.

Acupuncture helps some people.

Hypnosis can be an aid for some.

Dummy cigarettes, sometimes with a mint flavour, may be useful.

Sucking sweets helps some people; maybe sugar-free peppermints or chewing gum, maybe something with more specific anti-smoking claims.

Tablets to make smoking taste foul work for some.

Tobacco bags which you suck – some have been sold as Skoal Bandits – have attracted widespread concern among medical experts and are **NOT RECOMMENDED**: chewing or sucking tobacco carries the risk of cancer of the mouth, and perhaps other gum and mouth disorders.

Half-way houses

Cutting down is nowhere near as good as giving up. But it's better than nothing, and best seen as a step towards giving up altogether.

Switching to a lower tar cigarette may be some help in reducing the risk of lung disease – if you are careful not to smoke more, or inhale more deeply, to compensate (which many people do). But again, it's not nearly so good as giving up altogether. Its greatest benefit may be as a deliberate step towards giving up (people smoking the lowest tar cigarettes seem to find it easiest to give up).

Stopping in easy stages may be worth trying. Most people find it easiest to stop completely right away, but if you know that doesn't work for you, try giving up for just one day, then another, then another; a variation is to cut down by a set amount each day over several weeks, perhaps ticking off the number you smoke day by day on a chart; yet another is to fix smoke-free zones (either times or places where you don't smoke), and gradually extend them.

Helping smokers give up

It may be counter-productive to nag your nearest and dearest to give up. But there are ways you can help:
● **sponsorship** will show your heart's in it too, and may make the smoker determined not to lose face

● **keeping out of danger** is something you can help with – avoiding the people and places that encourage smoking
● **keep the smoker occupied**: don't let boredom creep in
● **make giving up a team effort** if you smoke too: mutual help is a great support. As a minimum, if someone in your home is trying to give up, try to avoid smoking in their presence
● **children** can be very effective in persuading their parents to give up – and if they do so are unlikely to start themselves.

The End

49

Gathering and Organising Ideas

You have seen how persuasive writing and speeches can be organised. You have seen some of the techniques used. Now you are ready to begin gathering ideas for a piece of persuasive writing for your assignment. The example below covers the topic of young people's health – you should use the activities in the example with a persuasive topic of your own choice. Some ideas for assignments are given on page 51.

1. With a partner

Take a few minutes to think of any points which relate to the health of young people. Try for a quick flow of ideas and don't worry at this stage whether or not the ideas are good – the aim is to have plenty to select from at a later stage. Jot down the ideas as they occur to you, using key words to jog your memory.

This method of gathering ideas is sometimes known as **brainstorming.**

If you are stuck, you might ask questions beginning with
WHO?   (for example: who are the different people and groups of people involved in the health of the young?)

WHAT?   (for example: what habits/life styles seem beneficial to health?)

WHICH?   (for example: which habits cause poor health?)

WHY?   (for example: why might you want to improve your health?
Why do you think that people do things which injure health?
Why is health important?)

Asking WHEN? and WHERE? questions can also be useful.

2. Stage two is the selection of ideas which seem relevant to the piece of writing you have in mind. Cross out the ideas which seem unimportant.

3. Next, try to find connections between the ideas you have left. Circle them and draw connecting lines and arrows between ideas which could be linked and/or developed in the same paragraph. By now your page might look something like this.

4. Fourthly, you could number the ideas according to where you want them to occur in the writing. Places where you need further examples, facts, or illustrations can also be marked.

Sources of information

These are suggestions for sources of information for your assignment. Can you think of other useful sources?

Use *your own experience*.
Talk to people about the issue.
Skim through lists of *television* and *radio* programmes to see if there is anything related to the issue.
Do the same with local and national *newspapers*.
See whether your school library has hobby or specialist *magazines* on the topic you have chosen.
Find relevant public information *leaflets* in post offices, libraries and schools.
Consult the *subject catalogue* in the library.
Consider your other *GCSE subjects*. For example, information from Biology or Home Economics may be relevant to an assignment on health.

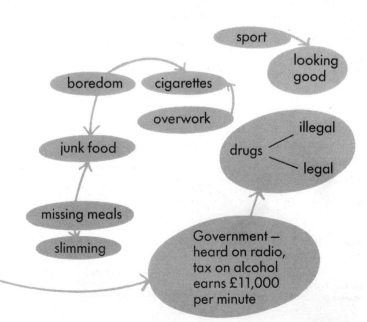

Considering students' work

A group of fifth years chose the following assignment on persuasive writing:

Topic: Dangers to health

Write an article for your school magazine to persuade readers to think more carefully of the dangers of smoking

OR drinking

OR another activity which can endanger health.

You should aim to make your readers aware of the dangers, without antagonising those who may smoke, drink alcohol, etc.

The *Which?* report on smoking was part of the material available for research. Here are the openings to two of the articles.

With a partner

- Read the openings aloud.
- Which would you prefer to continue reading? Give reasons for your choice.
- How well did the writers adapt the information in the *Which?* report for readers of the school magazine?
- What advice would you give to the writers?
- There are 3 spelling mistakes. Can you find them?

When did you last see your doctor smoking? It must have been a long time ago. Perhaps you haven't seen your doctor at all recently. That's a pity, because it is people of are generation who need to to be more aware of the dangers of cigerettes. A quarter of all fifteen and sixteen year olds have tried the habit. You are likely to have freinds who smoke, or smoke yourself, so let me give you a picture of the young smoker, inside and out.

Outside, the young smoker may look well, and some say it helps them to diet. Without even looking into the smoker's lungs, though, anyone can tell that smokers get out of breath in games and exercise, even after just one year of cigerettes.

Smoking is one of the severest problems of our day, a sad fact considering that resulting health problems could and should be preventable. In the first half of the twentieth century, advertisers encouraged people to smoke — it was a socially acceptable way to behave. Now that generation is paying the price in coronary heart disease and chronic lung disorders.

Compared with alcohol, smoking is the greater of two evils. It is the single main cause of lung cancer, a contributary factor in cardio vascular disorders — in addition the smoker will suffer chronic bronchitis, emphysema and other acute breathing problems.

Current research shows that the pollutants a smoker exhales are almost as injurious to health as active smoking when inhaled by non smokers.

The next steps

Below are comments from a teacher on the two openings you have read. Do you agree with the teacher's comments? Why or why not? How do they differ from your own?

Comments

OPENING ONE: the first writer addresses the reader directly (*You …*) and picks information to suit readers of his own age. The opening question gets the reader's attention. There are two spelling mistakes – *are* should be *our* in this context; *cigerettes* should be *cigarettes*, and the spelling mistake occurs twice, making a total of 3 errors.

OPENING TWO: the second writer has a mature vocabulary and makes no technical mistakes, but the article seems more suited to a medical journal than a school magazine. The writer tends to lift whole sentences out of the *Which?* report, rather than re-shaping the material for a new audience and purpose.

Assignment:

Persuasive Writing

Suggestions for assignments

1.   Write an article for your school magazine to persuade readers to share your views on one of the issues listed below.
2.   Design and write a pamphlet for either:
– pupils in your school
– users of the local library
– or another group of people of your choice
to persuade readers to share your views on one of the issues below.
3.   Write a letter to your local newspaper giving your views on an issue dealt with in its pages.
4.   Write a letter to a national newspaper giving your views on an issue dealt with in its pages.

5. Write a letter to either a radio or television station in support of the kind of programmes you would like to see broadcast more often.

6. A persuasive essay with the title:
'What I'd do about ...'

Giving up smoking

Under age drinking

The drugs problem

Legal age limits for young people

Leaving home

Graffiti – self expression or vandalism?

Rewards and punishments in school – do they work and are they fair?

Competition at school

Competition at work

Prejudice

Hooliganism in sport

Apartheid and sport

How important is pollution?

Nuclear arms

Everything in moderation is a fair rule for health

Taking up exercise

Junk food

Health food – common sense or a passing fad?

Should girls have the same education as boys?

Should sport and politics be kept apart?

Reviewing your work

Speaking: role play

Did you
● Select the right information?
● Organise your views so that your audience could follow them?
● Choose a style suited to the situation?
● Ask and answer questions? Listen to others?
● Could you be heard by your listeners?

Which of these do you think are your strengths?
Which would you like to improve?

Writing: persuasion

Did you
● Pick an assignment that was right for you and choose appropriate material for your research?
● Organise your ideas at the planning stage?
● Spend enough, or too much, time on preparation?
● Write in a style to suit your readers?
● Make clear when you were stating facts and when giving opinions?
● Use paragraphs and sentences?
● Check your work for spelling?

Which of these do you think are your strengths?
Which would you like to improve?

Unit 4 News: Television, Radio, Print

Aims: to see how news is selected and shaped, to create news items yourself for your assignment.

On the way: the activities include:
- considering ways that you learn about news
- organising a schedule for a news bulletin
- comparing the content and style of *John Craven's Newsround* and *News at 5.45*
- choosing headlines and captions for photographs
- following some ways that a news article can be developed
- commenting on newspaper articles for young people
- planning work on your own and in a group
- reading and commenting on a radio interview.

By the end: you will have looked closely at the ways news is presented. This will add to your understanding of written and spoken English and lead to a new type of assignment for your coursework folder. From now on you should have a better understanding of news in print, on radio and television.

Assignments include: presenting news and features in different ways for different groups of people.

MONDAY, MARCH 30, 1987

MANCHESTER AND LONDON 25p

No. 40,982.

Monday March 30 1987 TV: Page 20 *** 22p

Printed in London, Manchester and Portsmouth

Monday March 30 1987 25p

MONDAY, MARCH 30, 1987 20p

84234/163701 30p

Incorporating the Daily Worker – for Peace and Socialism

Thursday January 21 1988

Take a share in the Star

THURSDAY FEBRUARY 11 1988

TIMES

NEWSPAPER OF THE YEAR

THE INDEPENDENT

A News Schedule

A schedule is a list of things to be covered.

Activity

1. The following list of news items from one day was collected by a group of GCSE students. It formed part of their work in progress for a news programme to be recorded on tape, as if for a radio broadcast.

2. The list includes:

The HEADLINE – the news item summarised in a few words – in capital letters.
An OUTLINE – a brief outline of each story in brackets following the headline.

3. What to do

a) Pick out the items you would like to see in a news broadcast for people of your age.
b) Now select the items you would include in an existing news programme on radio or television, broadcast after 9 p.m. and intended for a general adult audience.
c) Which items would you include in a television news programme in the early evening, intended for viewers aged 12 and under?

Questions on what you did

What differences are there between your selections at a), b) and c)? Give reasons for the differences and similarities in your choices.

4. Group work

● In a group, select items from the following list for a television news programme for people of your age
OR adults
OR children.
● The programme must not last longer than 5 minutes.
● Place the items in the order they will appear in the programme.
● Decide how long you would give to each item.
● Give reasons for
a) your choice of news items
b) the order in which you placed them
c) the amount of time you gave to each.

5. Option

How would you present each item? For example, would you use outside broadcast, still photographs, several newsreaders, or one? Would you use graphs and diagrams? Would you include an interview with an expert and/or an eye-witness account?

To do this, make out a chart like the one below and fill it in.

ITEM	TIME	PRESENTATION/ DESCRIPTION	COMMENTS
Manchester air disaster	1½ minutes 1) 30 seconds 2) 1 minute	– presenter introduces story – eye-witness account by a survivor	

When you have completed the news schedule section:

● You will have learned something about **selection** in the news – not everything that happens makes the news.
● You will have learned more about speaking and writing for a particular **audience** by picking different news items for different groups of people.
● You will be able to use this for your news assignment later in the unit.

Items to choose from for your news schedule activity

BULLETIN (fill in the title of broadcast) ....
DAY: Wednesday (add date of broadcast) ....
NEWS ITEMS:

EXPLOSION IN PARIS
(A bomb exploded in the centre of Paris, killing four and injuring many others. There is a possible link with four previous explosions, part of a terrorist bombing campaign in the capital city.)

DEATH OF ACTRESS
(Pat Phoenix, who played Elsie Tanner in the long-running soap opera *Coronation Street,* died in her sleep this morning.)

CHOIR SINGS IN STATION
(The choir of Ely Cathedral sang in Liverpool Street Station in London today to raise money for repairs to the Cathedral.)

SOUTH AFRICAN MINE DISASTER
(Poison gas and a fire at a South African gold mine have killed 177 workers.)

USA EXPELS 25 RUSSIANS
(The American Government sent home 25 Russian members of staff of the United Nations who are based in New York, following the imprisonment of an American journalist in Russia on charges of spying.)

PRIME MINISTER VISITS GERMANY
(Mrs Thatcher is paying a visit to the German Government to inspect military manoeuvres of joint Anglo-German forces. The two armies are co-operating in NATO exercises. As part of her tour, Mrs Thatcher rode a tank on a mock battlefield.)

Margaret Thatcher on a British tank during Nato exercises in West Germany.

ROAD SAFETY CAMPAIGN
(A new campaign encourages children to help parents avoid careless driving. The campaign material features a cartoon character and a video game, both for use in schools.)

INQUEST ON MANCHESTER AIR DISASTER
(Investigations into the causes of the disaster continue. A fire in an aeroplane due to take off from Manchester Airport killed nearly all of the holiday-makers in the aircraft before the fire could be put out.)

Manchester air disaster, August 1985.

13 SETS OF TWINS AT ONE SCHOOL
(A record number of twins can be found at one Gloucester secondary school. The *Guinness Book of Records* reports that this is a record for Britain. A much larger school in America has 15 sets of twins.)

INCREASE IN DRUG SMUGGLING
(Customs Officers report that more hard drugs are being smuggled into airports and sea ports in Britain.)

SDP CONFERENCE
(At Harrogate, Dr David Owen revealed plans to reform the tax system to benefit low income groups.)

Comparing adults' and children's programmes

You are now asked to look in more detail at the way news items are presented for viewers of different ages.

There is a warm up activity first – it leads into the main activity.

Don't miss out the warm up because it helps you to focus on the ways we change words to suit the listeners. You will learn how different words are used for different audiences.

Warm up activity

● **FIRST**
Think of an accident, injury or mishap which happened to you or to someone you know – it doesn't have to be anything serious that might make the headlines, but it should be something that you don't mind talking about.

● **THEN, WITH A PARTNER**
1. Tell your partner what happened as you would to any friend of your own age.
Listen while your partner does the same.
2. Your partner is now a doctor – explain your accident to the doctor.
Listen while your partner does the same.

● **WHAT CHANGES DID YOU MAKE**
– in the things you included or left out?
– in the way you said it, your style and language?
– in the order of your account, what you put first, next and last?

● **OPTION**
Describe the accident to your partner as you would to a small child.
Listen while your partner does the same.
What changes did you make this time?

Activity: reading and making notes

A GCSE class made video-recordings, on the same evening, of *John Craven's Newsround*, a news programme on children's television, and *News at 5.45*. Small groups made written versions of these programmes, of what was said and how the items were presented. Their scripts follow.
1. Pick an item that was included in both *John Craven's Newsround* and *News at 5.45*.
2. Make notes on the differences you can see between the two treatments of the item in terms of
content – the actual items in the programme and the information given about them.
language – the words and phrases used in the broadcast; the 'level' of the language.
presentation – the way the material is presented e.g. use of graphics – photographs, charts, diagrams, maps; use of film specially shot for the news item.

style – the overall approach taken by the programme, the 'tone' of the broadcast – is it chatty or serious, long-winded or snappy, aggressive or laid-back? Is the approach aimed at the type of audience who would read *The Mirror* or *The Times?*

3.   Now consider the whole scripts of *John Craven's Newsround* and *News at 5.45*. What differences and similarities in treatment do you notice in terms of CONTENT, LANGUAGE, PRESENTATION and STYLE?

4.   How would you account for the differences?

Option

Watch different News programmes, such as those for local and national audiences, or those for adult and younger audiences. Make notes on the similarities and differences between the programmes. Use the above categories – content, language, presentation and style – to help you to make these notes. Report your findings to the class.

How does this help?

●   This unit began by asking you to select news items – you have now learned something more about CONTENT.

●   By comparing news programmes, you are learning how LANGUAGE, PRESENTATION and STYLE are shaped to fit different audiences.

●   You can use this in your news assignment later in the unit by selecting and shaping material to fit the audience that **you** have in mind.

John Craven's Newsround 5.00 – 5.05 p.m.

Presenter – John Craven

PRESENTER: Hello again. 'Think road safety for life.' That's the slogan of a major new campaign. Government has teamed with big business to stamp out the carelessness that causes so many deaths on the roads. The message of the two million project is: 'Think road safety for life.' It'll go out to 20,000 schools. A big insurance company is paying for the campaign.

The Transport Minister, Peter Bottomley, said that children could help in cars by keeping their parents on the right track.

(FILM OF TRAFFIC.)

Debbie Thrower reports.

(REPORTER FILMED AGAINST BACKGROUND OF TRAFFIC.)

REPORTER: The man they call 'Road' may have a white line for a nose (PICTURE OF CARTOON CHARACTER ON SCREEN, WITH REPORTER'S VOICE OVER.)

'Road'

… but it's hoped people will listen more readily when it comes to heeding advice. Four out of five road accidents are caused simply by carelessness. (FILM OF PAGES OF CARTOON BOOK FEATURING 'ROAD'. WITH PRESENTER'S VOICE OVER.) But now, thanks to a book, full of hints for survival, the cartoon character 'Road' hopes to teach children what their parents ought to know but often don't. There's also a road safety video game, soon to be played in schools.

(EXTRACT FROM ROAD SAFETY VIDEO.)

VOICE ON ROAD SAFETY VIDEO: Hi! Welcome to the Road Show, a brand new game that gives you the chance to make decisions that could save life.

(REPORTER'S VOICE OVER BACKGROUND OF FAMILIES WALKING DOWN A BUSY STREET.)

REPORTER: There'll be a poster competition in 20,000 schools and a hunt to find the family with the best road safety knowledge.

****

PRESENTER: In South Africa, they're counting the cost today of the country's worst ever gold mining disaster. One hundred and seventy-seven workers are now known to have died in a fire 2,000 metres underground. More than two hundred others are in hospital. (SIMPLE OUTLINE MAP OF SOUTH AFRICA, SHOWING POSITION OF JOHANNESBURG AND EVANDER, THE TOWN NEAREST TO THE DISASTER. PRESENTER'S VOICE OVER.)

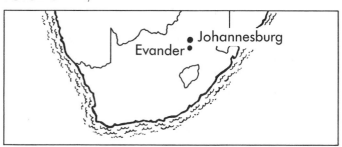

It happened in a mine at Evander, sixty miles south of Johannesburg. (DIAGRAM OF TWO LIFT SHAFTS IN THE MINE.)

In a passage between two lift shafts, a mistake with a burning torch set light to special foam covering the walls. A cloud of poisonous gas spread within minutes.

From the scene, Michael Burke reports.

(FILM OF REPORTER AGAINST BACKGROUND OF RESCUE OPERATIONS AT THE PIT HEAD).

REPORTER: The rescue teams were still working more than a mile under the pit head when dawn broke over the mine. By then they'd cleared through most of the two levels flooded by poison gas. Ambulances were kept waiting but the urgency had gone. Only a dozen or so miners had still to be found. There was no expectation now of discovering them alive. The poison gas had spread over several square miles.

****

PRESENTER: Reports are coming in of an exploision in the French capital, Paris. Several people are said to have been killed and about forty others injured. The explosion happened near a clothing shop in the Montparnasse area of the city. (SIMPLE OUTLINE MAP OF FRANCE, SHOWING ENGLISH COAST AND POSITION OF PARIS. PRESENTER'S VOICE OVER.)

It is not yet known whether the explosion was caused by a bomb. There have been four terrorist attacks in Paris over the last ten days, but police don't yet know whether today's incident is linked to these.

****

(ITEM ON SOUTHEND PIER.)

****

(PRESENTER AGAINST BACKGROUND PHOTOGRAPH OF PAT PHOENIX.)

Pat Phoenix

PRESENTER: Many tributes have been paid to the actress Pat Phoenix, who died today from cancer at the age of sixty-two. She made her first broadcast at age eleven for the BBC Children's Service. She became world famous for playing Elsie Tanner in the long-running ITV series, *Coronation Street*. (CLIP OF FIRST EPISODE OF *CORONATION STREET* WITHOUT SOUND. PRESENTER'S VOICE OVER MOVING PICTURES.) She appeared in this first episode in 1960 and became the show's greatest star. Twice a week, millions of fans tuned in to watch her. (CLIP OF LAST EPISODE IN WHICH PAT PHOENIX APPEARED, WITHOUT SOUND. PRESENTER'S VOICE OVER MOVING PICTURES.) She left in 1984. Viewers were told that Elsie Tanner had gone to live in Portugal. Pat went on to play other parts on stage and television, but she will always be remembered as Elsie Tanner.

****

(ITEM ON ELY CATHEDRAL.)

****

(ITEM ON TWINS AT A GLOUCESTER SCHOOL.)

(PROGRAMME ENDS WITH A VISUAL JOKE ABOUT SEEING DOUBLE – THE SCREEN IS SPLIT INTO TWO, AND JOHN CRAVEN IS SHOWN IN BOTH HALVES OF THE SCREEN, AS IF HE WERE TWINS.)

Opening to *News at 5.45* on the same day

NEWS READER: America has expelled twenty-five UN Soviet staff – the Administration denies it's retaliation for Daniloff.

America has this afternoon ordered out twenty-five Russian diplomats who work for the Soviet UN delegation in New York, but they say it has nothing to do with the expulsion of reporter Nicholas Daniloff on charges of espionage. The twenty-five members of the UN Russian delegation had been given until the end of the month to leave. Both Mr Daniloff and a Soviet scientist charged with spying were released from prison into the charge of their ambassadors in a bid to save the superpower summit.

Tim Ewart, in Washington, reports.

(REPORTER AGAINST BACKGROUND OF GOVERNMENT BUILDINGS IN WASHINGTON.)

REPORTER: The size of the Soviet UN delegation has long been a bone of contention with American Government officials, who claim that many of the representatives are spies, but as the announcement coincides with the arrival here of the Soviet Foreign Minister, the expulsion has been interpreted as increased pressure for the release of American journalist, Nicholas Daniloff, who has been charged with spying in Russia. Official spokesmen deny any direct link, but there are reported anxieties about the damage being caused by the Daniloff affair to negotiations for the proposed summit.

(SPOKESMAN FOR THE AMERICAN STATE DEPARTMENT AT A NEWS CONFERENCE IN WASHINGTON.)

SPOKESMAN FOR THE STATE DEPARTMENT: The longer the case festers, the greater the potential damage to US-Soviet relations.

(SPOKESMAN FOR THE WHITE HOUSE AT A NEWS CONFERENCE IN WASHINGTON.)

SPOKESMAN FOR THE WHITE HOUSE: The President wishes to emphasise, however, that Soviet treatment of Daniloff continues to limit severely what is achievable in bilateral relations between the two countries.

(REPORTER IN FRONT OF THE WHITE HOUSE.)

REPORTER: Reagan's position in dealing with the Russians is becoming increasingly difficult: leniency may lose him conservative support at home; if he gets tough, he puts the summit at risk.

This is Tim Ewart, in Washington, reporting.

****

NEWS READER: Within the last hour, another bomb has gone off in Paris, this time killing at least four people and injuring over forty others. The bomb – the fifth in ten days – was left on the pavement outside a clothes shop in the Montparnasse district. (STREET MAP OF MONTPARNASSE AREA OF PARIS. NEWS READER'S VOICE OVER.) The four other bombs which have exploded in the city since September the eighth have killed three and injured more than one hundred.

Paris, September 17, 1986 – aftermath of bomb explosion outside a clothing shop in the Montparnasse district.

(CHANGE TO PHOTOGRAPH OF SUSPECTED TERRORIST LEADER. NEWS READER'S VOICE OVER.)

All have been claimed by groups demanding the release of the suspected head of a terrorist organisation serving a four-year term of imprisonment in France on charges of possessing fire arms and false documents.

****

NEWS READER: Today, Pat Phoenix, who captured millions of viewers' hearts as Elsie Tanner of *Coronation Street*, lost her battle against lung cancer. "Her death was peaceful and completely pain-free", said a hospital spokesman. Her husband, Tony Booth, married to Miss Phoenix only last week, was at her bedside as tributes poured in …

A scene from *Coronation Street* – Elsie Tanner (Pat Phoenix) and Mike Baldwin (Johnny Briggs).

(ITEM OF MORE THAN FIVE MINUTES COVERING:)

Brief interviews with fellow-stars of *Coronation Street*.

Tribute from her theatrical agent.

Distraught fans crying outside the Manchester hospital where Miss Phoenix died.

Reporter pictured outside the hospital.

Library film of Miss Phoenix's marriages, with comments on a former husband's 'struggle against alcoholism'.

Library film of her meeting with former Prime Minister, Harold Wilson, with comments that Elsie Tanner was one of the 'sexiest women on television'.

Clips from an early episode of *Coronation Street* in which Elsie Tanner answered charges that she was 'living in sin'.

Clips from Pat Phoenix's last television role in *Hidden Truths,* a television play not yet screened, in which she played a dying woman.

Viewers were told that a special programme of tribute to Pat Phoenix would replace an advertised programme that night.

****

NEWS READER: Union leaders in South Africa have blamed bad safety standards for the gold mining disaster in which one hundred and seventy-seven workers were killed …

****

(ITEM ON SHOOTING IN BELFAST.)

****

(ITEM ON SDP CONFERENCE.)

(ITEM ON BANNED RUGBY PLAYER.)

****

(ITEM ON MRS THATCHER'S VISIT TO GERMANY.)

****

(FIRST PICTURES OF THE BOMBING FROM PARIS.)

****

(WEATHER, WITH PHOTOGRAPH OF A COUNTRY SCENE.)

****

Considering Ways that News is Broadcast

Television is not the only way that news is broadcast or disseminated. Some of the other ways include:

– national newspapers
– local newspapers
– national radio news
– local radio news
– talking with people you know.

Activity

1.   With a partner think of two items which have interested you in this week's news.
2.   How did you find out about them?
3.   Make a list of the ways in which you learn about news – name the specific programmes or newspapers if you can.
4.   As a class:
Report back to the class with your list, then decide on any advantages and disadvantages of presenting news in different ways.

How this helps

Your news assignment on p.64 asks you to present news in different ways. You can use your class list to help you to decide which way of presenting the news is most suitable for you and your audience.

Photographs and News

Options for assignments in this unit include writing your own newspaper articles – photographs can be a helpful way of getting started. The next activity shows you how to build a written article from a photograph.

Activity

1. Choosing a photograph

a) Choose one of the three photographs opposite.
b) Pick a caption for it or invent your own.

Questions

i) What aspect of the photograph does your caption emphasise?
ii) Does your caption give an opinion or a point of view?

CAPTION 1: Waste of potential – four young job-seekers after a tiring day looking for work.

CAPTION 2: Layabout city.

CAPTION 3: Young people in Wolverhampton, an area of high unemployment in the 1980's.

PHOTO 1

CAPTION 1: Police keep order as disgruntled protesters threaten the peace of the countryside.

CAPTION 2: Well-organised marchers do not rise to the bait of a heavy police presence.

CAPTION 3: The People's March for Jobs from Liverpool to London 1981.

PHOTO 2

PHOTO 3

CAPTION 1: The installation of robots has improved productivity and given precision that humans cannot match.

CAPTION 2: Job robbers – robots throw 400 car workers out of work.

CAPTION 3: Industrial robots perform the welding on an assembly line.

2. Building an article, stage by stage

By inventing details or researching them.

i) Give a HEADLINE to an article to go with your picture and caption.
ii) List the MAIN POINTS for your article.
iii) Add any MINOR POINTS.
iv) Add EXAMPLES to support your points.
v) Add any QUOTATIONS from people interviewed, experts on the subject, participants, eye witnesses.
iv) Decide on the best ORDER for these sections of your article.
vii) Now concentrate on the WORDING and phrasing of each paragraph in turn.

3. Group work

Join others who have chosen the same photograph and form a small group. Read out the articles. Compare and contrast the ways you have interpreted the photograph.

Uses

● You have learned to build an article from a photograph. You could choose an existing photograph or take a photograph yourself. You could then build an article from it as a way of achieving the aim in this unit – a news assignment for your coursework folder.

● Part of your aim in this unit is to get a better understanding of how news is selected and shaped. You can now look more critically at newspaper articles with photographs and ask yourself whether the words or the photograph came first and what contribution the picture makes to the article.

How a Feature Article is Built Up

As well as topical (day-to-day) news, many newspapers include features or special investigations. The article opposite is an example. Features have a more general interest over a longer peiod of time.

Activity

For this activity you will need a page of a newspaper. To help you to understand how a feature article is built up. An example is given opposite.

1. Read the example on the following page. It consists of an article and notes by the side.
2. Copy the labels below onto a sheet of paper and use them to analyse a newspaper article of your choice. Add a comment each time you use a label to show why the label applies to that part of the article.

HEADLINE

MAIN POINT

MINOR POINT

QUESTION

EXAMPLE

CONCLUSION

A further use

● You can use these labels as a checklist when writing articles of your own.

Activity

Here are some headlines from feature articles which appeared in newspapers published on March 14, 1988.

1. Choose two of the headlines.
2. For each headline:
a) Think of an article which might follow the headline.
b) Write a small headline or sub-headline which summarises the main point of the article.
c) Write a short paragraph which provides a specific example of the main point of the article.
(You may like to turn to the end of the book for a summary of what actually appeared under these headlines.)

Rich drive out young

The Fabulous Forties

Hot rock and the power it could deliver

Putting messages across without getting burned

Mountains of mystery

Russia poised to 'invade' Chunnel

Nice ad, shame about the product

Some TV commercials are better than the programmes. But do the watching millions get the message?

A PRETTY young woman in search of some routine banking service finds herself trapped in a nightmare of impenetrable robots.

Finally she emerges into the calm blue reassurance of Barclay's Bank. Relief is at hand.

It's an advertisement that has been made with all the skill of a first class feature film — which is not surprising, considering that it was created by Ridley Scott, director of Bladerunner and Alien.

In the early days of television, commercial breaks were the cue to leave the living-room to make a cup of Bovril before the resumption of, say, Take Your Pick or the Army Game.

Nowadays, the commercials are so slick that they are more arresting than most programmes.

But has the commercial message been drowned by the wave of images?

Advertising chief David Bernstein recalls the time he was on an awards panel and the international experts gasped in awe at several commercial concepts. Later, when they were asked the products's names, several responded with blank expressions. Nothing had registered.

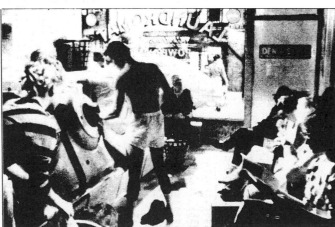

A SIZZLING SUCCESS: this Levi 501 ad won praise for director Roger Lyons

---

A Young Reader's Page

Activity

Opposite is a weekly page for young people from a national newspaper. Some of the writers are still at school — their work has been edited and set out by the staff on the newspaper.

1. Decide what should fill the three gaps in the *Young Guardian* page. An article or feature — on what? A photograph? An advertisement? Give reasons for your choices.

2. Divide the work between you and write the articles or describe the photographs.

The work for this activity could form the basis for your assignment on NEWS in the list on p. 64.

Why the lab test is a failure

GEORGINA FERRY on why girls dislike schools science

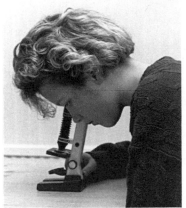
Eyes down — prospects not very clear

DESPITE all the effort to establish equal opportunities for men and women, in one of the top disciplines men are still overwhelmingly in the majority — science.

There are exceptions. Last month, Rita Levi-Montalcini won the Nobel Prize for physiology, for her discovery of chemicals in the body that influence growing nerve cells.

Another scientist who's had to fight authority is Alice Stewart of Birmingham University. In the 1950s, she showed that giving X-rays to pregnant mothers increased the risk that their children would develop cancer. No one believed her at first — now pregnant women are hardly ever X-rayed. At 80, she studies the effects of radiation from nuclear power stations; she's just been giving evidence the public in-

quiry into the nuclear reprocessing plant at Dounreay in Scotland.

But women like these are unusual. There are all sorts of reasons why it's more difficult for a woman to keep a scientific career going than it is for a man, but the problems start long before that. More girls than boys just give up science, especially physics and chemistry, as soon as they can.

There is no evidence worth talking about that boys are any better at science than girls, despite Bill Oddie's comments in Input.

There is, however, a great deal of evidence that the expectations of parents, teachers, and the students themselves differ. Accord-

ing to one survey, boys and girls find physics equally difficult. But boys are more likely to keep on with it because, they say, they want a technical career like engineering. Girls, on the other hand, see no link between the physics they encounter in school and the real-life problems they think are important.

In addition, girls are bombarded with subtle and not so subtle hints that undermine their confidence and persuade them that science and technology are "boys' subjects." In their early teens, many girls are preoccupied with establishing their femininity. They don't want to make choices that don't fit in with the feminine image

Imaginative teaching can help girls to take a more positive view of science, and many teachers and organisations have run successful projects to that end. Girls are choosing science in larger numbers, though they're still outnumbered by boys in physics and chemistry. But why does it matter whether girls do science or not?

It matters to girls. In a technical world it pays to be technically competent, whether or not you want to be a scientist. If you do eventually decide on a scientific career, no physics could mean no job, even in a mainly biological area. It matters to Britain, because whatever the unemployment figures may suggest,

British industry is desperately short of technically trained people at every level.

And it matters to society. While it's very hard to find evidence that more women would make science better, or even different — there aren't enough of them yet to test the idea — it's equally hard to believe that the interests of all society are best served by a science that's almost entirely controlled by its male representatives.

For more information: the Equal Opportunities Commission, Overseas House, Quay Street, Manchester 3; the Association for Science Education, College Lane, Hatfield, Herts AL10, 9AA; the Women's Engineering Society, 25 Foubert's Place, London W1V 2AL.

From Yops to the tops

SAMANTHA NORMAN on the rise of a football star

MITCHELL THOMAS was 16 when he signed on under the Youth Opportunities Schemes — to be a footballer for First Division Luton Town. Admittedly, he was only an apprentice, but now, still only 22, his pay has risen from his YOP's £50 a week to £50,000 a year. He is in the full England squad. And when manager David Pleat moved from Luton to the hot seat at Tottenham Hotspur, he took Mitchell with him, for a signing-on fee of £250,000.

Despite his move to Spurs, Mitchell still lives in Luton. " Well, I was born and brought up here," he says. His Jamaican-born mum and dad live just around the corner. He went to Lea Manor High School where he learnt a passion for football but little else. " Let's say I was easily distracted in lessons. After a few clips round the ear and the threat that they wouldn't let me play football if I didn't behave, I settled down. I got a lot of encouragement from my games teacher, Peter Clark. My parents aren't really interested in football; they're not bothered as long as I keep myself out of trouble."

He left school at 16 and was spotted by John Moore — now Luton's manager but then one of their scouts — who offered him a place as a YOPs (now Youth Training Scheme) apprentice. " On YOPs you get less time to prove yourself. An ordinary apprentice gets about two years. We only had six months." After only three months Luton made him an official apprentice. " I knew I had a long way to go before they signed me as a professional, so I kept working hard."

His is a marvellous success story but Micky Burns, education officer for the Footballers' Further Education and Training Society Ltd, is quick to point out that the Mitchell Thomas's are few and far between. " It's a very precarious career and a large proportion of kids drop out through injury. Mitchell was one of about 600 very talented youngsters on YOPs that year. Very few kids actually make it."

Mitchell Thomas in Tottenham strip — I kept working hard

How do you feel about unfairness at school?

CELIA KITZINGER is writing a book about how young people deal with injustice at school. She wants to hear from Young Guardian readers: especially those who have successfully protested about something unfair at school.

● Can you think of something unfair that happened at your school ? Please describe it. Why was it unfair ?

● How did you feel about it ?

● What did you do about it ?

● Looking back, what do you think you should have done ? If it happened again, what would you do ?

Over a thousand young people have already answered these questions, most writing about the commonplace, everyday aspects of school life

Please write to: Dr Celia Kitzinger, School of Education, 21 Unviersity Road, University of Leicester, Leicester LE1 7RF.

The Hit List

TOP TWENTY SINGLES

1	(7)	Take My Breath Away	Berlin
2	(1)	Every Loser Wins	Nick Berry
3	(2)	In The Army Now	Status Quo
4	(4)	Walk Like An Egyptian	Bangles
5	(3)	All I Ask Of You	Cliff Richard and Sarah Brightman
6	(15)	You Keep Me Hangin' On	Kim Wilde
7	(14)	Notorious	Duran Duran
8	(24)	Showing Out	Mel and Kim
9	(18)	Midas touch	Midnight Star
10	(10)	Don't Get Me Wrong	The Pretenders
11	(5)	True Blue	Madonna
12	(26)	Something Outa Nothing	Letitia Dean and Paul Medford
13	(6)	You Can Call Me Al	Paul Simon
14	(16)	Ask	The Smiths
15	(27)	Livin' On A Prayer	Bon Jovi
16	(11)	Don't Give Up	Peter Gabriel and Kate Bush
17	(36)	Breakout	Swing Out Sister
18	(9)	Suburbia	Pet Shops Boys
19	(12)	True Colours	Cyndi Lauper
20	(new)	Through The Barricades	Spandau Ballet

TOP TWENTY ALBUM

1	(new)	Every Breath You Take	The Police
2	(1)	Graceland	Paul Simon
3	(new)	Now Dance 2	Various
4	(2)	True Blue	Madonna
5	(3)	Silk and Steel	Five Star
6	(8)	Original Soundtrack of Top Gun	Various
7	(6)	Scoundrel Days	A-ha
8	(9)	Whiplash Smile	Billy Idol
9	(10)	Revenge	Eurythmics
10	(11)	Get Close	The Pretenders
11	(new)	No. 10 Upping Street	Big Audio Dynamite
12	(5)	Liverpool	Frankie Goes To Hollywood
13	(4)	Between Two Fires	Paul Young
14	(7)	The Chart	Various
15	(16)	Fore !	Huey Lewis and The News
16	(new)	Dreamtime	The Stranglers
17	(22)	A Kind Of Magic	Queen
18	(12)	London O Hull 4	The Housemartins
19	(29)	Reminiscing	Foster & Allen
20	(32)	Slippery When Wet	Bon Jovi

Compiled by Gallup for the BPI Music Week and the BBC based on a sample of 250 record outlets.

INKY by Ed McHenry

INKY THINKS I'M GOING DOWN WITH THE FLU, AND HE'S TOLD ME TO SPEND THE DAY IN BED

I WONDER WHAT HE'S UP TO ?

10p for the GUY

Assignments: Writing

Here are some suggested news assignments. Choose from them or invent your own.

1. Write a script for a short radio news bulletin, designed for a particular group of people, such as:

- children younger than yourself
- adults in your local area
- young listeners aged fifteen to twenty-five
- any other audience.

You could adapt existing news articles and broadcasts or invent believable news items of your own.

2. Choose a small number of news items or topical issues and present them in contrasting ways. Keep in mind the different media you will be using and the different audiences you aim to reach. Your choices might involve one or more of the following:

- local and national television programmes
- local and national newspapers
- local and national radio programmes
- young viewers, listeners or readers and adults
- a general and a specialist audience
- two different media, such as a printed article and a script for radio or television
- contrasting newspapers, such as a broadsheet and a tabloid.

3. Write, edit and set out a *Voice of Youth* or *Young Reader's* page. You can use a newspaper of your choice as a model, or you can set the style yourself and design your own layout.

Options: writing, speaking and recording

Script and present a news bulletin or short programme with a particular group of people in mind.

You could record it on audio-tape or perform it for the class.

You could use pre-recorded jingles, music, sound effects and interviews or eye-witness accounts.

Planning Work in Progress

A. You may need a variety of materials to compose and present your news assignment. You may be working within a small group, so you need to make sure that you are well organised.

To help you do this, complete the following statements:
1. The things I need are ...
(You may need major items like a cassette recorder, or smaller ones like a ruler and felt tip pens.)
Check that it is practical for you to use these things.
2. My audience/reader/listener is ...
3. I chose the following items/features for them because ...
4. My plan for actually doing the assignment is ...

EXAMPLE OF THE START OF A PLAN

PLAN / SCHEDULE.

Assignment : Number 3.
('Young Readers' page)

1. Decide on the newspaper in which the page will appear.

2. Research — ask a sample of students in school what information and features they would like to see on a page for young readers.

3. On the basis of their answers and my interests, decide on the main topics for the articles.

5. If working in a group, my particular tasks are ...

B. To help your coursework look its best

Newspaper staff check articles for misprints and mistakes but some still slip through.

This is just one example of many misprints in newspapers and magazines.

> **Richard Burton to teach English at Oforxd**

Be prepared to edit your work with a dictionary. The SKILLS section at the back of this book contains help with using dictionaries and with other aspects of checking your work.

News Role Play

The following JOB DESCRIPTION sheets are to help you with group work in creating a newspaper article or news broadcast.

The top of each sheet tells you the number of people involved in each group.

Activity

Hold an EDITORIAL MEETING in which the EDITOR in your group talks through your tasks with you – a time limit for the production of your article or broadcast makes the role play more realistic.

Editorial meeting at Independent Television News.

JOB DESCRIPTION – TELEVISION

Your aim is to prepare a news programme for television.

Name of programme _____

Time programme lasts _____

Group of 4 people

EDITOR
1. Prepare the 'news in brief' introduction to your programme.
2. Assist writer(s) with the preparation of items: do they fit in with the policy and audience of the programme?
3. Decide on the order of the items and form them into a script: are you going to run over time, how will you give variety? (An interview?)
4. Hold a rehearsal.

WRITER/PRESENTER
1. Write two main items and submit them to the Editor. Your first will be your own choice, after consulting with the Editor.
2. Rehearse your script.

INTERVIEWER
1. Research background information for an interview on a main news item after consulting with the Editor.
2. Prepare a schedule of questions.
3. Prepare an introduction to your interview.

INTERVIEWEE
1. Research background information to prepare for questions in interview on your involvement in a main news item.
2. Who will you be?
3. Will you give an 'eye-witness account'?

The programmes could be performed for the class, so that different groups can compare and contrast their treatment of the news.

JOB DESCRIPTION – RADIO

Your aim is to prepare a news programme for radio.

Name of programme _____ **Group of 4 people**

Time programme lasts _____

EDITOR
1. Prepare the 'news in brief' introduction.
2. Assist the writers with any re-wording, making sure the items are the right length and style for your audience.
3. Decide on the order of items and form them into a script.
4. Ensure silence and control the tape when recording.

WRITER/PRESENTER (1) and (2)
1. Write your two main items which you will read when the news bulletin goes out.
2. Give the draft items to your Editor for checking.
3. Practise the reading and timing of the items before recording.

ADVERTISING SECTION
1. Compose two advertisements, in keeping with the audience and policy of your programme.
2. Assist the Editor in all matters.

The programme could be performed for the class or recorded on audio cassette tape.

JOB DESCRIPTION – NEWSPAPERS

Your aim is to write the front page of a newspaper.

Name of newspaper _____ **Group of 5-9 people**

Size of page _____

EDITOR
1. Take charge of all equipment.
2. Give out the work for the day.
3. See that deadlines are met.
4. Keep staff informed on the newspaper's policy/audience.
5. Write the news in brief.
6. Make final decisions about the content and layout of the page.

SUB-EDITOR (1) and (2)
1. Make sure the Editor's instructions are carried out for your section of the newspaper.
2. Write your own article.
3. Proof read/check your journalists' articles. Consult the journalists for any changes to wording/headlines. Does the article have the right appeal for your audience? Are the pictures right?

JOURNALIST (1) (2) and (3)
1. Write your own article according to instructions from your Sub-Editor. You may be given new work by your Sub-Editor.
2. Give your article to the Sub-Editor for proof reading.
3. When returned to you, copy the final version of your article, so that it looks like one in a newspaper. For example, you might use large lettering for headlines.

ADVERTISING SECTION
1. Compose and set out two advertisements for the front page of the paper.
2. Select further advertisements in consultation with the Editor to fill up the spaces on the page.

The page could be displayed in class for others to read.

Understanding: A Radio Interview with French and Saunders

Introduction

a) Reading and understanding

Interviews in news bulletins on radio and television are usually short. This unit now moves away from news as such to look at a longer interview, which forms part of a radio programme. The following pages contain a radio interview with the comedy team Dawn French and Jennifer Saunders. It is a **transcript** of the interview – a written version of what was said.

Part of the GCSE syllabus is concerned with comprehension and understanding. You are required to show that you understand what you have read. The questions which follow the interview will help you develop this skill.

b) Listening and understanding

Some syllabuses ask you to listen as well as read. A tape recording is played and you are given a transcript to read. The transcript allows you to concentrate on understanding rather than on trying to remember what was said.

You can practise this by using the French and Saunders interview. Three members of your class can either record the interview or read it aloud. You can follow the interview from the transcript in this book.

c) Practice questions

The interview with French and Saunders lasted twelve minutes on radio. It will take about twenty minutes to read. To help you to concentrate, jot down answers to the following questions as you read the interview.
1.   Whom does Dawn French admire in comedy and why?
2.   The two women reveal things about their personalities, on and off stage. What impression do you get of Dawn French's character?

Jennifer Saunders and Dawn French.

<u>INTERVIEW WITH COMEDY DUO DAWN FRENCH AND
JENNIFER SAUNDERS, RADIO 4, SUMMER 1986.</u>
(The interviewer's first name is Sue)

1	Interviewer:	How do you actually work out who does what in the writing business? Jennifer?
	Dawn French:	You operate the kettle mainly, don't you?
5	Jennifer Saunders:	I mainly operate the kettle and buy the Maltesers and Dawn eats them and watches the video, and that's how we write together normally.
	Dawn French:	We have just managed to hire an office and that's the first real grown-up way of working that we've attempted, and we've moved into the office and it took us three days to put the plugs on the kettles and the fan and arrange flowers, put pictures of our beloveds on the wall and take them down and put other
10		pictures up, lift them …

Jennifer Saunders:	... and ring everyone and tell them exactly where we were ...
Dawn French:	Yep.
Jennifer Saunders:	... so that they could phone us at every hour of the day, making sure they knew where we were.
15 Dawn French:	We accept any packages, lick any envelopes – do anything other than work.
Interviewer:	But now that you are both married to your beloveds – and Dawn, you're married to Lenny Henry, and Jennifer is married to Ade Edmundson – is it harder to get together to work together?
20 Jennifer Saunders:	I think it's actually easier because when we shared a flat and lived in the same house, we very rarely used to ever bother to sit down and do any work together because we were always going out and missing each other or coming back and we didn't have time and that sort of thing. But I think with the office, erm ...
Dawn French:	Yes, er ...
25 Jennifer Saunders:	... we come to the office every morning and we sit down there and, you know, when we've had the coffee and the hour's worth of gossip, we actually sit down and do proper work.
Interviewer:	Have you been doing that today?
Dawn French:	We haven't had the chance to today, luckily. No, we've been at the costume fittings and things like that for a film we're about to do.
30 Interviewer:	Which is the bossy one of the two of you?
Dawn French:	Jennifer.
Jennifer Saunders:	Dawn. (Laughter)
Interviewer:	You're the bossy one Jennifer, and yet when one talks to you – 'when *one* talks to you' – I sound like royalty!
35 Jennifer Saunders:	Dawn says I'm the bossy one – I'm not really.
Interviewer:	You are the quieter one?
Jennifer Saunders:	Yes, you see, you've noticed.
Dawn French:	That's just not true. When we're on our own, there's just no stopping her, Sue.
Interviewer:	How did the two of you meet?
40 Dawn French:	At Drama College. Come on Mrs. Quiet One.
Jennifer Saunders:	Oh, all right. We met at Drama College and Dawn was very bossy and very chatty.
Interviewer:	This was the Central School of Speech and Drama?
Jennifer Saunders:	We didn't even like each other very much.
45 Dawn French:	Yes, we didn't hit it off immediately.
Interviewer:	What did you not like?
Dawn French:	Well, I had spent a year ...
Jennifer Saunders:	Her bossiness and chattiness mainly!
50 Dawn French:	I had spent a year in America and I decided to wear baseball caps and be very loud and say things like 'gross' and 'tacky' all the time.
Jennifer Saunders:	And 'let's have a cookie.'
Dawn French:	'Cookie', yes, I said plenty of that, and Jennifer had been in Italy and was being very refined. I came to college later than Jennifer – she'd been there for about

55	a week, and in that week she had managed to get a whole gang together, so by the time I arrived they just gave me filthy looks from the other side of the canteen and I knew that I was going to be sent to Coventry for most of the three years, which I was.
Interviewer:	Was it very useful training, at a proper Drama School, to do what you're doing now?
60 Jennifer Saunders:	Parts of it were. The teaching side of it wasn't really except, I suppose, we did sketches about kids and teachers, didn't we?
Interviewer:	I believe one of your teachers – one of your part-time teachers – was somebody who's going to appear later on in this programme, and that's Joan Washington, who is – what you would call her: a voice coach? – somebody who helps you with accents.
65	
Dawn French:	She's a terrific lady, very talented.
Interviewer:	What did she give to you?
Dawn French:	Well, funnily enough, I don't think she actually taught us accents or whatever she's doing now. She was mainly, er …
70 Jennifer Saunders:	… phonetics …
Dawn French:	And Drama teaching.
Jennifer Saunders:	One called 'Language and Learning' or something, one of those strange courses you do.
Dawn French:	But she was very good. She was very easy to relate to and she understood the problems of being a Drama teacher, and she gave us very practical help with teaching the kids we were going to be teaching.
75	
Interviewer:	Did you decide at that point that being funny was going to be your profession, or was it something you did because you weren't that interested in the straight theatre?
80 Jennifer Saunders:	Well, we were never aiming for the straight – for the theatre – at all.
Dawn French:	It was just complete luck, the whole thing. We actually … we started to show off at a revue at college, and we invented two American women that we did our best sketch about, and it took off from there really. I mean, we finished college still not intending to do anything like this. I went on to teach for a year then, and Jennifer went on not to teach.
85 Jennifer Saunders:	– to be unemployed.
Dawn French:	Yes, and she rang me after about six weeks after I started a teaching year and said, "There's this place called the Comic Strip in town and they're looking for female acts. Let's go down there and do this thing that we have done at the revue," and we did that, and it took off from there really.
90	
Interviewer:	Wasn't that very brave of you to do? Because the Comic Strip is in Soho and (not necessarily to do with stripping I think, or maybe it once was) is somewhere where you go in and you can get barracked by the audience and given the bird super fast.
95 Dawn French:	We – er – yes – but the Comedy Store was really the place that was like that. The Comedy Store at that time had a gong and the audience were encouraged to heckle and could actually gong you off if they didn't like you.
Interviewer:	As you are speaking, Jennifer is imitating –
Dawn French:	– the gong.
100 Interviewer:	Yes.

Dawn French:	That's means she's telling me to stop.
	(Laughter)
Jennifer Saunders:	No, no ... you see she gets on her own and it's 'chat, chat, chat' and I'm the one accused of being bossy!
105	(Laughter)
Interviewer:	Did you get the gong?
Jennifer Saunders:	No, we never did. We saw a few heading with that stick towards the gong and we just did our act in about thirty seconds and got off.
Dawn French: 110	We once did a twenty minute set in about seven-and-half minutes — it was very fast — nobody understood it but at least we didn't get gonged off.
Interviewer:	Who do you admire in the female comic world? Or, you obviously don't model yourselves on anybody, but are there people whose timing and whose dialogue you admire very much?
Jennifer Saunders:	Yes.
115 Dawn French:	Oh, yes.
Jennifer Saunders:	I think Victoria Wood is probably the best, definitely.
Interviewer:	And why?
Dawn French: 120	I think it's just because she's so true to life and she's basically just a very funny woman, and she hasn't slipped into a lot of, erm, the kind of conventional comic roles at all. She's doing what she thinks is funny. She hasn't felt obliged to do any kind of sexist humour or whatever. I mean, she escapes it all. She hasn't — she also hasn't been labelled as 'alternative' which we have which was a label that was given to us very early on and we've had to try and shake off.
Interviewer: 125	I don't actually understand this label — is it meant to mean that you are dealing with slightly rude areas of life, like sex, for instance? Or is it meant to be —
Dawn French:	No, because people —
Jennifer Saunders:	Well, I think originally it was to do with the venues because they were the alternative venues to standard clubs and stuff.
Dawn French:	Yeh.
130 Jennifer Saunders:	They were like pubs that put up a stage so you could do it in the corner, so it wasn't like — I think it was the alternative venue so we became alternative comics. I don't think originally it was anything to do with the material.
Interviewer: 135	The most testing part of your art is to stand up in an alternative venue or whatever, in front of a live audience and actually make them laugh. Is that still hard to do? Does it still take a lot of preparation?
Jennifer Sauders:	Takes a lot of nerve.
Dawn French:	Yes, it does.
Jennifer Saunders:	Everybody knows about it.
Dawn French: 140	Plus the kind of things we do — we do quite a lot of, sort of, gentle conversational humour which is quite hard to do in that stand-up situation, because the lights are on you and the microphone's in front of you and it's often the kind of place where you should be doing straight slamming-type humour.
Jennifer Saunders:	In the beginning, people just carried on talking.
Dawn French:	Yeh.
145 Jennifer Saunders:	And we'd go, "Sssh! There's a good bit coming up!"

Interviewer:	You have both made separate names for yourselves in television series and in one Jennifer notably played many parts, including quite an old lady. Is the hard thing now to establish yourselves as 'French and Saunders', as this double act?

. . . .

150 Interviewer:	Don't nod, because people can't see that!
Dawn French:	Let the quiet one have a go.
Jennifer Saunders:	All right Mrs. Quiet One.
Dawn French: 155	Yes, it is, because people don't know us as 'French and Saunders', funnily enough. They know us from the occasional sketch though. We did a 'special' once on I.T.V. but we're about to do a huge , wholloping great, incredibly funny –
Jennifer Saunders:	– spectacular –
Dawn French: 160	– show for the B.B.C. at the end of this year, which they're going to show at the beginning of next year, which is purely 'French and Saunders' which is what we've been doing in the clubs for ages and people will get the chance to see it all at last.
Interviewer:	And what will the material be? Anything that strikes your fancy?
Jennifer Saunders:	Yes.
Dawn French:	Lots of synchronised swimming.
170	(Laughter)
Jennifer Saunder:	Yes, lots of synchronised swimming.
Interviewer:	What about – you haven't got any sketches about ladies who do exercises have you? We're about to burst into a bout of that (the next item on the programme).

Practice questions and comments on

answers

You have now read the interview with French and Saunders and answered two practice questions. Below are the answers of a student who did the same as you.

Activity

- Read the answers and say how many marks you would give to each. Use your own answers to the practice questions to help you decide on marks. Give reasons for the number of marks you have given.
- Read the comments – they help you to see the skills that a marker looks for in an answer.

Question (1) Whom does Dawn French admire in comedy and why? (3 marks)

Student's answer:

Dawn French rates
Victoria Wood highly as a
comedy act.

What mark would you give to this?

Comment

The answer is fine as far as it goes. The student has glanced at the question, but she has not seen the second part which asks 'why?' Why does Dawn French look up to Victoria Wood as a comedienne? The student has not answered this part of the question. Reading the whole question and underlining one or two key words in pencil, or making a mental note of them, helps to avoid this sort of mistake. A complete answer might have added that Dawn thinks Victoria Wood's act is realistic (true to life) and avoids stereotyped jokes about women ('She hasn't felt obliged to do any kind of sexist humour or whatever.')

This answer would earn three marks.

The student's answer would probably get only one mark.

Question (2) The two women being interviewed reveal things about their personalities, on and off stage. What impression do you get of Dawn French's character? (6 marks)

Student's answer:

Dawn French jokes that she is quite shy in private, but she seems a very confident and talkative person — she admits that she was very 'loud' when she came back from America and she also answers a lot of questions in the interview. She also says she isn't bossy, but she prods Jennifer into answering a question, and her partner thinks that Dawn pushes herself forward more — she says this in a friendly way though.

I think that Dawn French must have nerves of steel too because she went on stage at places where the audience could shout and boo and 'gong you off' if they didn't like the comedy. As well as being brave, she seems an adventurous woman when she goes to America as a student when she must have been quite young, before she went to Drama College.

I think she must be original, unconventional, because the interviewer says that their act is original and Dawn French admires Victoria Wood for not being like everyone else. She can be serious, like when she says that her teacher was a 'terrific lady' but she is also clever and witty and enjoys a joke, like when she says there will be lots of 'synchronised swimming' in their new show, which makes them all laugh.

Finally, Dawn French must have had an interesting life because she has done lots of different things. She has been a student, a teacher, has been on many stages and to America and has got married.

Comment

The student has read the question more carefully this time. She has 'read between the lines' to decide what sort of person Dawn French seems to be from things she says, things she has done, and things other people say about her. We often take these things into account when getting to know a person we have only just met.

In this answer, the student backed up her views by letting the reader know where she got her ideas from — she made references to the interview and quoted some of it. This shows an ability to understand and apply what she has read. She also explained her views in her own words. The answer is written in paragraphs — each new stage is clear. But does the last paragraph answer the question quite so well as the first two? The student seems to be 'fishing around' for more points to make and strays off 'personality' into the 'life history' of Dawn French. All in all, however, this is a good answer and would probably get nearly full marks. An answer like this is not usually written straight off the top of the head — this student made brief notes before writing the final answer. This is helpful when the points you might want are spread over a long passage, article or interview.

Student's notes

DAWN. F.

'bossy' ... 'loud' (but different off stage?)
talks lots
on stage — need lot of nerve
'original'
done different things
likes a joke — wit.

A final point

These two questions did not ask you to go outside the interview and add opinions, experiences or knowledge of your own. Some GCSE questions ask you to comment on, add to or develop a piece of writing. Often you are asked to draw on your own experience and knowledge of the topic. If you were given an interview with a rock star, for example, you might be asked to write about the music you like. If you were given a newspaper article on punishments in school, you might be asked to write your views on punishments you think are fair or unfair.

Question 9 below provides an example of this kind of question. It asks you to go beyond the interview with French and Saunders and comment on other forms of comedy.

Now that you have:
– read the interview
– tried some practice questions
– seen comments on another student's answers

it is time for you to try some written answers and practise a longer activity.

How long do you have to answer the questions below?
If you are not set a time limit in class, allow 90 minutes (1½ hours) for this activity as it may be your first attempt at a long piece of written understanding.

Questions on the interview with French and Saunders (marks in brackets)

1. What new arrangements have French and Saunders made recently to help them to work? (2)
2. Sometimes during the interview, French and Saunders do not mean to be taken seriously – pick out an example where you think one of the speakers is joking.
3. The two women reveal things about their personalities, from their public and private lives, during the interview. What impression do you get of the character of Jennifer Saunders? (6)
4. Dawn and Jennifer met at Drama College, but they did not like each other at first. Why was this? (3)
5. The interviewer, Sue, is sometimes caught off gaurd and briefly drops her official role as interviewer. Where do you think this happens? Pick out an example and explain your choice. (3)
6. In what ways did their education at Drama College prepare French and Saunders for their present work? (3)
7. What does 'alternative comedy' mean to Dawn French?
8. Their first public appearances were not easy. Make a list of the difficulties that French and Saunders met with in trying to become successful in comedy. (8)
9. The two women have become successful in 'alternative comedy', but there are many other types of comedy which people enjoy.
Write about the type of comedy that you enjoy. You could consider films and comedy on television – you do not have to keep to comedy on stage – and you could also write about forms of comedy which you do not enjoy.

You may use things mentioned in the interview as a starting point, if you wish, and you should try to explain your views and feelings. (10)

Summing up so far: understanding

Here is a checklist of things to aim for in **understanding** or **comprehension**.

- Read the whole of each question.
- Underline key words in the question and in the piece of writing.
- Make notes before you write out the full answer.
- Questions can ask for different skills.
  Sometimes you are asked to
  – pick out facts
  – read between the lines/interpret
  – add related knowledge or experience of your own
  – summarise what you have read.

Make sure that you read the question carefully so that you know which skills are needed for a particular question.

- Try to put the answer in a straightforward way, in your own words rather than copying from the passage.
- Pieces of writing for understanding are often chosen to be **enjoyable and interesting.** They are not selected to trick readers. Try to enjoy them!

Unit 5 Poetry

Aims: to find poems which you enjoy, to develop your understanding of poetry, to help others to enjoy poetry.

On the way: the activities include:

● choosing a short poem
● using photographs to help in understanding poetry

Poems in outline: shapes and structures

● gathering ideas and memories
● filling in poetic outlines
● reading other students' work in progress
● putting a scrambled poem into shape

Poems in close-up: words and images

● 'interviewing' a poem
● asking your own questions and exchanging them with others
● filling in the missing details of a poem
● seeing how other students talk about poetry
● testing a 'guide' to a poem.

By the end: of the unit, you will have a poetry assignment which shows that you can work with this form of English. You will see that poetry can be an effective way to express thoughts and feelings. Some of the activities lead to poetry writing, and you could include your own poems in the coursework folder.

Assignments: Reading and writing

collecting poems which you enjoy and introducing your collection
writing poetry yourself
writing a 'guide' to a poem or poems, for other students.

Speaking and listening

reading aloud
talking in groups to re-arrange a poem or to fill in missing details.

Option

a tape-recorded 'guide' to a poem.

> I was angry with my friend:
> I told my wrath, my wrath did end.
> I was angry with my foe:
> I told it not, my wrath did grow.

William Blake – poet

> I'm going down, down baby,
> My nose is in the sand,
> A cloud of dust came over me,
> I think I'm drowning on dry land.

Poetry comes in many forms.

Albert King – blues singer

Starting Out

Many people are not used to reading poetry. They are more used to reading short stories, novels, magazines and newspapers. This section begins with two short activities to help familiarise you with poetry.

Choosing poems

The following poems were chosen by a GCSE English class as 'tasters' which they thought might interest you. Read the poems then complete the activity which follows.

Red Card

Right from the off,
straight into your penalty area
a quick one-two and it was all over
bar the shouting. Easy
Easy sang the terraces.
Half-time: I've given you a hundred per cent
and more. Two down, and I've got it all
to do again.

At the end of the day
the lap of honour. Your ribbons
round the Cup. I am
sick as a parrot. I am
over the moon you tell the cameras,
the waiting millions.
Back home I walk
alone.

Adrian Henri

This is just to say

This is just to say
I have eaten
the plums
that were in
the icebox

and which
you were probably
saving
for breakfast

Forgive me
they were delicious
so sweet
and so cold

William Carlos Williams

Pantomime Poem

'HE'S BEHIND YER'
chorused the children
but the warning came too late.

The monster leaped forward
and fastening its teeth into his neck,
tore off the head.

The body fell to the floor
'MORE' cried the children
'MORE, MORE, MORE

MORE

MOR

Roger McGough

The miracle of the burd and the fishes

ach sun
jiss keepyir chin up
dizny day gonabootlika hawf shut knife
inaw jiss cozzy a burd

luvur day yi?
ach well
gee it a wee while sun
thirz a loat mer fish in thi sea

Tom Leonard

Spring Onions

Decapitating the spring onions,
She made this mental note:
You can tell it's love, the real thing,
When you dream of slitting his throat.

Wendy Cope

Kick

Are you frightened?
Do you feel your throat tightening
like a drawstring purse, with
the air squeezed out?
Does your hair feel as though
it is slipping
Slowly
Off your scalp?
Do you want to run away?
Are your hands wet?
Is your life line distorted by rivulets of sweat?
Do you feel your face burning?
   Do you feel as though
   tens
   of
   thousands of sharp pins
   are jabbing you?
   Do you feel more alive?
   Don't say you don't like it.

Louise Orr (aged 15)

My Sock

My sock
is
round my foot.
My sock
is
in my shoe.

How can it
not only be
in two places
but 2 shapes?

Socks
are more cunning
than
they let on.

Ivor Cutler

Activity: with a partner

1.   Which poem do you like best?

2.   Read it aloud.

3.   What about the other poems? Read some of them aloud. Try using different accents, reading loudly or softly, quickly or slowly.

4.   Now make a final choice. Have you changed your mind? Explain to your partner why you liked the poem and what you found interesting about it.

Now that you have completed this activity:

●   You may have found something about poetry that appeals to you. Some people do not like poetry. Often they have never given it a fair try. At least you have now had a brief opportunity to enjoy poetry.

●   You may have found that reading poems aloud and talking about them helps you to understand, appreciate and enjoy poetry.

Photographs in Outline and Close-up

This activity will help you see poems in outline (their shape, structure, pattern) and in close-up (the object, event, experience, thought or emotion on which the writer focuses).

Questions

1.   In a sentence describe what you see in each of the photographs on the following page.

2.   The photographs can be interpreted in a number of ways. In a sentence describe another way of looking at each of the photographs.

3.   Two of the photographs show an outline, two show a close-up.

a)   List the advantages and disadvantages of viewing something in outline.

b)   List the advantages and disadvantages of viewing something in close-up.

Why look at photographs?

What has the above activity to do with poetry?

● First, a poem can be seen or interpreted in a number of ways – just like the photographs.

● Second, poems often focus closely on the details of an object, event, experience, thought or emotion – rather like a close-up in a photograph.

● Third, a poem has a shape or structure – rather like the two photographs which showed an outline or silhouette.

● When you read or hear a poem, think of these points:

– the different ways in which the poem can be interpreted

– the details on which the poet focused

– the outline or structure of the poem.

Poems in outline

These outlines or structures each fit one of the poems on pages 76-77.

1. Which poem does each fit?

2. Choose a further poem from pages 76-77 and draw an outline to fit it.

3. Why do you think writers use different outlines or structures for their poems?

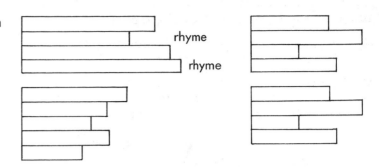

Shapes and Outlines

The next few pages contain activities to help you explore shapes and outlines for writing and reading poetry. You have looked at shapes in pictures – shapes can also be made with words. Remember the speeches you examined in Unit 3. The Martin Luther King speech on pages 32 – 33 used the repetition of the phrase, 'I have a dream'. This gave shape and structure to the speech. There are many basic word patterns which help to give shape, sense and meaning. Take the idea of time. We break it up, give it structure and meaning by using the simple patterns of words. Some are listed below.

Before	First	Spring	Past	Monday	Friday
Now	Second	Summer	Present	Tuesday	Saturday
After	Third	Autumn	Future	Wednesday	Sunday
		Winter		Thursday	

Like everybody else, poets use patterns of words to give shape and meaning to thoughts and feelings. Try to find word patterns in poems. This will help you to understand the structure of a poem – to see how it is put together.

Activity

Read the following two poems.

Poem 1, *My First Week at School* was written by an eleven year old in about ten minutes.

Poem 2, *Days* by Michael Swan is a sophisticated poem by an experienced adult writer.

The poems are very different but they share a common outline.

1. What is the common outline? (You may want to glance at the lists of word patterns above).

2. Choose one line from Poem 1 and write it as a verse (as in Poem 2).

3. Choose one verse from Poem 2 and write it as one line (as in Poem 1).

Now you have completed this activity, you can see how a similar outline or structure can be used in very different ways.

Poem 1

My first week at school

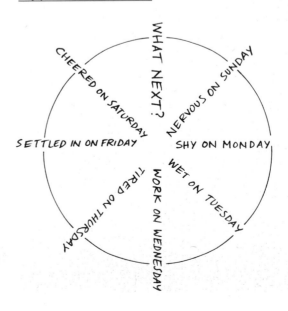

Poem 2

Days

MONDAY
You'd better not try anything
just don't try anything
that's all.
You're all the same
you days.
Give you an inch . . .
Well
I've got my eye on you
and I'm feeling light
fast
and full of aggro
so just watch it
OK?

TUESDAY
Listen, Tuesday
I'm sorry
I wasn't very nice to you.
It was *sweet* of you
to give me all those stars
when you said goodbye.
They must have cost a fortune
and they really were
just
what I've always wanted.

WEDNESDAY
Cracks, spills, burns, bills, broken cups, stains, wrong
 numbers missed trains:
you're doing it on purpose
aren't you?
Trying it on
to see how far you can go.
I swear to you
if the phone rings again
while I'm in the bath
I'll pull it out
and ram it down your throat.

THURSDAY
'A difficult day for Aries
caution is advisable
in business dealings
setbacks possible
in affairs of the heart.'
Thursday, my friend
if we've got to get
through all these hours together
we might as well do it
with as little trouble
as possible.
You keep to your side of the horoscope
and I'll keep to mine.

FRIDAY
Day like a shroud
ten feet down
black
in an airless coffin
you wrap me
in my own
clinging
loathsome
sticky skin.
I scream
and you laugh.

SATURDAY
Day
oh day
I love your perfume
(you put on daffodils
just for me)
and your yellow eye
sparkling
and the sexy way
you rub up
against me
day
I love you.

SUNDAY
Sunday and I
got drunk together
and you know
it turns out
we went to the same school.
He's a bit strange
at first
but actually
he's not a bad chap
when you get to know him
old Sunday.

Giving Shape to Memories

Places, people, songs, old toys or clothes spark off memories. To make these memories into a poem, we need to give them shape and order. Here are two successful attempts to do this.

Activity 1

It Was Long Ago was written by a student, aged eleven. The writer has used some simple but effective techniques to give shape to his memories. Firstly, he uses repetition to give a structure to the poem. Secondly, he organises and shapes his memories in terms of the five senses — he sees, hears, tastes, smells and feels.

1. a) Briefly describe the poet's use of repetition.
   b) Suggest why it is effective.
2. a) Show how the five senses are used in the poem.
   b) Do you think this is an effective way of giving shape and meaning to a memory? Give reasons for your answer.

It Was Long Ago

I'll tell you, shall I, something I remember.
Something that still means a great deal to me.
It was long ago.

The reds and yellows of the Wendy House, I remember.
The dark brown of the floor in the hall.
The teacher's red dress.

The sounds of the children in the playground, I remember.
The Headmistress shouting in the hall.
It scared me.

The taste of custard that was forced down me, I remember.
The stink of the wax floor cleaner in the hall.
It stank.

The butterflies in my stomach, I remember.
Scary thoughts whizzing round inside my head.
In my imagination.

Activity 2

The Choosing by Liz Lochhead

Before reading *The Choosing,* think of a person of your own age whom you have not seen since infant or junior school. You shared the experience of attending the same school, but you will both have changed since then. What do you think the person will be like now? How do you think that he or she will have changed?

Read *The Choosing* and answer the following questions.

1. Who are the main characters in the poem? List them.
2. In what ways were the two girls alike at junior school?
3. In what ways are they and their lives different now? Why do you think they have changed?
4. What does the writer feel about these changes?
5. Suggest reasons for the title, *The Choosing.*

The Choosing

We were first equal Mary and I
with same coloured ribbons in mouse-coloured hair
and with equal shyness,
we curtseyed to the lady councillor
for copies of Collins' Children's Classics
First equal, equally proud.

Best friends too Mary and I
a common bond in being cleverest (equal)
in our small school's small class.
I remember
the competition for top desk
at school service.
And my terrible fear
of her superiority at sums.

I remember the housing scheme
where we both stayed.
The same houses, different homes,
where the choices were made.

I don't know exactly why they moved,
but anyway they went.
Something about a three-apartment
and a cheaper rent.
But from the top deck of the high-school bus
I'd glimpse among the others on the corner
Mary's father, mufflered, contrasting strangely
with the elegant greyhounds by his side.
He didn't believe in high school education,
especially for girls,
or in forking out for uniforms.

Ten years later on a Saturday –
I am coming from the library –
sitting near me on the bus,
Mary
with a husband who is tall,
curly haired, has eyes
for no one else but Mary.
Her arms are round the full-shaped vase
that is her body.
Oh, you can see where the attraction lies
in Mary's life –
not that I envy her, really.

And I am coming from the library
with my arms full of books.
I think of those prizes that were ours for the taking
and wonder when the choices got made
we don't remember making.

Key words and phrases

Having answered the above questions, you probably feel you understand *The Choosing* – you know what the poet is trying to say. However, you probably didn't notice the shape of the poem – you took it for granted. Below is a worked example which shows how to analyse a poem's structure. It picks out the key words and phrases that give shape, order and meaning to thoughts and feelings. This can be a useful way of getting more out of a poem than you can from a first quick reading. The example uses *The Choosing* and picks out four key phrases and comments on them. Do you think this adds to your understanding of the poem?

Start as 'equals', the same ————

Long development of the section on 'then' – the past

Growing difference

Today/now – difference between them ————

The poem is like a circle – goes back to the 'books' at the start, and the 'choices' – how the past affects the present.

The Choosing

We were first equal Mary and I
with same coloured ribbons in mouse-coloured hair
and with equal shyness,
we curtseyed to the lady councillor
for copies of Collins' Children's Classics
First equal, equally proud.

Best friends too Mary and I
a common bond in being cleverest (equal)
in our small school's small class.
I remember
the competition for top desk
at school service.
And my terrible fear
of her superiority at sums.

I remember the housing scheme
where we both stayed.
The same houses, different homes,
where the choices were made.

I don't know exactly why they moved,
but anyway they went.
Something about a three-apartment
and a cheaper rent.
But from the top deck of the high-school bus
I'd glimpse among the others on the corner
Mary's father, mufflered, contrasting strangely
with the elegant greyhounds by his side.
He didn't believe in high school education,
especially for girls,
or in forking out for uniforms.

Ten years later on a Saturday –
I am coming from the library –
sitting near me on the bus,
Mary
with a husband who is tall,
curly haired, has eyes
for no one else but Mary.
Her arms are round the full-shaped vase
that is her body.
Oh, you can see where the attraction lies
in Mary's life –
not that I envy her, really.

And I am coming from the library
with my arms full of books.
I think of those prizes that were ours for the taking
and wonder when the choices got made
we don't remember making.

82

Activity 3

Select a poem of your own choice or use one that has been set in class. Pick out key words and phrases that give shape and meaning to the poem. Make comments in note form as in the worked example.

More uses of shape and structure

You have seen in a previous activity how numbers and days of the week can be used to give shape and meaning to thoughts and feelings. The section of verse which follows is from *As You Like It*, a play by Shakespeare. It uses a simple effective shape. Read the verse then answer the questions that follow.

All the world's a stage,
And all the men and women merely players;
They have their exits and their entrances;
And one man in his time plays many parts,
His acts being seven ages. At first the infant,
Mewling and puking in the nurse's arms;
And then the whining schoolboy, with his satchel,
And shining morning face, creeping like snail,
Unwillingly to school. And then the lover,
Sighing like furnace, with a woeful ballad
Made to his mistress' eyebrow. Then a soldier,
Full of strange oaths and bearded like a pard,
Jealous in honour, sudden and quick in quarrel,
Seeking the bubble reputation,
Even in the cannon's mouth. And then the justice,
In fair round belly with good capon lined,
With eyes severe and beard of formal cut,
Full of wise saws and modern instances,
And so he plays his part. The sixth age shifts
Into the lean and slipper'd pantaloon,
With spectacles on nose and pouch on side;
His youthful hose, well saved, a world too wide
For his shrunk shank; and his big manly voice,
Turning again towards childish treble, pipes
And whistles in his sound. Last scene of all,
That ends this strange eventful history,
Is second childishness and mere oblivion;
Sans teeth, sans eyes, sans taste, sans everything.

1. Describe the shape used in the verse.

2. Do you think it is effective? Give reasons for your answer.

3. The 'seven ages of man' begin as they end.

a) Briefly say what this statement means.

b) Suggest why this is an effective way of beginning and ending a verse or poem.

83

Writing a Poem

You may have done some acting, played a musical instrument or taken part in school sports days. But you would probably not see yourself as an actor, a musician or an athlete. However, these experiences probably mean you understand more about acting, music and athletics. The same applies to poetry. You might never become a famous poet but writing poetry – having a go – can add to your understanding of poetry. In fact there are a number of good reasons for trying to write poetry.

● It should help you appreciate, understand and analyse poetry.

● You might want to include a poem that you have written in your coursework folder.

● You might enjoy writing poetry and write more in the future.

Activity: group work

You will need a large sheet of paper for this activity. You are asked to choose a topic, plan the shape and select the content for a poem.

1. Choose a topic about which everybody in the group knows something – your first week at infant school, a school trip, asking somebody for a date.

2. Choose a shape or structure that seems appropriate for the poem. Make out a table on a large sheet of paper like this:

TOPIC	Driving a car
SHAPE	First impressions/Ideas
I wish . . . But . . . Therefore . . .	I could drive . . . and escape I can't afford it . . . I'll save up . . . and escape . . .

3. Think of anything and everything that might be used in the poem – words, phrases, impressions, ideas. Add them to your table.

I wish I could drive	I can't afford it	I'll save up
Freedom, fun weekends, holidays, sun, sea, camping, dates.	No job, pocket money insufficient. Fed up.	Get a job. Boring. No alternative. Worth it. Escape.

Examples

Here are two poems using 'I wish . . .' 'But . . .' 'Therefore . . .' as a structure. They were written in a lesson by a group of sixteen-year old students. They show how this structure can lead to two different poems.
Read the poems and give each a title.
Say which you prefer and why.

I wish I could drive
The power of transport
With the gift of freedom
Places to go and places to see
at leisure.

But I do not have the finance,
Money is what I require
To give me my freedom,
My key to the wide open spaces.

Therefore I shall work.
I will toil to find a result.
By my own effort I will drive
and escape.

I wish
That books wouldn't
Hide
In Libraries,

But would
See me first
And jump up to meet me,
Saying, 'I'm just the one,
You're looking for',
Not close their curtains
And turn down the t.v.
As if I were knocking
For money.

Therefore I shall stay
Indoors
Until I get their invitation card
The one with
'Overdue' on it.

Commenting on 'Work in Progress'

The aim of this section is to follow the process of writing a poem from first ideas to final version.

Three stages are shown here:

1. **NOTES** were made as a small group talked about memories of junior school. Each member of the group took away a copy of the notes to pick out what he or she thought was important.

2. **ROUGH DRAFT** — the notes were used to write a piece that looked more like a poem. But the student felt it needed improvements — additions, deletions, changing particular words, sharpening the focus.

3. **FINISHED POEM**
An important point is that the final poem was a result of talking, thinking, note-making and selection. Often you can find what you want to say if you do this, rather than staring at a blank page and waiting for a finished poem to appear.

Questions

Use these questions to help you follow the process of ideas and notes, making a draft, and achieving a finished poem.

1. In the notes, the student picked out five people or events from junior school: dinner times, a teacher, assembly, the Headmaster's office, a stink bomb.
Do you think that the student was right to cut out so much from the notes in moving on to the rough draft stage? Give reasons for your answer.

2. Pick out two or more words and phrases which the student used in the notes and kept in the rough draft. How effective do you find these words and phrases?

3. The finished poem concentrates on one incident. Briefly re-tell that incident in your own words.

4. What are the writer's feelings about the incident?

5. Do you think that the poem makes a point? If so, what is it?

6. What evidence can you find in the finished version that the student has borrowed some ideas from *The Choosing* by Liz Lochhead? Do you think that this matters?

7. What advice would you give the writer to improve the poem?

1. Notes

PEOPLE/EVENTS	DETAILS/THE FIVE SENSES	REACTIONS/FEELINGS
1. School dinners	watery cabbage like cut-up newspapers. Heavy puddings that pinned you to the chair.	I felt threatened — the dining hall was too noisy.
2. Teacher – Mrs Sharp:	very tall – wore high heels and her hair piled up. She loomed over you and her high heels clicked when she walked.	If you go back to junior school now, you can't fit in the chairs. The scale is different. Everything looks unreal and tiny.
3. Assembly:	Eric Jones sang rude words.	The teachers couldn't find out who it was.
4. Being sent to the Head's office:	Bald head. Got very angry and red-faced.	Sick with fear at first. I thought he'd cane me but he didn't.
5. The time when Lorraine stood on a stink bomb:	Awful smell. People holding their noses.	I can still smell it.

2. Rough draft

Two teachers . . . contrast them
Way I felt then and now
One teacher I liked and one I didn't
My teachers in the Junior School
The first tried to help me with my
'Daily Diary' and told me to write
about my pets and 'Spring' and
other pleasant things, that I was a
clever girl. Top of the class. I
think she wanted me to like her, to
be 'a good girl'. She never told me
off. But I couldn't help noticing
when she sat by me how her skin was
like pale pastry and the pink showed
through her blonde hair on her head.
She always wore mauve lipstick smelled
of lavender, not cigarettes like Mr
White of the Top Juniors. When I
scribbled a rude word in my Diary,
she didn't tell me off, but sent me
to the Head. As he talked at me, the
red crept up his face and over his
bald head.
I was so fascinated I forgot to feel
afraid. So I noticed he was old too.
His old face, like hers, an old,
bald man of sixty-five. He looked
almost upset – the good girl had let
down the shabby school. I felt
rotten and shameful, worse than
getting the cane.
That's the clearest thing I remember,
how bad I felt. Why I didn't get the
cane I still don't understand.

3. Finished poem

I remember best my Daily Diary at the Junior School –
A dull yellow book with rough paper and wide lines.
I think we were supposed to write about 'Our Pets'
And 'Spring' and 'Visits to the Zoo'.
Once I wrote a swear word,
Just to see what would happen.
I had to see the Head. He stood behind his desk,
And as he shouted, first his cheeks grew red –
The crimson spread up to his ears and boiled
Over his bald head.
I was so fascinated, I forgot to be afraid.
When there was no fear I saw his face,
An old face, a bald old man of sixty-five,
That I had let him down,
Let down the shabby school.
He didn't raise his cane or hand,
And that's what I remember worst –
The squirming guilt I didn't understand.

Uses

- You have seen that writers often start with notes and jottings. They refine and rework this jumble of ideas before getting to the final product. This should give you confidence in your own writing. So don't worry if all you have to start with is a similar jumble of notes and jottings.

- Thinking ahead to your assignment on poetry – one option is to include your own poems in your folder. You can use the stages of gathering ideas, notes and rough drafts to help you get to the finished product.

Some Suggestions for Beginning and Developing a Poem

Gathering ideas yourself, with a partner or in a group:

OBJECTS – focus on an object

– a real object that you bring to class

– a picture of an object

– an object from memory that was important to you.

Be as detailed as you can – it is often the individual, precisely recalled details as much as the 'fine phrases' or 'poetic words' which make a piece memorable.

– look at the object from unusual angles.

– what story might the object have to tell, e.g. the story of the desk at which you are sitting – who might have sat there before?

FLY ON THE WALL – if you have sometimes wished you could eavesdrop on a situation, imagine that you can – what can you overhear and see?

OUT OF THE WINDOW – write down everything you can see – fill up a page. You can select from it later.

AT THE BUS STOP – carry out some discreet detective work observing people. There may be a number of children, women and men waiting for the bus – what makes one of them distinct from the rest, an individual? Have you heard any characteristic sayings of the person? Where might they live? What would be the first thing they say when they get home.
Make notes when you can, perhaps on the bus, or as soon as you get home.

COMPARISONS AND CONTRASTS – striking metaphors and similes can occur as you develop a piece of writing, but they can also be the starting point. How is one thing like another – Saturday like a good friend?

Being in a bad mood like a winter's night?
Make a random list of nouns that interest you. Try different pairs of nouns to see how many similarities you can get. Some might seem unlikely, but famous poems have been based on seemingly outrageous comparisons such as being in love and a pair of compasses and the act of trying to write a poem and the approach of a fox (John Donne, *The Compasses;* Ted Hughes, *Thought Fox*). Try looking for points of difference between things or people which are usually thought of as similar.

Comparisons and contrasts

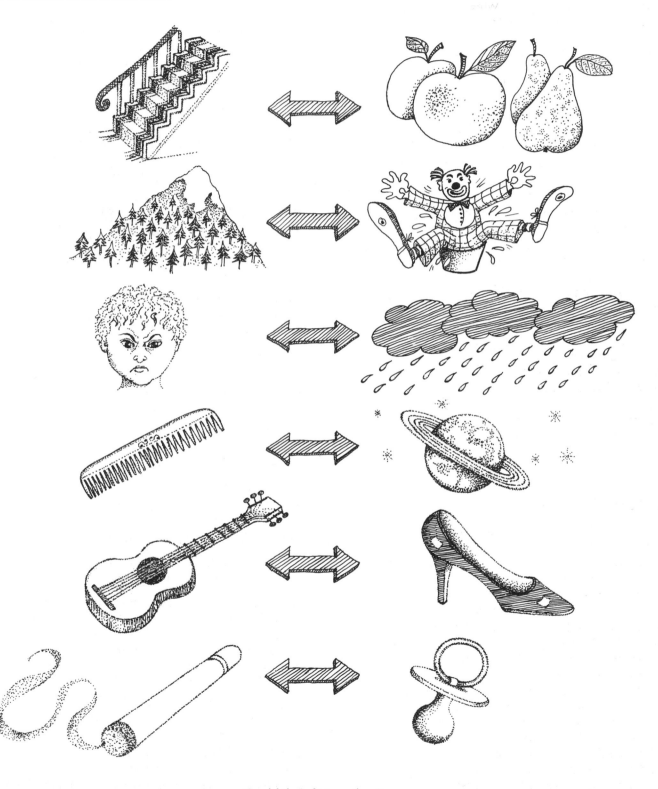

Could they fit together?

'FINDING' POETRY – take any printed page that you are allowed to cut up, such as an old newspaper or magazine, or even the clues to a crossword. Cut out a collection of individual words and keep choosing and re-arranging them until you get a line or phrase you like. Then use that line as a starting point for your own writing.

OBSESSIONS – your fascinations or worries. Brainstorm all the associated words and phrases you can think of.

BRAINSTORMING – many of the ways of getting started involve filling a space of paper with your first ideas – any ideas – and selecting from them later. More ideas and details occur as you write, select and re-draft. Writers usually find that it is better to have something on paper early on in composition. Trying to get the whole thing perfect before putting pen to paper can mean a start is never made.

Shapes and structures

SEQUENCES – of colours, numbers, days, times, seasons, months can be used to begin lines, sections or verses of a poem.

A sequence

From pine cone to newspaper

Sequences of types of words can also be used, e.g.

PREPOSITIONS – words like to, by, near, under, above (see Ivor Cutler's poem on 'socks' at the opening of this chapter).

QUESTIONS/QUESTION AND ANSWER – lines beginning with interrogatives or question words like 'When?', 'Why?', 'Who?', 'How?', 'Does?', (see *Kick* on page 77).

THE FIVE SENSES – in describing a place or experience, one section could deal mainly with sights, another with smells, another with sounds, another with tastes or textures (see the eleven-year old's poem *It Was Long Ago* on page 81).

PATTERNS OF RHYME AND RHYTHM – look again at the poems in this unit or those you have chosen yourself. Do they have a repeated pattern of rhyme? A distinctive rhythm? Song lyrics often have memorable patterns of rhyme. Rap, whether to music or spoken, has a distinctive beat or rhythm. You could pick a pattern of sound or rhythm and shape your own ideas to fit it.

LANGUAGE PATTERNS/'THOUGHT SHAPES' – try starting each section with sequences like:

I wish . . . If only . . . Suppose . . . Imagine
But . . .
So . . . Therefore
I was . . . Once . . . Then
I am . . . Now
I shall be . . .

Try adapting and combining these shapes, or inventing others.

FINDING RHYMES – suppose that you need a word to rhyme with 'remain'. You will need a piece of paper – write the alphabet down one side – and a dictionary to make sure that your words have meanings and are spelt correctly.

Fill in the alphabet with words with the same sound in the last syllable, e.g. 'ain', 'ane', 'ein', 'eign':

a –	aim	attain
b –	bane	became
c –	cane	contain
d –	deign	domain

Using Your Skills

Putting a scrambled poem into shape

You have worked on order, shape and sequence in poetry. Now is a chance to put what you have learned into practice.

The following poem entitled *Out, Out . . .*, by the American poet Robert Frost, has been mixed up or scrambled. It has a strong narrative or story.

Out, Out . . .

A

The buzz saw snarled and rattled in the yard
And made dust and dropped stove-length sticks of wood,
Sweet-scented stuff when the breeze drew across it.
And from there those that lifted eyes could count
Five mountain ranges one behind the other
Under the sunset far into Vermont.

B

So. Bet the hand was gone already.
The doctor put him in the dark of ether.
He lay and puffed his lips out with his breath.
And then – the watcher at his pulse took fright.
No one believed. They listened at his heart.

C

And the saw snarled and rattled, snarled and rattled,
As it ran light, or had to bear a load.
And nothing happened: day was all but done.

	Letter
1	
2	
3	
4	
5	
6	
7	
8	

D

No more to build on there. And they, since they
Were not the one dead, turned to their affairs.

E

At the word, the saw,
As if to prove saws knew what supper meant,
Leaped out of the boy's hand, or seemed to leap
He must have given the hand. However it was,
Neither refused the meeting. But the hand!

F

The boy's first outcry was a rueful laugh,
As he swung toward them holding up the hand
Half in appeal, but half as if to keep
The life from spilling. Then the boy saw all –
Since he was old enough to know, big boy
Doing a man's work, though a child at heart –
He saw all spoiled. 'Don't let him cut my hand off –
The doctor, when he comes. Don't let him sister!'

G

Little – less – nothing – and that ended it.

H

Call it a day, I wish they might have said
To please the boy by giving him the half hour
That a boy counts so much when saved from work.
His sister stood beside them in her apron
To tell them 'Supper'.

Choices:

A. Reassemble the poem in one of these ways:

1. In table form – copy the above table and use it to record the order of the segments by using the letters attached to them – if you think 'A' is first, record the letter 'A' in Box 1. Read the poem in the order you have chosen then write it down.

OR

2. Copy the segments of the poem on to scrap paper. Cut out the segments and try arranging and re-arranging them until you arrive at an order which satisfies you. Read the poem through in the order you have chosen. Stick the final version in your book or file.

Whichever method you chose to reassemble the poem, the shorthand term for what you have been doing is **sequencing.**

B. You now have a complete poem in your book. Make notes in the margins to show why you have arrived at that particular order. Include comments on at least two lines which interest you and explain why you think they are effective.

In doing this, you are moving towards the details of the poem, having first got an 'overall impression' of the whole structure.

C. Compare notes with others and add to your notes afterwards.

Example

A student of fourteen who completed this activity gave the following order at the end of the poem. It differs from the poet's original, but the student justified his choice as follows:

Little – less – nothing – and that ended it.
And the saw snarled and rattled, snarled and rattled,
As it ran light or had to bear a load.
And nothing happened: the day was all but done.
No more to build on there. And they, since they
Were not the one dead, turned to their affairs.

D. Compare this version with yours. If it differs from your version, do you feel it is better or worse? Give reasons for your answer.

Boy's heartbeat slowing, getting quieter.

Everyone has forgotten about the saw. These verbs suggest the saw is a living thing, with a malicious life of its own is carried on after the boy is dead and may kill again.

Adults? They were supposed to take care of the boy. They use him and callously turn back to their business affairs.

Thinking ahead to your assignment

One possibility is to construct a sequencing exercise like the one above for other students to complete. Use your own choice of poetry and provide materials and instructions. Include an explanation of how the activity may help students to understand and appreciate the poem.

'Interviewing' a Poem

You have probably seen an interview with a well-known person on television. They are usually asked a series of questions about their experiences and opinions. After the interview you may well feel that you know the person a little better.

The questioning technique of an interview can be used to get to know a poem in more depth.

Why do this?

- Poems are often shorter than other forms of writing. But there can be a lot in them! A poem is a concentrated form of writing, which sometimes needs to be read and re-read to get the most out of it. Taking on the role of an interviewer and 'interviewing' a poem, helps you to look at poetry in a new way. Details you might have missed before may now become important.

- A mock interview is an enjoyable way of talking about a poem with a partner.

- An interview starts with questions – being able to ask relevant questions is essential to understanding not only poetry but any other form of English.

Activity A: reading and writing

1. Suppose that you are a reporter. You have been asked to investigate a death for your newspaper. Using a poem as evidence for your report, decide who you would interview and what questions you would ask. Choose from *Out, Out . . .* (page 89), *Limbo* and *The Important Man* (page 91). All these poems deal with a person

dying. List the evidence from the poem about the cause of death and who or what was to blame. What message or moral, if any, would you want to point out to your readers from the incident? What angle would you adopt for the article? What factors would you emphasise for readers?

Option: with a partner. One of you is the reporter and one an eye-witness or a character in the poem. Using your questions about the death, hold an interview. You could include quotations from the 'eye-witness' in your article. Give the article a headline.

2. Now write the article based on the poem, for one or more of the following:

- a paper local to the area where the death took place
- a serious daily newspaper
- a Sunday magazine
- a tabloid newspaper.

Option: What questions would you like to ask the poet who wrote *Out, Out . . ., Limbo* or *The Important Man*. Make a list that you would include in a letter to him or her. Write the letter.

Limbo

Fishermen at Ballyshannon
Netted an infant last night
Along with the salmon.
An illegitimate spawning,

A small one thrown back
To the waters. But I'm sure
As she stood in the shallows
Ducking him tenderly

Till the frozen knobs of her wrists
Were dead as the gravel,
He was a minnow with hooks
Tearing her wide open.

She waded in under
The sign of her cross.
He was hauled in with the fish.
Now limbo will be

A cold glitter of souls
Through some far briny zone,
Even Christ's palms, unhealed,
Smart and cannot fish there.

Seamus Heaney

The Important Man

Bothered by his wife
From a good dinner,
The lock-keeper goes down
To his ponderous water's edge
To steer in the new corpse.

A bargee, shouting to be let through,
Stumps over the bulging lengths
Of his hatches,
Cursing the slowness
Of water.

The lock-keeper bends and pulls her out
With his bare hands.
Her white eyes, rolled upwards,
Just stare.

He is an important man now.
He turns to his charge:
The water flows uphill.

Jeffrey Wainwright

Activity B: note-making/asking questions

1. Choose a poem in this chapter or one of your choice. Write a list of questions which
   A. test 'factual' knowledge of the poem or word-meanings, identify features of style such as metaphors, similes, rhyme, repetition, e.g.
      1. *Out, Out . . .* what does the word *ether* mean?
      2. *Limbo* – name the place given in the poem where events happen.
   B. ask for personal feelings and ideas about the poem, more general impressions. Such questions often start with words like
      How . . .?
      Why . . .?
      When . . .?
      Tell me more about . . .?
      What did you think about . . .?

2. Exchange the questions with someone else in your class. Answer those you have received while yours are being answered. Talk through the answers together and compare notes on the poem.

   Some of the questions that students have found useful for many poems are:

   WHO is the main character in the poem?
   WHO is spoken to/about? WHAT are their feelings?
   WHERE does it take place?
   HOW is it put together; WHAT is its shape?
   HOW does it sound?
   WHAT details seem to work best/do you enjoy?

Thinking ahead to your assignment

One possibility is to write a news article or interview based on one or more poems which you have chosen.

Filling in some Missing Details

Compared with many other forms of English, poems are quite short. There is little room for mistakes – every word must count. The next activity will help you to look in more depth at particular words and phrases and the work they do – their effect.

Activity: with a partner

Innocence by Thom Gunn follows the life of a boy from school to joining the army and on to World War Two. The poet questions how someone can watch a person being burned alive without being horrified.

1. Read the poem and discuss it with your partner. Fill in the seven gaps from the list of words. There are five more items in the list than there are gaps.

2. With your partner, decide on possible reasons why the poem is titled *Innocence*.

(The process of filling in gaps is sometimes called **cloze** or **cloze procedure**.)

Innocence

He ran the course and as he ran he grew
And smelled his fragrance in the field. Already
Running, he knew the most _____
The egotism of a healthy body.

Ran into manhood, ignorant of the past;
Culture of guilt and guilt's vague heritage,
Self-pity and the _____ ; what he possessed
Was rich, potential, like the bud's tipped rage.

The Corps developed, it was plain to see
_____ , endurance, _____ , and skill
To a morale firm as morality
Hardening him into an instrument, until

The finitude of virtues that were there
Bodied within that swarthy uniform
A compact innocence, childlike and clear,
No doubt could penetrate, no act could harm.

When he stood near the Russian partisan
Being burned alive, he therefore could behold
The ribs wear gently through the darkening skin
And sicken only at the Northern cold,

Could watch the _____ burn with a violet flame
And _____ only at the smell,
And judge that all pain finishes the same
As melting _____ by his boots it fell.

List

loyalty	feel digusted
courage	quietly
man	he ever knew
patriotic feeling	with sickening violence
fat	soul
notice	spiritual feeling

Thinking back

You probably tried to fit words and phrases into the gaps to see if they sounded right. Sounding right can mean having the right rhyme where rhyme is used in a poem, e.g. 'grew' and 'knew' in the first four lines. The length of

the word or phrase can matter too. If the last line read:
'As melting *with sickening violence* by his boots it fell'
it would make sense, but it would sound too long and clumsy after the previous lines.
The choice of exactly the right word or phrase in a poem is very important. There are often several words which would do to make sense. Only one sounds right, however. Only one is perfect.
In the last verse:
Could watch the man burn with a violet flame would just about do, but
Could watch the fat burn with a violet flame is much better. *Fat* has a spitting sound, like the noise of burning, and *fat* is less personal and human than *man*.

When you next read a poem:
Find three or four interesting words or phrases in it.
Ask yourself:
– Why does that word or phrase sound right?
– Why is it better than other possible words or phrases
   that have similar meaning?

Talking about Poems – Comparisons

This section looks at two poems:
A Poison Tree by William Blake and
Tamer and Hawk by Thom Gunn.

The purpose of the activities is:

1. to learn about another interesting and important aspect of poetry – the use of comparisons;

2. to let you see some 'work in progress' by other students – a finished poetry assignment doesn't just happen. You should gain confidence from seeing that others have to work through various stages.

The two poems involve extended comparisons – the writers see one thing in terms of another. *A Poison Tree* compares nursing poisonous hatred for an enemy with nurturing a tree with deadly fruit. (Though this is not the only way of interpreting the poem.)
A small group of eleven-year-olds was given this poem to discuss. They were not given any guidelines about what to discuss. The start of their discussion follows the poem below.

Activity

Read the poem several times, aloud if you prefer, before going on. As you read the group's discussion, make a note of:

1. where you think they need some help,

2. where the group seem to be getting somewhere,

3. the help you would suggest for the group, the questions they might ask, the words they might look up.

4. Imagine you are their teacher. Which good points in their discussion would you tell the children to write down?

A Poison Tree

I was angry with my friend:
I told my wrath, my wrath did end.
I was angry with my foe:
I told it not, my wrath did grow.

And I water'd it in fears,
Night & morning with my tears;
And I sunned it with smiles,
And with soft deceitful wiles.

And it grew both day and night,
Till it bore an apple bright;
And my foe beheld it shine,
And he knew that it was mine,

And into my garden stole
When the night had veil'd the pole:
In the morning glad I see
My foe outstretch'd beneath the tree.

A Poison Tree: Discussion

A. I'll read it out then.

B. Come on.

A. 'I was angry with my friend:
    I told . . .'
'My friend?' . . . 'my wrath:' – Who's 'my wrath'?

B. 'I told my wrath . . .'

A. It's weird, this.

C. Yeah it's . . . (A. carries on reading aloud)

A. 'I was angry with my foe:
    I told it not, my wrath did grow.

    And I watered it in fears,
    Night and morning with my tears;
    And I sunn'd it with smiles,
    And with soft deceitful wiles.

    And it grew both day and night . . .'

B. That's the tree.

A. Yeah, right, er . . . (A. carries on reading to the end of the poem.)

A. Right, er, I think it's about this friend, right? And he gives him this apple and then he sees him under his tree, like in his garden, 'cos it says he was 'outstretched'.

B. Yeah.

A. The friend's asleep under the tree, and it's sunny, like in the summer when it's hot and you lie under a tree. That's what it means.

B. And he eats an apple. A big red apple.

A. Yeah, um, sometimes it's night though.

A. Wait, 'day and night . . .' 'When the night . . .'. Yeah.

B. (Reads out) And it grew both day and night,
                till it bore an apple bright;
                And my foe beheld it shine,
                And he knew that it was mine.
    Foe, foe – that's someone else . . .

C. So he doesn't give the apple to his friend.

A. He gives it to his enemy.

C. Yeah.

A. No, wait, the enemy stole it though.
    (A. reads last verse)

B. When . . . right . . . he's glad about it. He wants this foe to eat the apple . . . because he's greedy and . . .

A. He gets revenge . . . He's glad to get revenge on the foe.

C. Um . . . it's been eating away inside of him and he wants to get revenge.

Testing a students' guide

Three sixteen year old students completed the activities in this unit. They used what they had learned to write a guide to a poem entitled *Tamer and Hawk*. The guide was intended to help others understand and appreciate the poem.

The activity below asks you to read the poem and say how useful you found the guide. It shows how one group of students began to work towards a poetry assignment by making notes on their discussion. The acitivity will also help you to learn more about comparisons in poetry, something you looked at in the previous section.

Activity

1. Read *Tamer and Hawk* several times, aloud if you prefer.

2. As you read make a note of your questions about the poem and things that interest or puzzle you.

3. Then, read the guide, commenting on how helpful you found it. Did it:

— answer any of your questions about the poem?

— pick up any of your points of interest?

— add anything you had not thought about?

— make you want to read the poem again?

Tamer and Hawk

I thought I was so tough,
But, gentled at your hands
Cannot be quick enough
To fly for you and show
That when I go I go
At your commands.

Even in flight above
I am no longer free:
You seeled me with your love,
I am blind to other birds –
The habit of your words
Has hooded me.

As formerly, I wheel
I hover and I twist,
But only want the feel,
In my possessive thought,
Of catcher and of caught
Upon your wrist.

You but half-civilize,
Taming me in this way.
Through having only eyes
For you I fear to lose,
I lose to keep, and choose
Tamer as prey.

Thom Gunn

A guide to *Tamer and Hawk* by Thom Gunn

Students: Andrew, Danny, Karen.

Notes: 1. 'seeled' is a special word used in training birds of prey like hawks. The bird is blinded or blinkered so it concentrates on its trainer's wishes.

2. 'habit' can be a covering for the head as well as an action you are used to.

This short poem caused some arguments, because when we read it at home, there were two different views – Karen thought it was about a hawk being trained and Danny thought the 'training' was a way of thinking of a relationship between a man and a woman, a metaphor in other words. After talking, and re-reading the poem, we decided that both views were valid. The hawk is also a man and the tamer or trainer is also a woman, and the 'taming' is their relationship.

In thinking about who is in the poem, there is 'I' and 'you', as you can see from the first two lines:

'I thought I was so tough
But gentled at your hands . . .'

('gentled' is unusual . . . a shorter version of 'made gentle', perhaps – the poet often does this, packing in lots of meaning and cutting out unnecessary words so that readers have to think.)

The hawk tells of how the trainer has taught him to fly on command and has 'imprisoned' him in the habit of these commands (a play on words – 'habit' as a covering for the head and a familiar action).

The hawk's emotions are of pride and eagerness. Once, the hawk was completely free. Now, he goes through the motions of his former actions for the tamer, not himself:

'As formerly, I wheel,
I hover and I twist . . .'

but he always comes back to the tamer's wrist because he would rather lose his freedom than lose her:

'Through having only eyes
For you I fear to lose,
I lose to keep . . .'

Danny felt that the poem was a metaphor, a way of a man thinking about how his relationship with a woman has changed him. The term for a clever comparison developed over a whole poem is 'a conceit'. The man is held in captivity by the woman – possibly that captivity is marriage, but he doesn't want to lose her love, whether they are married or not. He feels very possessive about the tamer.

'I am no longer free:
You seeled me with your love . . .'

Some lines which convey the two aspects of the poem (hawk and man) are:

'You seeled me with your love,
I am blind to other birds.'

'Seeled' is a special word from falconry – the hawk can't look for other birds to hunt, but the man is 'blinded' from looking at other women too, 'birds' being slang for girls or women. This is another play on words. Most of the poem is about the tamer's effect on the hawk. The last verse reverses it, and asks about the effect of the hawk on the tamer. She is also his prey – when you think of hawks hunting and killing small birds, you wonder whether he will harm her, mentally or otherwise.

A lot has been compacted into small lines, such as:

'I lose to keep . . .'

(I lose my freedom to keep your love) but if you try re-writing the line as we did, you will see it is very difficult to be so neat and sharp. The words are sharp and simple, right for a message about strong basic emotions of possessive love and feeling trapped. The lines are short and the same rhymes occur very often, again and again in a set pattern. Some lines have rhymes and repeated words inside them as well as at the end, like 'show', 'go' and 'go' near the start. All the rhymes make the poem

seem very tight, like a parcel bound up with a lot of string. We think this is deliberate, to give a sense of captivity. Some questions were left at the end, like whether the ending was a surprise or not. So we thought this poem was clever. It is more unusual and deep than you might think at first.

Thinking back to your aims

● Enjoying poetry? In the last activity, you have seen extensive notes on one short poem from a group of sixteen-year-olds. They obviously thought it was worth spending time on the poem, and they enjoyed doing it.

● Learning ways of working with poetry?
In the unit, you have:
  – chosen poems
  – read them aloud
  – talked about poems
  – made notes on them
  – looked at shapes and structures
  – worked on the details of individual words
  – considered comparisons in poetry.
  You could do some or all of these things for your own choice of poems.

● Working towards an assignment?
By choosing poems from this unit or elsewhere and working on them in the ways you have practised, you are half way to your assignment.

Poetry Assignments

Some suggestions for your poetry assignment. Choose one or invent your own.

Reading and writing

1.   Make a collection of poems you enjoy.
They could be:

– on a similar subject, or contrasting ones
– with similar or contrasting themes or messages
– with similar structures or details
– by the same writer or a group of writers.

Write an introduction to the collection, explaining the interest and appeal of the poems you have chosen. Aim to help readers understand and enjoy the collection.

2.   Include some of your own poetry in the collection. Explain to readers how you arrived at your ideas and made choices in writing. You could include some of your early versions or first drafts and show where and why you made changes.

3. Pick one or two poems which interest you and write a guide to help other students understand and enjoy the poetry you have chosen. There is a section from a students' guide in this unit. You could also look at *Cole's Notes, Brodie's Notes, York Notes* for ideas. They provide published guides to poetry and literature.

4. Design an assignment for future GCSE students on poetry. Decide which poem or poems you will include and how you would like students to get to know them — on their own or in groups, by reading or writing, for example. You could use a 're-arranging' activity or ask students to 'fill in gaps', as in this unit. Whichever activity you design, you should explain why you think this would help students enjoy and appreciate the poetry you have chosen.

5. Base some of your own poetry on recent news.

6. Write a news article or an interview based on one or two poems. You could include a mock interview with the poet or with one of the characters in the poem.

7. From a poem that interests you, choose a character who does not speak in the poem. Write the poem from his or her viewpoint.

8. Write an extract from that character's diary.

9. Write a modern version of the poem, ten years on . . . twenty years on . . . or whatever time seems suitable.

Speaking and listening

1. Talk in groups to compare and contrast two poems. Re-arrange a scrambled poem or fill in missing details. Read the completed poem and discuss your results.

2. Read aloud to a small group, to your class or another class. You could pick two contrasting poems, or the same poem read in two different ways, to show different interpretations of it.

3. Choose a poem containing different speaking parts and read it aloud in a group. You could also add sound effects.

4. Prepare and hold a mock interview with a poet or a character in a poem. Perform it for a group or the rest of the class.

Option
Prepare and tape-record choices 2 or 3 in SPEAKING AND LISTENING. A personal collection or a guide for other students could also be prepared as tape-recorded assignments, in the style of a radio review.

Unit 6 Facts and Opinions

Aims: to distinguish fact from opinion,
to understand information based on facts and opinions,
to be able to clearly express fact and opinion.

On the way: the following activities will help you to
achieve these aims:
- examining two versions of a student's profile
- advising the student, using information from the profile
- looking at fact and opinion in newspapers
- examining ways in which information about males and
  females is presented
- understanding factual information using the topic of
  young people and leisure
- learning how to express facts and opinions — example,
  a student's speech
- making decisions based on fact and opinion
- understanding information from leaflets

By the end: you will have two assignments for your
coursework folder, one on understanding and one on
writing. There is also an assignment on speaking and
listening which could be used as part of your assessment
in oral English.

Assignments: Understanding — using and
adapting information on leisure activities.

Writing — a leaflet; a consumer report.

Speaking and listening — decision making; a talk;
a debate.

Facts or opinions?

Considering a Student's Profile

This unit is about facts and opinions. A **fact** is something that we know to be true. Think about your school report — it probably contains information about your age and sex. These are facts — there is no dispute or argument over whether or not they are true. An **opinion** is a judgement, or a belief about something. It is a point of view.

Returning to your school report, statements such as *a reliable pupil, a helpful boy, a hardworking girl,* are examples of opinions. There is no certainty that such statements are true. The *hardworking girl* may be seen as *making no effort* by another teacher. Opinions are not based on certainty. They are often disputed — people often disagree with the opinions of others.

There is, however, a connection between fact and opinion. People often base their opinions on facts. For example, a student may have received a grade B for English. This fact can lead to various opinions about her attainment. One teacher may see it as praiseworthy, feeling that the student has made real progress. Another teacher may view it as a poor result, feeling that the student is capable of a higher grade. Facts can be interpreted in various ways. They can lead to different judgements, to different opinions.

Activity

Below is an imaginary, but fairly realistic, student profile. It contains facts about the student and opinions based upon those facts. There are two versions of a tutor's comments on the student's performance. Read the profile carefully, then answer the questions which follow.

Student Profile

April 19....

STUDENT DETAILS

NAME: L. Rimmer

FORM: 5T

AGE: 16 years 1 month

ATTENDANCE: Fifth year: Term 1: 98%
Term 2:100%

PUNCTUALITY: Term 1: On time for registration 75%
Term 2: On time for registration 78%

SUBJECTS STUDIED: GCSE

English
Maths
Craft, Design Technology
Physics
Economics
Home Economics
Spanish

STUDENT'S PREFERENCES:

HIGH INTEREST

CDT
MATHS

MEDIUM INTEREST

ENGLISH
PHYSICS
ECONOMICS
HOME ECONOMICS

LOW INTEREST

SPANISH

TEACHERS' ESTIMATED
GRADES AT GCSE:

FOURTH YEAR COURSEWORK

English	B	C
Maths	C/D	C
CDT	A	A
Physics	C/D	D
Economics	D	D
Home Economics	D	D
Spanish	G	G

INTERESTS: tennis, badminton — school first teams in both.
Out of school: tennis, visiting friends, listening to records and tapes.

PERSONAL PROFILE

TUTOR'S COMMENTS (VERSION A)

ATTENDANCE: Excellent, rarely absent and then only with good reason.

PUNCTUALITY: Is able to be on time and we have talked about being quicker when changing after tennis practice in the lunch hour, and I hope that continued improvements will be made.

ADAPTABILITY: Adapts easily and enjoys the challenge of new situations. Does not get anxious when routine disturbed.

SELF-RELIANCE: Able to set own goals and tasks in some subjects — needs guidance in others and responds to firm direction when necessary.

TUTOR'S COMMENTS (VERSION B)

ATTENDANCE: Good, but spoilt by some afternoons at the dentist's.

PUNCTUALITY: Must learn that punctuality matters — late half the time in the afternoons.

ADAPTABILITY: Butterfly mind — poor concentration on the essential routine tasks of school life. Too easily distracted by the new and different.

SELF-RELIANCE: Some complaints — particularly in Spanish — about this student's lack of ability to get down to work and get on with it.

Questions on the profile

1. If this were your profile, which version of the tutor's comments would you prefer? Why?

2. What is similar in the two sets of comments?

3. What is different?

4. Suggest how and why it is possible for different tutors to hold different opinions which are based on the same set of facts.

Facts can be checked, verified (shown to be true) and, if necessary, corrected. On the student's profile the grades for fourth year coursework can be checked and any mistakes put right. However, opinions cannot be verified. They are judgements rather than facts. They are, however, very important. A tutor's opinion about a student can determine whether she/he is entered for a particular examination and it appears on references to employers. Important decisions are based on opinions.

Role play based on a student's profile

The following activity asks you to examine facts, form opinions, and make decisions based upon those facts and opinions.

Activity

Role play
What to do

1. Divide the class into two halves, X and Y.

2. Set a time limit of 10 or 15 minutes for the whole class.

3. Form small groups as shown in the diagram.

4. Imagine that the profile on the previous page was written about a fifth year student called L. Rimmer.

5. Each group is a panel of teachers. You are meeting to decide what advice you will give to L. Rimmer on courses, training and careers after the fifth year.
What should L. Rimmer do? For example, should she/he stay on at school, take 'A' levels, if so in which subjects, etc.

6. You have the information available from the profile, apart from one detail.
X groups - turn to page 119 for this detail.
Y groups - turn to page 142 for this detail.

Courses/ Training		Careers	
X	Y	X	Y
1. 'A' levels	1. apprenticeship	1. mechanic	1. clerk
2. BTEC	2. secretarial	2. nurse	2. surgeon
3. etc.	course (RSA)	3. etc.	3. etc.
	3. etc.		

3. Examine the range of qualifications/training L. Rimmer has been advised to obtain. Why do you think they differ?

4. a) How many careers chosen by Y groups are similar in pay and status (prestige) to those chosen by X groups?

b) How many are different?

c) Why do you think they are different?

5. It may have become clear at this stage that some groups were advising a girl and some a boy. Rejoin your groups and discuss why the differences in advice occurred.

a) How much of the advice was based on facts about L. Rimmer?

b) How much was based on opinions about L. Rimmer?

c) How much was based on opinions about suitable training and careers for boys and girls? What are these opinions?

Reporting Back

1. Report back to the rest of the class, with one spokesperson per group.

2. Make lists of the recommended courses/training and careers for L. Rimmer, as shown above right.

Newspapers - Facts and Opinions

Newspapers are supposed to contain facts. The editorial section in newspapers contains comment and opinions — judgements on the news. However, as the following activities will show, the division between fact and opinion is not as clear cut as it might appear.

DAILY NEWS

Public wants grants for school students

POST

SURVEY ON BILL TO GIVE GRANTS TO CHILDREN AT SCHOOL

IN FAVOUR OF BILL AS IT STANDS 28%

IN FAVOUR OF BILL WITH AMENDMENTS 22%

AGAINST BILL 31%

DON'T KNOW 19%

DAILY ECHO

Public says NO to grants for school pupils

Activity 1

Look at the two newspaper headlines on either side of the billboard. They are based on the same facts — the results of a public opinion poll on a Bill to give grants to all children of school age. A BILL is a proposal which M.P.'s discuss in Parliament to decide whether to make it law. AMENDMENTS are changes to a Bill before it becomes law. They could be small changes, e.g. children from families earning over £100,000 year will not receive grants. Or, they could be major changes, e.g. only pupils from families with six or more children will be eligible for the grant.

Question

WITH A PARTNER
Explain how the two newspapers could arrive at different headlines.

Comment

People tend to see 'figures' as 'facts'. Putting information in the form of numbers makes it appear factual. However, you must be wary of seeing figures in this way. You may have heard the phrase 'lies, damn lies and statistics'. This means that statistics can be used to lie convincingly. As you have seen from the newspaper headlines, statistics can be interpreted in very different ways. It is also important to see how the statistics have been collected. Have they been based on 'leading questions' which lead people to particular answers, e.g. 'You do think grants for school children are a good thing, don't you?' Are the people questioned those who are likely to hold a particular view, e.g. parents with children of school age? Statistics are not always what they seem.

"I'm a 'don't know'! 'Don't know' whether to smash your face in or not."

Activity 2

(You will need a newspaper for this activity.) Opinions can be expressed in such a way as to appear convincing, to seem like facts. Some of the techniques for doing this are shown below.

a) 'OBVIOUSLY...' by using words like *obviously*, *clearly* or *plainly*. e.g. It is obvious that the country cannot afford to give grants to school students.

b) GENERALISATION... by making sweeping claims which cover a wide range of people, things or ideas. e.g. All humane and intelligent people know that school students should get more financial support.
A generalisation ignores what may be important differences between people.

c) EMOTIONAL APPEALS... by using words/phrases which bring out feelings of approval or disapproval. e.g. Why should honest taxpayers give grants to young hooligans?

d) ASSOCIATION... by linking the opinion to a famous person who may or may not have any special expertise on the subject, or by claiming that the opinion is not yours but a famous expert's, or by associating the view with pleasant experiences.
e.g. The Prime Minister says abortion is wrong. A leading heart specialist recommends exercise. The family must be preserved - think about family outings, Christmas and birthdays with the family.

e) REPITITION... sometimes an opinion can be made to stick in the mind and become accepted as 'fact-like' by simply repeating it often enough.
e.g. Young people have too much money - just look at the money they waste on clothes and music. Young people have too much money for their own good.

1. Look at the editorial section (*Editorial, Comment, Viewpoint*) of a newspaper. See how many examples of the above techniques you can find. You could do the same with the *Letters/Correspondence* section.

2. Select one or more news items and see how many examples of the above techniques are used.

3. Examine a news item and an editorial. They should be roughly the same length. How many examples of the above techniques does each contain?

Option

Working with a partner, get two rival newspapers for the same day.

1. Find a subject which **both** papers cover and on which they have different opinions.

2. Cut out the two articles.

3. List the facts common to the two articles.

4. What is **your** opinion about the subject, based on these facts?

5. What other facts would you like to know?

6. How do the two newspapers use the same facts to support their different opinions?

Uses

READING AND LISTENING

You can pick out techniques like repetition and emotional appeals when you are:
- reading an article in a newpaper or magazine
- listening to a speech, debate or interview
- watching a documentary
- watching or listening to news on television or radio.

Presenting Information

Facts and Opinions on Girls and Boys, Women and Men

Information is presented in many different ways: — it is broadcast via television and radio, printed in words and pictures in newspapers, magazines, leaflets and books, it is exchanged in conversation, it appears in a variety of statistical representations — tables, bar charts, pie charts and line graphs.

This section examines a range of facts and opinions about males and females which has appeared in print. It shows some of the ways in which information can be presented. You can make a similar collection on a subject of your choice as part of a coursework assignment.

Activity 1

The four pictures, shown opposite, are taken from primary school reading books published in the 1960's. Your parents may have learned to read from these books.

1. If you asked the girl in picture 3 what she wanted to do when she grows up, what do you think she would say?

2. If you asked the boy in picture 4 the same question, what do you think he would say?

3. Pictures often put forward a point of view. What do these pictures suggest is the proper role for girls and boys, women and men?

4. Judging by these pictures, which would you rather be — a girl or a boy? Give reasons for your answer.

5. If you were illustrating a reading book to be used today, what changes would you make to the pictures? Give reasons for your answer.

1

6b We like to help

The Ladybird Key Words Reading Scheme

2

3

Activity 2

Read the following newspaper article. It contains facts and opinions. The facts are used to support the author's opinions.

1. Write a short paragraph which summarises the point of view presented in the article.

2. Why does the author use facts about children's toys to support her argument?

3. Do you agree with the author's view that the treatment of girls is unjust? Give reasons for your answer.

The girl who always says yes
by Jacqueline Penrose

In a high street toyshop I picked up a catalogue. It states — and I think rightly — that 'babies are ready to start to learn about the world right from the start... The right toys will provide the stimulation they need...'

And they learn that certain types of toys are suitable only for boys, and others for girls. There's Judy and Velvet, her pony: 'This pretty pair are tipped for the top...' What boy would be caught dead with that? There are 'dolls' for boys:

'The Cosmic Command defence forces. These brave heroes...' And Tommy Gunn, 'a man of many roles. He is trained as a medic, but can use a gun...'

For the girls: 'Sweet Baby. Advice for young mothers from Auntie Brenda. Dear Auntie Brenda — I want to be sure to keep my baby warm this winter, but it is also very important that she has pretty clothes...' And there's Rachel Ballerina, 'of great beauty and grace but she is also a young lady with a tremendous interest in fashion'.

Even when children themselves want to experiment with a wider range of toys, this hard sell makes it very difficult. So does the packaging. I saw a large chemistry set in the window, a boy and a girl shown on the box. The boy was eight inches high, the girl only two. Before the Renaissance artists would make the most important figure in the picture the largest; children's own work follows the same principle and they can recognise it when they meet it on a box. This toy is for boys.

In another shop I picked up a selection of children's birthday cards, which will be chosen by adults, presumably to conform to their notions of what children are like — or ought to be like.

First, for the newborn boy. His cot is trimmed with blue. Inside it says: 'A baby boy — you must be proud; and very happy, too...'

The baby girl is dressed in pink, with a ribbon in her hair. Inside: 'Bet she's even sweeter than you ever dreamed she'd be...'

Sons one is proud of, daughters are sweet.

For the four-year-olds: the girls' card shows a girl in a flounced pink dress, flowers in her hat. She pushes a pram and carries a handbag. The four-year-old boy is dressed in jeans and trainers, and he is fishing.

At eight the girl is wearing a dress (with a tiny waist) made entirely of pink roses. There are roses in her long fair hair — but she does nothing. Inside it says: 'For a sweet young Miss who is eight today and growing up in such a lovely way...'

The eight-year-old boy is on a racing bike, in a T-shirt, jeans and trainers.

Such examples abound. They show that girls are still expected to be sweet, demure, pretty and passive, destined only for domesticity and motherhood. They are reminded of it wherever they look. It is not a matter of choice. Hard luck if they are born with a creative, dynamic intelligence. Parents and teachers need to be more aware of the problem if the unjust and arbitrary division of people into active and passive roles is to stop.

(from *The Guardian*, April 6, 1982)

Activity 3

In this activity information is presented in three forms — a line graph, bar charts and a newspaper article. Read the article, examine the graph and charts, then answer the questions which follow.

Women's earnings as a percentage of men's 1970-1985

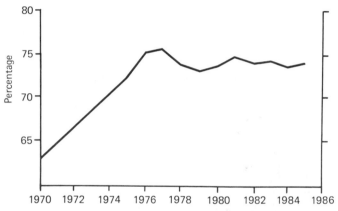

Maths genius Ruth scores again

**By JOHN IZBICKI
Education Correspondent**

RUTH LAWRENCE, the 14-year-old mathematics genius who managed to pass with flying colours an Oxford University maths degree at First Class Honours level in two instead of three years, has done it again.

Because Oxford rules forbid anyone to graduate in less than three years she was made to spend one year in an academic limbo, and rest is something this child finds unbearable.

She decided to have a bash at Oxford's gruelling physics degree course. This she completed in one year instead of three, and last night the University confirmed her second First Class degree..

She will now be the only undergraduate to go through the graduation cermony to receive two degrees, completed in half the normal six years.

That will not be all, for Ruth returns to her college, St Hugh's, in October to take up her special scholarship and study for a D Phil. If she manages to go through in a year she will be the youngest Doctor of Philosophy in modern times: Dr Ruth Lawrence, aged 15.

Ruth is not the only prodigy in the family. Her younger sister, Rebecca, 12, is at Chetham's, the famous School of Music at Manchester, where she holds a scholarship for her brilliance as a pianist.

Last year Rebecca passed her O-level maths exam five years earlier than normal having passed her Grade Eight piano examination at nine, a phenomenal achievement.

(from *The Daily Telegraph*, July 5, 1986)

104

School leavers with higher grade results at 'O' level or CSE[1] in selected subjects: by sex, 1970/71 and 1985/86

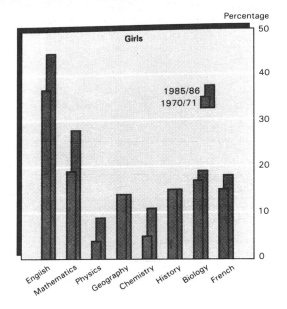

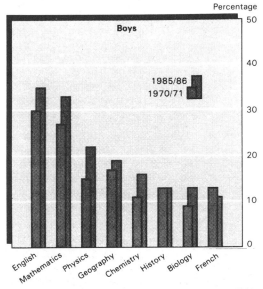

1 'O' level grades A-C, CSE grade 1. Excludes 'O' level passes on 'A' level papers.

(from *Social Trends 18,* HMSO, 1988.)

1. Briefly summarise the trends shown in the graph on women's pay compared to that of men.

2. From the bar charts:

a) Name two subjects in which girls have more passes than boys.

b) Name two subjects in which boys have more passes than girls.

c) In subjects where boys have more passes than girls, is it:

(i) Because more boys than girls enter the subject?
(ii) Because more boys than girls passed the subject?
(iii) A mixture of (i) and (ii)?
(iv) Impossible to tell from the information in the bar charts?
Give reasons for your answer.

3. The information in the graph and charts could have been presented in the form of words. Why do you think words would be a less effective method of presentation?

4. The article makes news both because of the child's age and because she is a girl. Using information from the bar charts, suggest why Ruth's achievements are particularly unusual for a girl.

5. From what have you learned so far, suggest why women's average earnings are only three quarters of men's average earnings.

Activity 4

Read the following poem by John Agard.

Rainbow

When you see
de rainbow
you know
wha he doing —
one big smile —
across the sky —
I tell you
God got style
the man got style

When you see
raincloud pass
and de rainbow
make a show
I tell you
is God doing
limbo
the man doing
limbo

But sometimes
you know
when I see
de rainbow
so full of glow
and curving
like she bearing child
I does want know
if God
ain't a woman

If that is so
the woman got style
man she got style

1. The poem contains an interesting speculation. What is it?

2. A number of books have been written claiming that the first supernatural beings which people worshipped were female. In particular they were fertility goddesses. Where in the poem does John Agard link the idea of fertility and a goddess?

3. Why might a poem be more effective than an academic book filled with facts and figures in putting forward the view that God might be female?

Activity 5

Look at the following cartoons.

1. What viewpoint do you think each cartoon expresses?

2. How effective do you think each cartoon is in expressing its viewpoint?

3. What advantages do you think cartoons have compared to other ways of presenting a point of view?

Young People and Leisure - Facts and Statistics

Facts are often represented in statistical form in tables, charts and graphs. This section looks at information in these forms using the topic of young people and leisure. The activities allow you to practise **understanding** factual information. This skill is part of your GCSE English course.

Activity 1

WITH A PARTNER
The following **pie charts,** based on research in the U.S.A., show times spent by children on various leisure activities for a typical weekday.

Children's Free Time

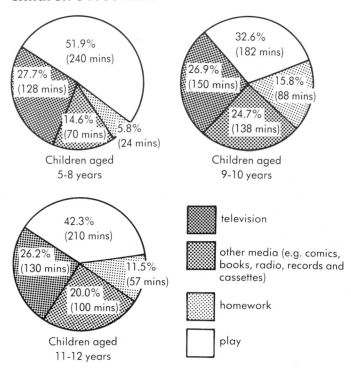

Children aged
5-8 years

Children aged
9-10 years

Children aged
11-12 years

▓ television

▒ other media (e.g. comics, books, radio, records and cassettes)

░ homework

□ play

Questions

1. Ask your partner these questions. Your partner will use the PIE CHARTS to answer verbally.
— Which age group spends most TIME watching television?
— Which age group spends the largest PROPORTION of its free time watching television?
— Describe the changes in time spent watching television and using 'other media' such as comics and books, as children get older.

2. Now your partner will ask you these questions. Use the PIE CHARTS to answer verbally.
— Which age group spends most time playing?
— Which age group spends the largest proportion of its time playing?
— Describe the changes in the pattern of playing and homework time as children get older.

3. Write a brief account of how children spend their free time, pointing out the similarities and changes as children get older. Use the information in the PIE CHARTS. Do not include any OPINIONS at this stage.

4. Draw a PIE CHART showing how you spend your leisure time on a typical weekday.

5. How far do the above charts reflect your memories of how you spent free time when you were younger?

6. How far do the charts fit in with your OPINIONS on how children's free time SHOULD be spent?

Options

1. a) How much time do you think you spend on various activities such as homework and watching television?

b) Check your impressions against the facts by keeping a diary for a week.

c) If others (e.g. friend, Headteacher, possible employer) were going to see the diary, what changes to the 'facts' would you make? Why would you make these changes?

2. List the things you do in your free time. Make a note of the amount of time spent on each and present the information in chart or table form. Are you surprised by the results? If so, why? Compare your results with those of another student. What are the similarities and differences?

3. FOR DISCUSSION

a) Do you think that children should be allowed to watch what they like on television? Why or why not? Note the use of fact and opinion in you discussion.

b) A lot of attention has been given to the possible effects of television on young people, especially with developments such as cable and satellite stations. Some argue that life was more violent before television; others that violence in society has grown as the screen shows more bloodthirsty acts. What is your view? On what information do you base your view?

Activity 2

This activity allows you to compare two ways of presenting the same information. The table and bar chart were compiled from a nationwide survey. They show the percentage of 16-19 year olds taking part in various leisure activities, other than watching television.

Version A   Table

Activity	% 16-19 year-olds who did the activity in the month before they were interviewed
Indoor sports	
Snooker/pool	20
Darts	17
Outdoor sports	
Football	12
Fishing	2
Spectator sports	
Watching football	7
Other activities	
Cinema	33
Dancing (discos)	34
Football pools	6
Listening to records	92
Reading books	56
Listening to radio	94

(adapted from *Social Trends 12,* HMSO, 1982)

Version B   Bar Chart

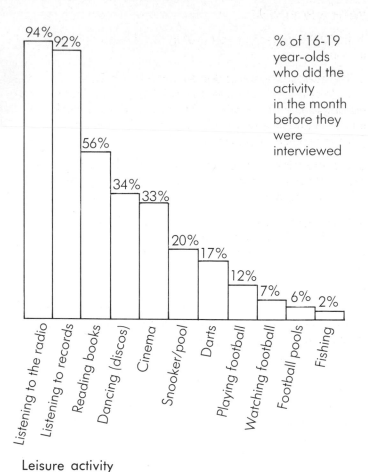

% of 16-19 year-olds who did the activity in the month before they were interviewed

Leisure activity

1. Which form of presentation — the table or bar chart — do you prefer?
Give reasons for your answer.

2. Using the bar chart, record your own leisure activities as a percentage of the total time available to you for leisure in one week.

Facts and Opinions in Speech

One of the aims of this unit is to help you to clearly express facts and opinions yourself. This section helps you to do this for your speaking assignment. It looks at a speech written by a student aged sixteen. The speech was delivered to a large audience of Manchester business people, as part of a speaking competition. There was a choice of topics. The student concerned chose to write about being sixteen.

Activity 1

WITH A PARTNER

1. Read the speech. If you prefer, one of you could read it aloud.

2. The speaker has included facts on what young people can and cannot legally do. He has then related his opinions and feelings to these facts. Do you think this is an effective way of using facts and opinions? Give reasons for your answer.

3. Do you think the speech contains the right balance of fact and opinion - too much of one, not enough of the other, or about right? Give reasons for your answer.

4. Many speeches do not simply present facts and opinions. Speakers often seek to amuse and entertain. Do you think the speech below has succeeded in this respect? Give examples in your answer to support the points you make.

5. Pick out a phrase or sentence which suggests that the speech was written for an audience of business people. Briefly explain your selection.

By his moustache ye shall know him! Yes I've been acquainted with the fig tree for some time, because Adam had to use the leaf — I've heard about temptations because Eve sank her pearly teeth into the apple, but last Saturday I received my personal symbol of masculinity — an electric shaver. I was 16.

The shaver, however, is representative of the dichotomy of this coming of age. Why anyone felt I had need of this article is a mystery to me, because the only moustache I possess has a plastic nose with spectacles attached. In fact for a few delirious seconds I had expected a remote control T.V. to mark the event, but then it would have put them in hock with the bank manager. Yes, I was 16 and along with the razor was bestowed on me the legal right to purchase and smoke cigarettes, to get married, to have sex and to pay full-fare on the buses — but, of course, NOT the right to vote. How on earth could anyone expect a 16 year old to have political opinions? Nor must I purchase alcohol because it is so much more damaging to health than smoking — isn't it?

Obviously the machinery of state decrees that I am supposed to be different now that I have reached this age milestone, but to be truthful no one seems to notice this new man who walks the street with legal rights and designer stubble. I certainly do not feel any different at all. There has been no miraculous transformation from acne-plagued adolescence to the Sylvester Stallone look alike that I had anticipated. Possibly I should have been prepared for this disappointment for I clearly remember that on my 15th birthday I felt that 1986 was going to be the year when it all came together. I would be popular with the girls, maybe even the life and soul of the party — perhaps, I thought, I might even get invited to one. In fact, since my 16th birthday not even the first formers have noticed my new status. I've grown taller since the day I joined my school but my ego has not swelled as I've climbed the school's ladder — rather I suggest that mine developed a slow puncture.

Undisputedly I have acquired more information in the last year. Now I really know the French past historic — so useful to my future. I know about isotopes, atomic fusion, Shakespeare and the rat's reproductive system. I am aware that girls are not caught as easily as a cheeky grin and "Hi want to dance?" I know the blonde pocket-venus that I fancy is not the one my mother wants me to take home. But the real me is just the same — no more ready to bring up a family or stomach the violence the cinema allows me to witness than I was two weeks ago.

It is patently obvious that this age-limit business is not based on common-sense! Project my dilemma forward two years. Technically I could with the demise of a long lost uncle, be the head of the family firm, drive my two children to play-school in my B.M.W. and even buy a bottle of wine for the dinner party I would be holding to celebrate my eighteenth in my Surrey mansion. I am of age — you see — the machinery of state decrees that this is so.

May I respectfully suggest that the state is misinformed. What we need is not evidence of a birth certificate, but evidence of responsibility — this may I add, does not occur over-night. A responsible citizen's test should be a compulsory element of each pupil's education, maybe in the form of community service. In fact I would go so far as to say problems arise because the barriers are lifted too suddenly. Deaths on the road are highest in the 17-19 year-old age group and it is true to say that the average 18 year-old gets well and truly ratted on that great birthday.

Perhaps we should learn from other countries. In some Canadian provinces, for example, compulsory driving lessons are given in schools and in France children accompany their parents outside the home and drink wine, under parental supervision from an early age. Thus the age barrier becomes less significant, the forbidden fruits less desirable because the seeds have been carefully nurtured.

As Oscar Wilde once said, "The book of life begins with a man and woman and ends with Revelations". Yes I am 16; I am a man but I still await the revelation as to the logic.

Ages of responsibility - the facts

Many of you might have found lists of facts dull and boring when you have had to learn them for an examination. However, facts can be very interesting, particularly if they are relevant to your own life. You may well find this from the list on the following page which gives some of the rights and responsibilities of young people according to the law in 1987.

Activity

Prepare a speech relating your own experience and opinions to some of the facts listed below. Bear in mind the type of audience for whom the speech is intended. If you have the opportunity, deliver the speech to the intended audience.

Ages of responsibility

At 10   You can be convicted of a criminal offence if it is proved you knew what you were doing was wrong. If you are detained by the police, you will be old enough to be strip searched, fingerprinted, photographed.

At 12   You can buy a pet.

At 13   You can get a part-time job (but you can't work for more than two hours on a school day or on a Sunday).

At 14   You can go into a pub but you cannot buy or drink alcohol there.
You can posses a shotgun or air pistol.

At 15   You can see a category 15 film.
You can open a Post Office Girobank account (but you'll need a guarantor).

At 16   You can probably leave home without your parent's consent.
A girl can consent to sexual intercourse.
You can marry with your parents' consent.
You can leave school.
You can claim supplementary benefit.
You can apply for your own passport.
You can drink beer, cider or wine with a meal in a restaurant.
You can buy liqueur chocolates.

At 17   You can be used by another person in order to beg in the street.
You can hold a licence to drive most vehicles.
You can become a street trader.
You can hold a pilot's licence.

At 18   You become an adult (in the eyes of the law). You can vote, serve on a jury, change your name, make a will, enter a betting shop, be tattooed, donate your body to science, pawn something.

Before children's rights: original illustration for *Oliver Twist* by George Cruikshank.

For discussion

● Which items in the list do you find surprising?.
● Which do you agree with?
● Which do you disagree with?
● What changes, if any, would you make in ages of responsibility?
Give reasons for your answer.

Assignments: Speaking and Listening

Here are three types of ORAL ASSIGNMENT. You could try all three and pick the type with which you feel most confident for your oral assessment in GCSE English.

Remember the GCSE gives you the chance to show your abilities in speaking and listening as well as in writing.

1. Decision making

Imagine that the three teachers opposite have applied for the job of Pastoral Care at your school. The position involves counselling students, preparing references for them and giving advice on careers. In a group of 4-6, hold a meeting to decide which of the applicants you would give the job to.

You can be:
(i) Yourselves — a pupil panel.
OR
(ii) An appointment panel — Headteacher, School/Parent Governor(s), Pupil Representative(s), Deputy Head(s).

The information on which you must base your decision consists of photgraphs of the applicants plus a short description of each. The description contains both fact and opinion. You should bear this in mind when reaching a decision.

Report your decision and the reasons for it to the rest of the class. State to what degree your choice was influenced by (1) facts and (2) opinions about the candidates.

This assignment emphasises skills in working as part of a group and your ability to use information to make decisions.

OPTION

Hold interviews — divide your group into two halves, one half is the interviewing panel and the other half the job applicants. The panel should prepare a list of questions for the applicants. The applicants should each, separately, try to anticipate questions and think of 'background' information about themselves based on the information provided. Interview each applicant before you reach your decision.

Report your decision and the reasons for it to the rest of the class. State what degree your choice was influenced by (1) facts and (2) opinions about the candidates.

Candidate: Carmel Jones

Mrs Jones is 29 and has been teaching Maths and Computer Studies for eight years. After gaining a Degree in these two subjects from Leeds University, she taught in two schools, one in London and one in Manchester - both were large comprehensive schools. At her second school, Mrs Jones was in charge of Careers and was also a Fifth Year Tutor. She became interested in Pastoral Counselling through this work and has been on two courses recently, one on records of achievement for students and one on counselling students who are having difficulties at school. She would like to run a computer club. Her teaching colleagues say that she works hard at her job, and is a fun-loving person. She does not have strong views on many subjects.

Candidate: June Wallis

Ms Wallis is 36 and has taught Business Studies and Economics for twelve years, firstly in a Further Education College for five years, secondly in a comprehensive school in the Midlands for four years. Her present school is also a comprehensive in the Midlands, where she has taught for three years. After qualifying with an Economics Degree from Birmingham University, she worked for two years as a Research Assistant with a radio station on news and current affairs programmes, but says in her application that she finds much more job satisfaction in teaching, and much more scope to advise, direct and lead others. At her present school, she is Head of Sixth Form and in charge of Business Studies throughout the school, where she has introduced many new courses, sometimes despite opposition at first. Her job as Head of Sixth Form involves student counselling.

Her colleagues say that she is very well-organised and totally reliable, that she is tirelessly energetic and determined. She expects and gets high standards from her students. Her colleagues add that she is very strong-minded and prepared to risk unpopularity to see through new developments in which she believes.

Candidate: Simon Kerr

Mr Kerr is 36 and has taught German and French for fourteen years - his Degree is in Modern Languages from Oxford University. He taught at one school, where he ran many clubs, including Music Appreciation and Chess. His present school is fee-paying, and his application says that he wishes to join a school in the state system and to teach a wider range of students. His colleagues say that he is a quiet person, a good listener who is always willing to help anyone interested in his subjects. His colleagues think of him as an intellectual — he speaks many languages effortlessly and has won many chess championships. He thinks of himself as an idealist with strong views on the development of talent in everyone and on fair play.

2. A talk

Choose a subject about which you know something, which interests you and which you think would interest others. Your subject might be a leisure activity like those discussed in this unit. Decide who your audience will be:
— the rest of the class?
— a smaller group?
or if you have checked with your teacher that it is practical to arrange other audiences
— other students in your school — your year or younger?
— parents or other adults?
— beginners or people who are already interested in the subject?

Decide on the purpose of your talk — to provide a balanced view of the subject, to support a particular viewpoint, to inform, to interest, to entertain, etc. Where possible, support your opinions with facts and try to develop a consistent argument which leads to a conclusion. Try to make clear to your listeners when you are stating facts and when you are expressing opinions.

Give your talk, invite, and be ready to answer, questions from your listeners.

A talk emphasises your awareness of an audience and your ability to respond to their interest (or lack of it) and to questions.

3. A debate

In a group of 5-6, choose a subject that you would like to debate. The subject could be one dealt with in this unit, or another of your choice. Turn the topic into a motion, starting with the words:
'We believe that...'
If you pick the topic of girls and boys from this unit, you might form a motion that: 'We believe that girls and boys should study the same subjects at school', or 'We believe that a woman's place is in the home'.

Each side in a debate introduces a range of facts to support its viewpoint.
This is a useful exercise for discovering how facts can be used to support opinions. You might even find that both sides use the same facts to support opposing viewpoints.

A debate emphasises your ability to take on a role in a more formal situation of speaking and listening.

Decide who will be:

1. **Chairperson** — to introduce the motion that the speakers will support or oppose. To keep order and make sure the debate runs smoothly.

2. **Proposer** — to make a short speech in favour of the motion.

3. **Seconder** — to add further points in favour of the motion and support the proposer.

4. **Opposer** — to make a short speech against the motion.

5. **Seconder** — to add further points against the motion and support the opposer.

6. If there is a sixth person in your group, they are the Questioner, who 'cross-examines' the Proposer, Opposer and their Seconders.
Each person in the group needs to research the topic and form facts and opinions into a well-organised and interesting speech to convince listeners to vote for them.

Many formal debates are held like this:

1. Chairperson sits in the centre, facing audience — the rest of the class.
Proposers sit to right, Opposers to left.

2. Chairperson introduces the proposal and invites each speaker to contribute in this order:
(i) Proposer
(ii) Opposer
(iii) Seconder FOR the motion
(iv) Seconder AGAINST the motion

3. The Chairperson invites questions from the audience.

4. The members of the audiences vote, for or against the motion.

Leaflets

Leaflets come in all shapes and sizes and are produced for a wide variety of purposes. Government departments such as the Department of Health and Social Security produce millions of public information leaflets each year. (Some of these are so badly written that an organisation has been formed to translate them into plain English.) Local authorities, charities, trades unions, banks, building societies and a range of other organisations produce masses of leaflets on practically every subject under the sun.

Your aim in this unit is to understand fact and opinion and to consider the forms of English used to transmit information. Leaflets have a number of advantages for realising this aim:
— there are a wide variety
— they are usually written with a specific audience or group of people in mind
— they usually have a clear and limited aim
— they are easy to obtain: libraries, post offices, banks, shops, careers conventions and other public places usually have displays of leaflets
— they are usually free (check, though, before you take any)
— the language they use varies from the incomprehensible to the plain, simple and direct
— they often contain information presented in a variety of forms - maps, charts, graphs, photographs, cartoons, comic strips, pictograms.

A public information leaflet produced by a local authority

Activity

As you will need to go to a library for this activity, you will probably have to carry it out for homework.
How effective is the *Finding Out* leaflet above?
To test it out:
● go to the library
● read the *Finding Out* leaflet when you are there
● use points 8 to 12 to find the title of a book you have not seen before on any subject which interests you.
You have now CONSUMER TESTED the leaflet.

Uses

If you choose to design and write a similar leaflet for your assignment, consumer test the draft/rough version on someone else to see if they can use it. Change your draft accordingly, if you think their comments are useful, before writing the final version.

A leaflet produced by a charity

Activity

Read the leaflet entitled *Living on the Edge of the Desert*. Pay close attention to the design (the way it has been set out), the illustrations, the choice of language and the information it provides.

1. What is the purpose of the leaflet?

2. Does the leaflet achieve its purpose? If your answer is 'yes', how does it achieve its purpose? If your answer is 'no', what changes would you make in order for its purpose to be achieved?

LIVING ON THE EDGE OF THE DESERT

WAR ON WANT at work with the farmers of the Sahel »

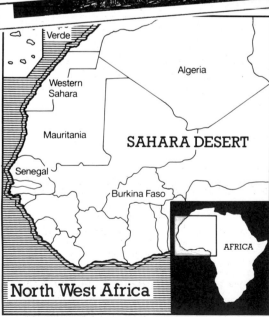

North West Africa

WAR ON WANT is involved in a number of successful projects. They are aimed at strengthening peasant associations and helping the individual peasants to improve and diversify their food production.

The Senegal River Valley

In one project, War on Want has helped to introduce improved seed varieties, animal traction for ploughing and a vegetable gardening scheme. Now the villagers are growing more food for themselves – and earning a cash income by selling their surplus produce.

In another project, we provided pumps, piping and a tractor for clearing land, so that a group of 13 village associations could start their own irrigation scheme. This will give them the protection against drought.

The Network for Integrated Development

In Thies, 30 miles inland from Dakar, War on Want is backing a series of projects sponsored by the African Network for Integrated Development – who have devised a new irrigation scheme for the area in collaboration with village co-operatives and government authorities.

Twenty village associations are now involved. Training and advice is given to farmers on market gardening, appropriate equipment and maintenance. And loans are made to co-operatives to provide working capital.

Cereal Banks in Burkina Faso

In Burkina Faso, one of the world's poorest countries, War on Want supports a project which is sending agricultural extension workers into the villages. These are training men and women who teach the local people literacy and basic management skills.

Farming in the neighbourhood of famine and drought.

Cultivating the desert. Sahrawi women grow vegetables to help feed a refugee camp.

A community project in Cape Verde. Young people from the cities learn to work the land with local women and men.

The same project is also supporting local initiatives such as cereal banks, which provide an alternative source of cereals to that of private traders and reduce the risk of speculation in grain.

Co-operatives in Cape Verde

Off the coast of north west Africa in Cape Verde, we are working with the Instituto Nacional des Cooperativas (INC). With loans for new piping and pumps to improve the irrigation system and cheaper supplies of seeds and fertilisers, we are helping local farmers to rebuild their agriculture, which has suffered badly from over-exploitation of the land. We are helping to support small-scale fishing co-operatives with boats and equipment.

War on Want also supports a youth organisation, Juventude African Amilcar Cabral which runs annual camps. Here young people from urban backgrounds work alongside local women and men on community projects, particularly tree planting, and the building of dykes, terraces and water barriers for water conservation.

Overleaf: How your help can defeat famine...

Growing food in the hostile desert.

IN THE SAHEL region of north west Africa – a semi-arid belt of land on the edge of the Sahara Desert – life has always been desperately hard.

And in the last ten years the Sahel has suffered recurrent drought and two devastating famines. The people are being pushed literally to the margins of existence.

But now farmers of the Shahel are fighting back.

They are taking the initiative to improve their food production and raise themselves and their families out of desperate poverty. And they are doing this with War on Want's active support, by organising themselves, making use of modern equipment and techniques, and adapting the centuries-old traditional methods of farming.

The Traditional Foods

Sorghum
Related to sugar-cane, this is one of the most successful crops in the Sahel because of its ability to grow in very arid regions. It not only provides a nutritious source of food but its long stalks provide plentiful supplies of animal fodder.

Millet
Another traditional crop which can grow well without rain. This tall, spear-like cereal shoots up and matures in only 11 weeks and is one of the Sahel's dominant crops.

Vegetables
The Sahrawi people have proved that is is possible to grow fresh vegetables in desert conditions. They have had success with foods which are resistant to high concentrations of salt in the soil, such as tomatoes, beetroot, potatoes and onion.

Trees
Massive deforestation in the Sahel has upset the ecological balance by exposing the delicate but vital top soil to the elements. To make the land fertile again new drought resistant trees are being nurtured in special nurseries.

You can help the farmers of the Sahel take control of their future.

Without the help of our supporters, War on Want could not have done so much to help the farmers of the Sahel in their efforts to take control of their own lives.

Now there is so much more work to be done – and we need your support to succeed. The hostile climate is still a fact of life and the threat of famine is ever present.

Please send what you can today. You can be sure your gift will be used where it is most needed.

Thank You!

WAR ON WANT

WAR ON WANT, Room 91C, FREEPOST, 37-39 Great Guildford Street, London SE1 0YU. Tel: 01-620 1111.

Activity

1. Make a collection of leaflets.

2. Pick out several contrasting leaflets and for each decide on:
a) its audience
b) its aim
c) the method used to achieve its aim
d) how successfully it achieves its aim.

3. It is said that a good leaflet or poster should have 'AIDA', that is:
Attract — a word/phrase/colour/illustration to attract the eye

Interest — words/diagrams to keep the reader's interest
Desire — creating the desire to become involved; pointing out what is in it for the reader
Action — a reply slip/address/telephone number or other ways readers can follow up their reading of the leaflet or poster.

Which of the leaflets you have collected uses each of these features most successfully?

Assignment: Understanding

The assignment which follows gives you the chance to use the skills you have learned in this unit to produce a piece of work for your coursework folder.
● This assignment is based on READING AND UNDERSTANDING. It uses information about what people do in their spare time. The information is in a variety of forms — a chart, a table, a cartoon and a piece of writing.
● You may be given this assignment by your teacher to do in class, within a fixed time. In this case you will be working under 'controlled conditions'. At other times there may be no time limit and you may be allowed to complete your work at home or in a library. This means that your coursework folder gives an indication of the way you write in different circumstances.
● If you are not set a time limit, allow one hour for this assignment.
● If your course includes an examination, working under controlled conditions provides examination practice.
● This assignment includes charts and tables. Should they form part of English? Aren't they just for Maths, Science and technical subjects?
If you look at a:

— magazine
— instruction manual
— recipe
— textbook
— poster
— advertisement
— newspaper
— leaflet
— comic
— Teletext
— computer screen
— application form
— brochure

facts and opinions are not only presented in words, but also in pictures, charts and tables. This is English in real life. Different ways of presenting information must, therefore, be understood if you wish to select information, follow instructions, form opinions and, most importantly, be aware of the world around you.

Understanding: leisure time

Questions (total possible marks in brackets)
A. 1. Using the bar chart write a brief outline in two or three sentences of how participation in sports has changed over the three years shown. (5)
2. Using the table, write several paragraphs comparing and contrasting the leisure interests of teenagers and pensioners. (10)
3. Using the extract on page 118, make two lists of opinions on the future of leisure. The first list should be headed: *Hopes for the future*. The second list should be headed: *Fears for the future*. (10)

B. Suppose that your local council is making plans for new leisure facilities in your area.
Write a letter to your local newspaper giving your views on the leisure facilities that you would like to see provided. (15)
OR
Write the speech you would give at a public meeting held by the local council Leisure and Planning Committee, at which members of the public are invited to give their views. (15)
OR
Write a report to the Chairman of the Leisure and Planning Committee in which you argue for the type of leisure facilities that you think would be best for young people in your area. (15)

If you wish, you may use information from the chart, table and extract for Section B.

Participation[1] in indoor and outdoor sporting activities: by sex, 1977 and 1980

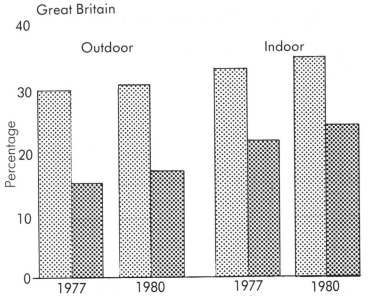

Great Britain

 Males
Females

[1]Percentage of the population aged 16 or over engaging in sporting activities in the 4 weeks before interview (annual averages). Source: *General Household Survey,* 1977 and 1980.

Participation[1] in selected social and cultural activities: by sex and age, 1983.

Great Britain — Percentages and numbers

	Males					Females				
	16-19	20-34	35-59	60 or over	All aged 16 or over	16-19	20-34	35-59	60 or over	All aged 16 or over
Percentage in each age group engaging in each activity in the 4 weeks before interview										
Open air outings										
Seaside	4	7	8	5	7	8	10	8	5	8
Country	1	2	3	3	3	2	3	3	3	3
Parks	2	4	3	2	3	3	8	3	2	4
Entertainment, social, and cultural activities										
Going to the cinema	17	13	5	1	7	25	13	5	2	8
Visiting historic buildings	6	8	9	7	8	6	9	10	7	8
Going to the theatre/opera/ballet	2	4	4	3	4	5	5	7	4	5
Going to museums/art galleries	2	3	3	3	3	3	4	4	2	3
Amateur music/drama	6	4	3	2	3	6	3	3	2	3
Attending leisure classes	1	1	2	1	1	1	2	3	2	2
Going to fairs/amusement arcades	4	2	1	–	1	5	3	1	–	2
Going out for a meal[2]	39	47	42	31	41	44	46	44	29	40
Going out for a drink[2]	68	82	65	41	64	72	67	49	18	46
Dancing	25	13	9	4	10	41	15	11	4	12
Home-based activities										
Listening to records/tapes[2]	93	81	65	40	65	94	80	67	32	62
Gardening[2]	20	39	58	59	50	13	36	49	37	39
Needlework/knitting[2]	3	2	2	2	2	34	49	54	44	48
House repairs/DIY[2]	31	55	61	39	51	12	31	30	13	24
Reading books[2]	44	49	51	51	50	62	62	62	59	61
Sample size (=100%) (numbers)	722	2,314	3,509	2,199	8,744	727	2,650	3,841	3,088	10,306

[1]Annual averages of participation of people aged 16 or over.
[2]The high participation levels are partly attributable to the fact that these items were prompted (see Appendix, Part 10: General Household Survey).

Source: General Household Survey, 1983

The future of leisure

With the development of microtechnology the optimists look forward to a golden age of leisure. The 5 day, 40 hour week will be a thing of the past. Save for the occasional spell of work, people will have the freedom to enjoy a life of leisure. This will not of course happen overnight. People will have to be educated for leisure and there needs to be a large investment in sport and leisure facilities.

But, unemployment is not the same as leisure. There are few if any signs that the unemployed regard their situation as leisure. At present they do not appear to be compensating for unemployment with 'leisure activities'. Employment appears to provide a type of status, identity and sense of personal worth that leisure activities cannot offer.

The pessimists are forecasting an age of enforced unemployment for a large section of the population. Part of the workforce will enjoy the fruits of the new technology while the rest will be unemployed, their skills unwanted and unneeded. The following rather pessimistic note is sounded by the famous science fiction writer Arthur C. Clarke, author of 2001.

> In the world of the future, the sort of mindless labour that has occupied 99% of mankind for much more than 99% of its existence, will, of course, be largely taken over by machines. Yet most people are bored to death without work — even work that they don't like. In a workless world, therefore, only the highly educated will be able to flourish, or perhaps even survive. The rest are likely to destroy themselves and their environment out of sheer frustration. This is no vision of the distant future: it is already happening, most of all in the decaying cities. So perhaps we should not despise TV soap operas if, during the turbulent transition period between our culture and real civilisation, they serve as yet another opium for the masses. The drug, at any rate, is cheap and harmless, serving to kill time for those many people who like it better dead.

(quoted in 'Society Today' p.1, in *New Society,* 29 November 1979)

The future of work and leisure?

Assignments: Writing

Here are suggestions from which you can select. Alternatively, design your own.

A. Leaflets

1. Research, design and write a leaflet for one of these purposes, or for a purpose of your choice:
— to publicise a club, organisation or society to which you belong or would like to start,
— to make people more aware of a service or facility in your area
— to give information on how a particular group (e.g. pensioners, young women, younger people, owners of bicycles, pet owners) can help protect or advance itself.

OR

B. Consumer Reports

1. Select a product or service for which you have an advertisement. Write a consumer report on the product or service, taking into account the claims of the advertisement and how far they are justified.

OR

2. Choose two similar products or services (e.g. two types of canned drinks, training shoes, calculators) and write a consumer report which compares the two.

OR

3. Write a consumer report on a product or service of your choice.

For these assignments, you should think carefully about who is going to use your report. People of your own age for a report on training shoes? Housewives for washing powders? Children for comics?

Adapt your writing style and presentation to the intended audience.

Thinking Through Your Work

The aims of this unit are to understand and express facts and opinions. Collecting information for an assignment can be a lengthy process. Careful planning can save time and energy. You have considerable freedom of choice in the subjects you select. Use this freedom well — it will show you can work independently.

Starting

It is usually better to start from something you know, something that interests you. You are more likely to ask relevant questions and know about the information available and where to find it. You are less likely to become bored with the topic.

Planning and research

Planning saves time, organises your research and gives direction to your work.

Here is an example of a plan which you might find useful.

Subject ....
Aim of leaflet/report ....
Audience for leaflet/report ....
What I need to find out
1.
2.
3.

Where and how I can find it out
1.
2.
3.

A time limit for completing the assignment should be built into your plan. Research can go on and on and on. If you are writing for information, be sure to post your requests well before the deadline for handing in your assignment.

Role play, student's profile
(from page 100)
X groups — his name is Leslie Rimmer

Unit 7 Novels and Plays

Aim: to enjoy and appreciate novels and plays.

On the way: activities include:

Novels
- looking at covers and reading 'blurbs'
- describing impressions from opening pages
- keeping a reading log
- understanding characters
- thinking about style
- making a storyboard

Plays
- appreciating words
- understanding stage directions
- outlining a play.

By the end: you will have sampled a variety of writing styles and completed at least one assignment for your coursework folder.

Assignments: Novels
1. Putting yourself in their shoes.
2. Standing back; assessing; analysing.
3. Helping others to enjoy reading.
4. Further ideas.

Plays
A choice of writing and speaking assignments.

Novels

First impressions

First impressions are important. On the basis of first impressions you may decide to make a friend, to watch a T.V. programme, to buy a record or read a novel. First impressions of a novel are usually based on the cover and the first few pages. Can you judge a book by its cover? Are the title and the description on the cover important? This section seeks to answer these questions by examining the covers of several novels.

Choosing novels

The course outline or syllabus for GCSE English asks students to read whole works of literature. This is a real opportunity to get to know a novel or a play. Through novels and plays you can learn about life in other times and places and develop your understanding of people and their behaviour.

On your course, the teacher may give you a novel to read or you may be given a list of books to choose from. So, let's start where most people do — looking at the covers of books.

Activity

Here is an example of a cover you might find.

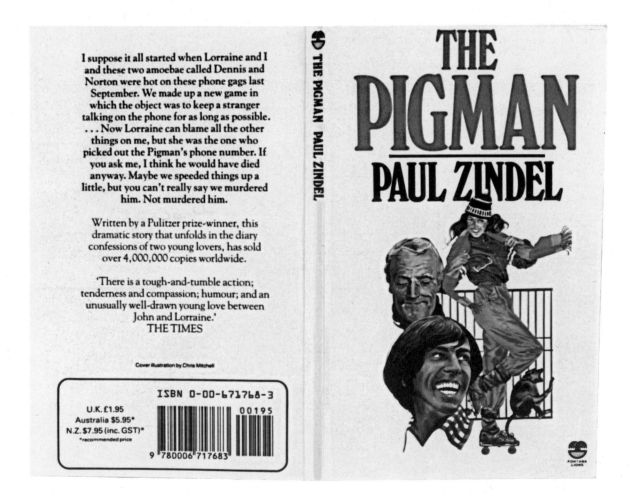

I suppose it all started when Lorraine and I and these two amoebae called Dennis and Norton were hot on these phone gags last September. We made up a new game in which the object was to keep a stranger talking on the phone for as long as possible. ... Now Lorraine can blame all the other things on me, but she was the one who picked out the Pigman's phone number. If you ask me, I think he would have died anyway. Maybe we speeded things up a little, but you can't really say we murdered him. Not murdered him.

Written by a Pulitzer prize-winner, this dramatic story that unfolds in the diary confessions of two young lovers, has sold over 4,000,000 copies worldwide.

'There is a tough-and-tumble action; tenderness and compassion; humour; and an unusually well-drawn young love between John and Lorraine.'
THE TIMES

Cover illustration by Chris Mitchell

ISBN 0-00-671768-3

U.K. £1.95
Australia $5.95*
N.Z. $7.95 (inc. GST)*
*recommended price

9 780006 717683   00195

THE PIGMAN PAUL ZINDEL

THE PIGMAN
PAUL ZINDEL

Questions

1. What are your first impressions of the book from the front cover?

2. Who and what would you expect it to be about?

3. What effect does the title have on you?

Here is one view of the cover. How does it differ from yours?

The cover illustration suggests that the novel will be concerned with three people, an older man, a boy and a girl. The girl looks very active and lively. The smiling faces suggest that the reader might expect some laughs from the book. The older man is shown with a more reflective, sadder expression. He is looking down — is his expression a sad smile? The reader might expect some unhappiness in the older man's life.

The 'blurb', on the back cover in this case, confirms what the front cover suggests. 'Blurbs' usually give a very brief description of plot, character and setting, with praise given to the novel by reviewers in newspapers and journals, by other novelists or perhaps by readers.

The 'blurb' is another place to look when choosing a novel. But remember, it is written to attract readers or buyers of the book, so it is bound to be complimentary.

Can you judge a book by its cover?

Don't be put off by a cover which looks unexciting. Often, the author does not design or choose the cover, so you may not give his or her writing a fair chance. A popular book may be printed several times in new editions, with a new cover for each edition.
Here are two covers for the same novel.
Which do you think it the more recent edition?
Why?
What are your first impressions of the book from each cover?

Starting points

You have looked at three starting points — and their limitations — for choosing a novel and beginning to get to know it:

● the cover
● the title
● the blurb

Use these starting points in libraries or bookshops to help you choose a novel. But remember — first impressions are not always correct.

The Opening Pages

Your aim is to get to know a novel. Give it a fair try. The cover and the blurb do not tell the whole story by any means. It is the inside that counts. In many ways the first few pages are the most important. If you enjoy them, you will probably read on. If not, you may well stop there.

This section examines the openings of five novels.

The Pigman

Read the first page of *The Pigman*. (The cover of one edition of this book is shown on page 122). Read the comment which follows.

a) Does the comment reflect your understanding of the opening? Give reasons for your answer.

b) Does the opening page make you want to read on? Explain your decision.

The Pigman

Chapter 1

Now, I don't like school, which you might say is one of the factors that got us involved with this old guy we nicknamed the Pigman. Actually, I hate school, but then again most of the time I hate everything.

I used to really hate school when I first started at Franklin High. I hated it so much the first year they called me the Bathroom Bomber. Other kids got elected G.O. President and class secretary and lab-squad captain, but I got elected the Bathroom Bomber. They called me that because I used to set off bombs in the bathroom. I set off twenty-three bombs before I didn't feel like doing it anymore.

The reason I never got caught was because I used to take a tin can (that's a firecracker, as if you didn't know) and mould a piece of clay around it so it'd hold a candle attached to a fuse. One of those skinny little birthday candles. Then I'd light the thing, and it'd take about eight minutes before the fuse got lit. I always put the bombs in the first-floor boys' john right behind one of the porcelain unmentionables where nobody could see it. Then I'd go off to my next class. No matter where I was in the building I could hear the blast.

If I got all involved, I'd forget I had lit the bomb, and then even I'd be surprised when it went off. Of course, I was never as surprised as the poor guys who were in the boys' john on the first floor sneaking a cigarette, because the boys' john is right next to the Dean's office and a whole flock of gestapo would race in there and blame them. Sure they didn't do it, but it's pretty hard to say

you're innocent when you're caught with a lungful of rich, mellow tobacco smoke. When the Dean catches you smoking, it really may be hazardous to your health. I smoke one with a recessed filter myself.

Comment

Someone is addressing us directly. He or she 'hates school' and could be the school-age John or Lorraine of the cover. Whichever it is, the claim to fame is rather out-of-the-ordinary: 'I got elected the Bathroom Bomber', so the reader's curiosity is aroused by this 'anti-hero' or 'anti-heroine'. Most of the words are ordinary, but some, like 'guy', 'Franklin High' 'boys' john' and 'G.O. President' suggest that the character is American.

The nickname is the title of the novel — the character who addresses us has become involved with 'The Pigman'. Perhaps, then, the rest of the novel will look back to how they met and what happened when they did. The 'I' who 'hates school' is looking back to something important in his or her life.

Empire of the Sun

Read the opening of *Empire of the Sun* and the comment which follows.

a) Does the comment add to your understanding of the opening?
Give reasons for your answer.

b) Would you have written a similar comment? What points would you have made which are not included in the comment?

c) *Empire of the Sun* was a bestseller when it was published in 1984. Would you buy or borrow a copy having read the first page? Give reasons for your answer.

Empire of the Sun

The Eve of Pearl Harbor

Wars came early to Shanghai, overtaking each other like the tides that raced up the Yangtze and returned to this gaudy city all the coffins cast adrift from the funeral piers of the Chinese Bund.

Jim had begun to dream of wars. At night the same silent films seemed to flicker against the wall of his bedroom in Amherst Avenue, and transformed his sleeping mind into a deserted newsreel theatre. During the winter of 1941 everyone in Shanghai was showing war films. Fragments of his dreams followed Jim around the city; in the foyers of department stores and hotels the images of Dunkirk and Tobruk, Barbarossa and the Rape of Nanking sprang loose from his crowded head.

To Jim's dismay, even the Dean of Shanghai Cathedral had equipped himself with an antique projector. After morning service on Sunday, 7th December, the eve of the Japanese attack on Pearl Harbour, the choirboys were stopped before they could leave for home and were marched down to the crypt. Still wearing their cassocks, they sat in a row of deck-chairs requisitioned from the Shanghai Yacht Club and watched a year old *March of Time*.

Thinking of his unsettled dreams, and puzzled by their missing sound-track, Jim tugged at his ruffled collar. The organ voluntary drummed like a headache through the cement roof and the screen trembled with the familiar images of tank battles and aerial dogfights. Jim was eager to prepare for the fancy-dress Christmas party being held that afternoon by Dr Lockwood, the vice-chairman of the British Residents' Association. There would be the drive through the Japanese lines to Hungjao, and then Chinese conjurors, fireworks and yet more newsreels, but Jim had his own reasons for wanting to go to Dr Lockwood's party.

Comment

This time the chapter has a title — *The Eve of Pearl Harbour.* This places the novel in time — just before the Japanese bombing of the American fleet in Pearl Harbour, after which the USA entered World War Two.

'The Eve of ...' creates interest and suspense — we are on the brink of something. 'Jim' does not address the reader so directly as in the opening to The Pigman. 'He' is referred to rather than 'I', but we seem to be quite close to the things that concern Jim, the events of his life and his thoughts.

'At night, the same silent films seemed to flicker against the wall of his bedroom in Amherst Avenue.' Jim seems to be disturbed by the war in this imaginative comparison of his worries to silent films of battles. The reader might expect, then, a novel which concentrates on the effects of a world-wide event on one person, one way of looking at a war which changed everyone's lives. The 'gaudy city' might intrigue the reader, who could learn something of unfamiliar places and times by reading on.

Pride and Prejudice

Read the opening of *Pride and Prejudice.* Do **not** read the comment which follows yet.

a) Write a comment on the opening.
Now read the comment in the book.

b) How does it differ from your comment?
What are the points of agreement and disagreement?

Pride and Prejudice

Chapter 1

It is a truth universally acknowledged, that a single man in possession of a good fortune, must be in want of a wife.

However little known the feelings or views of such a man may be on his first entering a neighbourhood, this truth is so well fixed in the minds of the surrounding families, that he is considered as the rightful property of some one or other of their daughters.

'My dear Mr Bennet,' said his lady to him one day, 'have you heard that Netherfield Park is let at last?'

Mr Bennet replied that he had not.

'But it is,' returned she, 'for Mrs Long has just been here, and she told me all about it.'

Mr Bennet made no answer.

'Do not you want to know who has taken it?' cried his wife impatiently.

'*You* want to tell me, and I have no objection in hearing it.'

This was invitation enough.

'Why, my dear, you must know, Mrs Long says that Netherfield is taken by a young man of large fortune from the north of England; that he came down on Monday in a chaise and four to see the place, and was so much delighted with it that he agreed with Mr Morris immediately; that he is to take possession before

Michaelmas, and some of his servants are to be in the house by the end of next week.'
'What is his name?'
'Bingley.'
'Is he married or single?'
'Oh! single, my dear, to be sure! A single man of large fortune; four or five thousand a year. What a fine thing for our girls!'
'How so? How can it affect them?'
'My dear Mr Bennet,' replied his wife, 'how can you be so tiresome! You must know that I am thinking of his marrying one of them.'
'Is that his design in settling here?'

Comment

The novel opens with what appears to be a blunt statement of fact, something which everybody knows, a 'truth universally acknowledged'. It soon becomes clear that the writer, Jane Austen, is using the word 'truth' in an ironic sense. Truth is simply the wishful thinking of scheming families. The author takes a cool look at their motives and laughs quietly at them.

Mrs Bennet is seen in this ironic light. The rich young man has not even moved into the area, but this 'large fortune' is so attractive that Mrs Bennet already expects him to marry one of her daughters.

From the opening we might expect the novel to deal with schemes for getting people married. With characters as foolish as Mrs Bennet, we might expect a lot of things to go wrong along the way.

Setting the Scene

The opening pages of a novel introduce people, places and plots. They may also touch on the author's main ideas or 'message'. Openings create expectations — readers expect something to happen next.

Below are the openings of two novels. Read them carefully then answer the following questions for each opening.

1. **Who** are the main characters?

2. **Where** are the events taking place?

3. **What** do you think will happen next?

4. Are there **points of interest** or mystery which might make readers curious and encourage them to read on?

The Nature of the Beast

Chapter 1

JOBS BLOW FOR HAVERSTON   Hope for Stone Cross

DOUBLE TRAGEDY FOR LOCAL FARMER

THE HAVERSTON BEAST STRIKES AGAIN!

REWARD OFFERED FOR
HAVERSTON BEAST   Beast's Last
Victim

Oh, I remember the headlines, but they don't tell the whole story — newspapers never do. They don't know the half of it. Not one half! And even if they did, I reckon they wouldn't care — not about Dad or Chunder, or the trouble I'm in.

I'll give them headlines! I'll hammer them with headlines until I make this town squint! But I bet you a pound to a pinch of salt that they still won't see the thread. No, they'll not see that all these things are connected up, just like knots in a length of thread . . .

And here's me, Bill Coward, Ned Coward's son and Chunder's grandson — nobody. Nowt. And I'm the only one who really knows about the Beast. But they'll never listen. Maybe you'll not listen either, but I'm telling you it started on that cold January evening when Dad came home from work.

He wasn't walking properly. He held onto the edge of the door, and then onto the sideboard, and he walked very very slowly to his chair, as if he was drunk. I thought he was drunk. He had a letter in his hand. That was about six o'clock. Then Chunder came round about an hour later, and Dad had never moved from his chair, and he hadn't touched the mug of tea I'd made for him.

Chunder *was* drunk. He went out into the backyard to pee in the drain — he was that far gone he didn't fancy climbing the stairs to the bathroom. He sat opposite my dad, but not before pulling a screwed up letter from his pocket and chucking it into the grate. He put his head in his hands and propped his elbows on his bony knees and watched the letter burn. Then he just sat watching the coals burning into red caves and sparks and black soot, and his face was red in the firelight, like a red skull with black eyes. He's very thin in the face is Chunder.

I thought there was some funeral on or something, but I didn't know what I was seeing — just my old man come home from work and Chunder round visiting. Chunder often comes round to watch the telly, especially in winter when there's not much doing on the allotment. Nowt strange in that, except they said nothing, at least not while I was there.

I must have gone out. I can't remember what I'd been up to. Something and nothing . . . Wait on . . . I do remember. Me and Mick Dalton were pelting the phone box with snowballs, well, slushballs. The snow was melted except for lumps by walls and yellow gritty bits. And Mick and me were lobbing handfuls at Angie Thomson in the phone box just to make her mad.

But the thing was — no one made us come in. We could have stayed out all night, we almost did, with our fingers freezing. Nobody yelled for us to come in, nor for any of the other kids.

Lord of the Flies
Chapter One
The Sound of the Shell

The boy with fair hair lowered himself down the last few feet of rock and began to pick his way towards the lagoon. Though he had taken off his school sweater and trailed it now from one hand, his grey shirt stuck to him and his hair was plastered to his forehead. All round him the long scar smashed into the jungle was a bath of heat. He was clambering heavily among the creepers and broken trunks when a bird, a vision of red and yellow, flashed upwards with a witch-like cry; and this cry was echoed by another.

"Hi!" it said, "Wait a minute!"

The undergrowth at the side of the scar was shaken and a multitude of raindrops fell pattering.

"Wait a minute," the voice said, "I got caught up,"

The fair boy stopped and jerked his stockings with an automatic gesture that made the jungle seem for a moment like the Home Counties.

The voice spoke again.

"I can't hardly move with all these creeper things."

The owner of the voice came backing out of the undergrowth so that twigs scratched on a greasy wind-breaker. The naked crooks of his knees were plump, caught and scratched by thorns. He bent down, removed the thorns carefully, and turned round. He was shorter than the fair boy and very fat. He came forward, searching out safe lodgements for his feet, and then looked up through thick spectacles.

"Where's the man with the megaphone?"

The fair boy shook his head.

"This is an island. At least I think it's an island. That's a reef out in the sea. Perhaps there aren't any grown-ups anywhere."

The fat boy looked startled.

"There was that pilot. But he wasn't in the passenger tube, he was up in the cabin in front."

The fair boy was peering at the reef through screwed-up eyes.

"All them other kids," the fat boy went on. "Some of them must have got out. They must have, mustn't they?"

The fair boy began to pick his way as casually as possible towards the water. He tried to be offhand and not too obviously uninterested, but the fat boy hurried after him.

"Aren't there any grown-ups at all?"

"I don't think so."

The fair boy said this solemnly; but then the delight of a realized ambition overcame him. In the middle of the scar he stood on his head and grinned at the reversed fat boy.

"No grown-ups!"

The fat boy thought for a moment.

"That pilot."

The fair boy allowed his feet to come down and sat on the steamy earth.

"He must have flown off after he dropped us. He couldn't land here. Not in a plane with wheels."

Using this section

In this section you have looked in detail at the openings of several novels. You will not be commenting in so much detail on every page of the novel you will read. However, you will be discussing many of the same things — the characters, settings, points of interest, and so on. Your comments in this section can be seen as mini-versions of discussions of novels as a whole. The lessons you have learned here can therefore be applied to the novel you have chosen.

Keeping Track of Your Reading

A personal reading log

An aim of this unit is to get to know a novel **for yourself**.

A personal reading log can help achieve this aim. It allows you to organise your thoughts and feelings about a novel as you are reading it. You can refer to the log when answering questions, planning assignments and in group discussions. The log may be kept in:

— a note book
— the back of an exercise book
— a section of your English file.

What to do

After reading each section or chapter of the novel, jot down your first impressions of anything that seems interesting and important:

● a turning point in the plot
● a vivid description
● an interesting, intriguing or puzzling event
● the author's point of view or 'message'
● a character's reasons for doing something
● your thoughts on the author's style
● page references for your notes.

Do not spend too much time writing ideas in your log. Remember, your notes are first impressions, not a final product to be presented as part of your coursework. They are a store of ideas from which to develop your assignment.

Other students' work

Looking at logs written by other students can help you to improve your log. A class of GCSE students was asked to read the novel *Lord of the Flies* by William Golding, during a holiday. (The opening of this novel is on page 127). The students were asked to jot down their first impressions, likes and dislikes, as soon as they had finished the novel. Extracts from their logs are given below. These extracts are the start of responding to a novel — they are notes rather than carefully written essays. Read them and answer the following questions.

1. Which student seems to have enjoyed the novel? Why do you think this?

2. Which student seems to dislike the novel? Give reasons for your answer.

3. What advice would you give to the students to improve their logs?

4. What have you learned from the extracts that will help to improve your log?

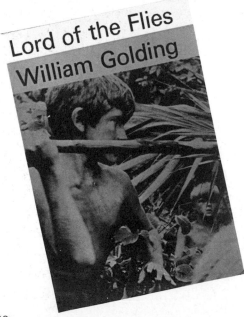

The start of a log: example 1

I read this book in the summer holidays and though it takes place on a desert island, it seems true to life. The children soon get bored; the 'coral island' type glamour starts to fade. Like the summer holidays, it feels great for a few weeks to have all that freedom, then you exhaust ways of amusing yourself, so you sit down, doing nothing, being bored. The glamour is starting to fade by chapter two, when a child dies in a fire. If the children on the island had acted more seriously and had been more organised they would have known the name of the boy killed in the fire. It occured to me that this is why we have fire drill. I suppose the incident proves the need for a school register. It shows the need for things like fire drill in normal life.

Chapter 4 — children really start to 'crack up'. ALL the glamour of the island has faded.
e.g — swimming in the pool, gathering fruit, climbing the mountain aren't interesting any more.
Some show signs of going mad, resorting to violence,
e.g — Jack kills the pig more out of wanting amusement and adventure than wanting

the pig meat. Jack becomes blood-thirsty.

The small children sit in the sand all day singing to themselves, humming or crying or shouting for their mothers. You felt afraid for them. What would I have done? I don't know, but I might have been more organised. Ralph is probably the hero – he tries to make rules, everyone ignores them though, even after they missed the ship that could've rescued them and Ralph tried to make a new set of rules.

There are incidents trying to represent life – the whole book is, really – like getting bored and resorting to violence (soccer hooliganism???) Why do things go wrong on the island and fall apart? At the start, everything is perfect for the children, such as: sandy beaches, sunshine, a warm pool, plenty of fruit to eat. Then things start to go wrong – the children start to mention a 'beastie' – it could be many things; I haven't made my mind up yet.

At the beginning, it seems like an adventure story that could be for quite young children, but there is violence and blood-lust, and the incidents represent things, like I was told that the

murders of boys on the island stand for World War 1 and World War 2.

The 'beastie' is mentioned as a serpent, like in the Garden of Eden where everything went wrong. All the rules that Ralph makes and the rules of normal life being broken are like the 10 Commandments. When Ralph was hunted down and the whole island destroyed by fire, then the naval officer arrives on a ship – this could be like the end of the world. William Golding is pointing out, how man is destroying the world. It isn't a book with many laughs, but it makes you wonder. The hunting of Ralph and the fire could be like World War Three.

The start of a log: example 2

1/ At the beginning of the novel, the author doesn't describe the plane crash very well. The opening is therefore confusing because you don't know exactly where these children are or how they got there.

2/ I don't see why the fat boy, known throughout the book as 'Piggy', would want to tell Ralph his nickname, especially if it was insulting. Piggy is ashamed of his nickname and so he would not reveal it to a complete stranger.

3, I don't think that Ralph should be the chief or 'Governor' of the children. Sometimes his character is not suited to his responsibility He is immature and silly when he rolls about laughing on the floor when he hears Piggy's nickname. Ralph also pretends to be an aeroplane. I think Jack is more capable. Jack does have reasons for what he does. When he kills the pig, it is for meat.

4/ Why is Piggy praised? The reader keeps being told how intelligent Piggy is. 'Only Piggy could have the intellectual daring....' 'Ralph claims he can't think. Not like Piggy.' I find these examples of Piggy's intelligence incredible — all he did was suggest that the fire should be moved.

5/ I dislike the twins, Sam and Eric. I can't tell the difference between them. When they are speaking, so what is the point of having two of them?

The young children are far too accepting when they speak — on page 75 of the book, there is 'And if he had been told that the other boy had gone home on an aircraft, he would have accepted the statement without fuss or disbelief.' William Golding is describing a boy presumably of about seven years of age. All the seven year-olds I've ever met would miss their parents and would ask many questions as well, so I think that the child on the island would want to know how someone got home, so he could see his parents again.

A structured log

An alternative method for keeping a log is to organise your notes for each section or chapter of the novel under headings such as those below.
This gives a clearer structure to your log.

1. Where is it set? (e.g. a room, a circus, a city street)

2. What is the main event?

3. Who are the new characters?

4. What are your views on them?

5. Points of interest.

6. Comments on style.

7. Likes and dislikes.

Using a log

Logs are meant to be used. Many students have found them extremely valuable. They can be used:

● to plan and prepare an assignment
● in a discussion
● to compare first impressions with later thoughts
● to recall ideas, feelings and questions that arose as the novel was being read.

Characters

Every novel has a cast of characters. A successful author brings these characters to life. They seem real and believable to the reader. They are memorable. The aim of this section is to understand characters in novels — to gain insights into their personalities and to appreciate their motives.

Activity 1

1. Think of a person you know.

2. In a paragraph, describe his or her personality.

3. Explain why you described the person in this way. For example, if you described the person as honest, friendly, selfish or vain, what is it about their behaviour that led to this description?

Assessing characters

Your answer to part 3 shows some of the ways in which personality is judged and assessed. Our thoughts about a person derive from the way he or she behaves towards ourselves and others. We may observe this behaviour ourselves or hear about it from other people. Impressions of people also come from their appearance, the clothes they wear, their tone of voice, the colour of their skin, their age, sex, social class, their hobbies and interests and a multitude of other factors.

However, the way we see other people says as much about ourselves as it does about them. Think of your best friends. Some peoply may dislike them, though you enjoy their company. Why? Probably because there is something about your personality that makes you like them. You may see someone as amusing and ambitious. Others may see them as sarcastic and pushy. The same behaviour can be judged in very different ways.

Getting to know a character in a novel is similar to getting to know a person in real life. The author describes a character and gives him or her a role to play in the story. As we read, we form judgements on the character's personality. These judgements are influenced by many of the factors we use in everyday life — the character's words, actions, manner, appearance and so on. But there is an important difference. In a novel the author has an opinion about the character. Authors try to influence the reader to see a character in a certain way. This is apparent from Jane Austen's use of irony when introducing Mrs Bennet in the opening of *Pride and Prejudice* on page 125.

Activity 2 : describing characters

It is sometimes difficult to put your impressions of a character in a novel into words. Here is an activity which may help.

1. Each person should have a dictionary.

2. Write the alphabet down the left-hand side of a sheet of paper.

3. Each person is given one letter of the alphabet. Some letters like A, D or U could be given to more than one person. X and Z may be left out since, apart from 'zany' and perhaps 'xenophobic' there are very few appropriate words for this activity which begin with these letters.

4. Look up in your dictionary words which describe personality or character. They will be describing words or adjectives and will probably have 'adj.' next to them. Read the whole entry for each word you choose and make sure it applies to personality.

5. Write the words by your letter as in the example below.

6. When everybody has at least two words, report back to the class.

Fill in the rest of the chart as you listen to the reports. Check spellings (and meanings if necessary) in your dictionary.

	Character and Personality
A	amiable, arrogant
B	bossy, boisterous
C	cunning, cantankerous, conventional
D	decisive, deceitful, dour
E	earnest, eccentric
F	frank, fastidious, fussy
G	greedy, grasping

Uses

● You now have a table of words to help to describe characters in a novel.
● When you use such words, always check for evidence to support your choice. If you describe a character as cunning, provide evidence from his or her behaviour.

Activity 3 : profiles

Teachers write profiles in which they assess students' characters and abilities. You might find this technique useful for describing a character in a novel.

1. Copy the profile form below.

2. Choose a character from the novel you are reading. You are his or her teacher. The character can be an adult — increasing numbers of adults are returning to education or undertaking training.

3. Fill in the profile for the character you have chosen. Check that the points you make about your 'student' are accurate by re-reading relevant passages in the novel.

School/college profile

Name of Student (the character you have chosen)

....

Age and sex ....

Interests ....

....

....

Abilities ....

....

Strengths and weaknesses ....

....

Areas for improvement ....

....

Training/career advice ....

....

....

If you feel an educational profile is not appropriate for a character, invent an alternative assessment form such as a police report or an employer's reference.

Reading minds

To get to know characters in novels you need to discover their motives, the reasons for their behaviour. This involves understanding their personalities, their roles in the stories and relationships with other characters. Often you have to 'read between the lines' to appreciate why something is said or done. The following cartoon provides a simple example. The employer's real motive for rejecting the candidate is not apparent from what he says.

Activity 4

A friend tells you what she did at the weekend. You reply, "Really?" This reply might be spoken with interest and enthusiasm or with uninterest and apathy. The real meaning of your response is not contained in the literal meaning of the word but in your manner and tone of voice. Dialogue in novels must be viewed in the same way. It requires interpretation; it does not speak for itself. In order to understand a character's meaning and motives you must get below the surface and discover what is really being said.

1. Select a conversation or an argument between two characters in a novel.

2. For each stage of the dialogue, write what each character really means.

3. Briefly explain your interpretation of the dialogue.

Thinking about Style

Two authors write a description of a thunderstorm. They are both describing the same thing but they do so in very different ways. The authors have different styles of writing. Style in a novel refers to the **way** an author describes objects and events, the **way** she develops a story, the **way** she constructs dialogue, creates moods, conveys feeling and portrays characters. In a novel all these things must be done with the written word. This section looks at how an author's choice of words and phrases creates a particular style of writing.

Activity 1

Read the following passages. The first is an extract from the novel *Cold Comfort Farm* by Stella Gibbons. The second is an alternative version of the first passage, written in a different style. Answer the questions which follow.

Cold Comfort Farm

In the large kitchen, which occupied most of the middle of the house, a sullen fire burned, the smoke of which wavered up the blackened walls and over the deal table, darkened by age and dirt, which was roughly set for a meal. A snood full of coarse porridge hung over the fire, and standing with one arm resting upon the high mantel, looking moodily down into the heaving contents of the snood, was a tall young man whose riding-boots were splashed with mud to the thigh, and whose coarse linen shirt was open to his waist. The firelight lit up his diaphragm muscles as they heaved slowly in rough rhythm with the porridge.

He looked up as Judith entered, and gave a short, defiant laugh, but said nothing. Judith slowly crossed over until she stood by his side. She was as tall as he. They stood in silence, she staring at him, and he down into the secret crevasses of the porridge.

"Well mother mine," he said at last "here I am, you see. I said I would be in time for breakfast, and I have kept my word."

His voice had a low, throaty, animal quality, a sneering warmth that wound a velvet ribbon of sexuality over the outward coarseness of the man.

"Cur," said Judith levelly, at last. "Coward! Liar! Libertine! Who were you with last night? Moll at the mill or Violet at the vicarage? Or Ivy, perhaps, at the ironmongery? Seth — my son..."

Her deep, dry voice quivered, but she whipped it back, and her next words flew out at him like a lash.

"Do you want to break my heart?"

"Yes," said Seth, with an elemental simplicity.

Judith's breath came in long shudders. She thrust her arms deeper into her shawl. The porridge gave an ominous, leering heave; it might almost have been endowed with life, so uncannily did its movements keep pace with the human passions that throbbed above it.

The porridge boiled over.

Judith knelt, and hastily and absently ladled it off the floor back into the snood, biting back her tears.

Cold Comfort Farm - alternative version

The kitchen was large. It took up most of the middle of the house. A dull fire spread smoke up the blackened walls and round the wooden table, dark with age and dirt. The table had been clumsily set for a meal. A pot of thick porridge hung over the fire. A tall young man stood, resting one arm on the mantelpiece. He looked moody and stared into the bubbling porridge. He wore muddy riding-boots and a rough linen shirt, unbuttoned to the waist. His stomach muscles moved slowly in time with the porridge.

As Judith came in he looked up and laughed defiantly. She walked over and stood beside him. There was silence. She stared at him. He stared into the porridge. At last he spoke.

"Well mother, here I am. I said I wouldn't be late for breakfast and I've kept my word." There was a sneer in his smooth, deep, manly voice.

"You dog," said Judith. "Coward! Liar! Womaniser! Who were you with last night? Moll at the mill, Violet at the vicarage or Ivy at the ironmongery? Seth — my son..." Her voice quivered and she said angrily, "Do you want to break my heart?"

"Yes", said Seth, simply.

Judith shuddered and wrapped her shawl around her.

The porridge heaved in time with her emotions.

The porridge boiled over.

Judith knelt down and scooped it back into the pot. She fought back her tears.

Questions

1. Which passage do you prefer? Give reasons for your answer.

2. Compare the descriptions of the young man's voice in the two extracts. Which description do you feel is most effective? Explain your answer.

3. How did each passage make use of the porridge to convey mood, atmosphere and emotion? Which passage was most effective? Give reasons for your answer.

4. How were Judith's feelings conveyed to the reader in the two passages? Which passage conveyed them most effectively? Give reasons for your answer.

5. The atmosphere was thick with emotion! Which passage best fits this description? Briefly explain why.

6. Consider the first version. It resembles the highly emotional style often found in romantic novels. What evidence can you find which indicates that the writer is making fun of this style?

Activity 2 : style in detail

As you have seen from the previous activity, the choice of words and phrases and the way they are used shapes an author's style. The activity which follows will develop your understanding of words and style. It can be done by yourself or with a partner.

● The following passage is the opening of *Cider with Rosie* by Laurie Lee.

● There are gaps in the text. From the words and phrases provided, choose one from each pair to fill the gaps. Your choice should fit the style of the passage. In each case briefly explain your choice of word or phrase.

● For example both 'towered' and 'stood' could be used to fill the gap in line 6. Both are verbs, both make sense in the sentence. However, the word 'towered' conveys much more meaning. It makes the grass seem threatening, the boy very little and vulnerable. It fits well with the 'bewilderment and terror' of the three-year-old boy from whose viewpoint we see things. 'Stood' is adequate and might well fit another style of writing. But for this style - rather poetic, larger than life, vivid and vital - the word 'stood' is plain and flat.

First Light

I was set down from the carrier's cart at the age of three; and there with a sense of bewilderment and terror my life in the village began.
The June grass, amongst which I stood, was taller than I was, and I wept. I had never been so close to grass before. It _____ above me and all around me, each blade tatooed with _____ of sunlight. It was knife-edged, dark, and a _____, thick as a forest and alive with grasshoppers that chirped and _____ and leapt through the air like _____.
I was lost and didn't know where to move. A tropic heat oozed up from the ground, rank with sharp odours of roots and nettles. Snow-clouds of elder-blossom banked in the sky, showering upon me the fumes and flakes of their sweet and _____ suffocation. High overhead ran frenzied larks, screaming, as though the sky were tearing apart.
For the first time in my life I was out of the sight of humans. For the first time in my life _____ in a world whose behaviour I could neither predict nor fathom: a world of birds that squealed, of plants that stank, of insects that sprang about without warning. I was lost and I did not expect to be found again. I put back my head and howled, and the sun hit me smartly on the face _____.
From this daylight _____ I was awakened, as from many another, by the appearance of my sisters. They came scrambling and calling up the steep rough bank, and parting the long grass found me. Faces of rose, familiar, living; huge shining faces hung up _____ between me and the sky; faces with grins and white teeth (some broken) to be conjured up like genii with a howl, brushing off terror with their broad scoldings and affection.

towered	I was present	like shields
stood	I was alone	like evil masks
stuffy	wicked green	rays
giddy	bright green	tiger-skins
nightmare	like a bully	springs
sleep	like a boxer	monkeys
nattered		
chattered		

Making a Storyboard

When planning a television commercial, a film or a television drama, the director must decide what will be shown in each 'shot' or picture.
Storyboards have been used to do this. A storyboard is rather like a strip cartoon. It shows a series of events in still, snapshot form, with directions for the actors, camera crew and lighting operators.
You can use storyboards to help you visualise parts of a novel or play. This may give you a different perspective and help you see details of description or the significance of certain events that you might otherwise have missed.
Storyboards are particularly useful for turning a novel or a play into a film or television drama.

Activity

1. Choose an interesting section from a novel — about one page in length.

2. Use the headings below to make notes on what would appear in each shot.

3. You may use outline drawings as in the example below. However, you do **not** have to be able to draw to make a storyboard — written notes will do.

LOCATION
DIALOGUE
DURATION OF SHOT
DESCRIPTION OF SHOT
COMMENTS

Example
Storyboard for opening of *The Pigman* (see page 124)

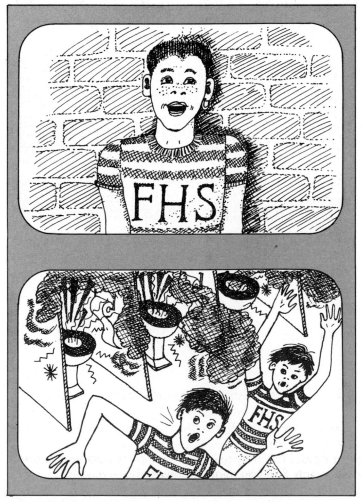

SHOT 1

Location: Franklin High school toilets
Dialogue: Boy talks about his reasons for setting off bombs.
Duration: 20 seconds
Description: Teenage boy faces camera against background of grey wall.
Comments: Boy talks directly to camera.

SHOT 2

Location: Franklin High School toilets
Dialogue: Shouts of fear/ surprise as boys run out of toilets.
Duration: 10 seconds
Description: Pall of smoke from explosion. Two boys run out of toilets.
Comments: Sound effects — explosion, coughing, running feet.

Assignments: Novels

The following assignments are divided into four sections:

- putting yourself in their shoes
- standing back
- helping others to enjoy reading
- further ideas

with an option for tape-recorded coursework.

You may choose one of these assignments or invent your own.

A. Putting yourself in their shoes (identifying with characters and situations; writing in the style of a novel you enjoyed).

1. Select a character who interests you, but who does not have a major part in the novel. Explain how he or she sees the main character.
OR
Re-write a major episode in the novel from the standpoint of a minor character.
OR
Interview any character from a novel. Write the questions and invent the replies. You may choose a radio or television programme or a newspaper or magazine for which the interview is intended. Bear in mind the style of the programme or publication and the audience you intend to reach. Describe how you designed the interview to suit the audience.

2. An alternative ending. If you feel that the ending of a novel was unsatisfactory, write your own version.
OR
Do the same for the opening of a novel.

3. Write a short story in the same style as a novel you have read.

4. Ten years on. Write the opening chapter of a sequel (follow-up) to a novel. A re-union could form the basis of your chapter.
OR
Son of/daughter of ... Choose a child or young person in a novel. Write an opening chapter in which he or she is now an adult and is the main character in the novel.
OR
Write a short 'prequel' to a novel. A prequel is set **before** the events in a novel start. (Some of the *Star Wars* films are prequels.)

5. Write a parody of part of a novel. A parody is a comic imitation or 'send-up'. You will find a section on parodies in most libraries. Use the guide to libraries on page 113 to help you to find it.

B. Standing back; assessing; analysing

1. Select a major incident from a novel. Write newspaper articles based on this event for two contrasting newspapers with different styles and viewpoints. You may choose actual newspapers, e.g. *The Sun* and *The Guardian* or invent your own. For example, you might write about the death of Boxer in *Animal Farm* for a newspaper controlled by the pigs and an alternative version for a paper supporting the opponents of the pigs' regime.

2. Look at the last section or chapter of a novel. Is it an effective and satisfactory ending? Write your comments and criticisms.

3. Look at the opening chapter or section of a novel. How well does it prepare the reader for the rest of the novel?

4. English teachers often meet to discuss which novels to select for their students. Write in support of a novel for a teachers' meeting. Your aim is to convince those attending the meeting that students should read this novel as part of their coursework.

C. Helping others to enjoy reading

1. Write a review of a novel. Your aim is to help other students to decide whether or not they would like to read it. You may design a cover for the novel and include illustrations and/or diagrams.

2. Choose one or two pages you particularly like from a novel. Imagine you have been asked to read this section aloud to the class. Discuss how you would read it, with your teacher or a partner. Copy the section and write an explanation of why you chose it and how it relates to the rest of the novel. Include comments from your discussion about how it should be read to the class.

3. Some novels are enjoyed by all age groups, e.g. *Animal Farm* and *The Secret Diary of Adrian Mole Aged 13¾*. Does the novel you have read fall into this category? If so, write two reviews, one for young readers and one for adult readers. Point out what would appeal to each age group and write in a style suitable for each group. Find some examples of library and bookshop bulletins, e.g. W. H. Smith's monthly book bulletin, as part of your research for this assignment.

D. Further ideas for assignments

1. There is crisis in the publishing world — cutbacks in expenditure must be made. Your editor tells you that you must cut out about fifteen pages of a novel you have written, in time for the next edition. Write a letter to your editor saying which chapter or section you would

omit and why. Alternatively, if you feel any cuts would spoil the novel, write a letter defending your refusal to make cuts.

2. A local newspaper has received a letter which objects to a novel which forms part of your GCSE English course. The writer objects to bad language and the portrayal of the main character whom the letter-writer sees as a bad example to young people. Write a letter to the newspaper which argues that the novel is suitable for school pupils.

3. Look at the section on storyboards on page 135. Choose a short dramatic episode from a novel and present it in a storyboard form. With reference to the rest of the novel, explain why you focused on these events. Also explain why you chose particular effects and lighting and why you included certain parts of the dialogue.

OR

Re-write this section of the novel as a script for a radio programme designed for students studying the novel.

4. Choose an activity from this unit. Design a similar activity based on a novel you have read. Explain how it might develop students' appreciation and understanding of the novel.

Option: tape-recorded coursework

1. Choose a short section of a novel or a short story for students of your own age who, for whatever reason, are not able to read easily. Record it on to audio-tape along with an introduction written by yourself. You may use other voices and sound effects.

2. You have been asked to prepare a review of a novel for a radio programme. The review is to last five minutes. Outline the plot (don't give it all away), describe the characters, the author's style and anything else that might interest your listeners. You may include short quotations from the novel. Design your review for a particular audience, e.g.

a) A programme for Radio 4 for an adult audience who are buying books for their children.

b) A local radio programme for listeners of your own age.

You might like to record two reviews, each for a different audience.

You may collaborate with up to three other students and make a full programme. Include an introduction and link passages, e.g. are there any links between the novels you have chosen?

Before doing this assignment, you should listen to a range of review programmes on radio.

Plays

Plays are written to be performed. They are performed live in the theatre, recorded on video tape for television and on audio tape for radio. Travelling companies of actors perform plays in community centres, church halls and schools. Amateur dramatic societies across the country stage performances in their local communities. And you may well have played a role in a school production before an audience of students, teachers and parents.

Plays are not written to be studied for GCSE English. However, studying a play can add to your enjoyment of an actual performance. The second part of this unit looks at ways of developing your understanding and appreciation of plays.

Little words mean a lot

The two main ingredients of a successful play are the words of the playwright and the performances of the actors. Using the author's words and stage directions, actors convey a range of emotions with voice, facial expression and gesture. Emotions such as love, hate, fear and excitement do not necessarily require long speeches to be expressed effectively. They can be conveyed with simple, apparently insignificant words like 'yes', 'no', 'really', 'perhaps'. The following activity allows you to try this for yourself.

Activity 1

With a partner.

1. Here is a short conversation.

Character 1 : Money.
Character 2 : Perhaps.
Character 1 : Money.
Character 2 : Perhaps.
Character 1 : Please.
Character 2 : Maybe.
Character 1 : When?
Character 2 : I don't know.
Character 1 : ....
Character 2 : ....

2. You are a parent (Character 2) and your partner is a child (Character 1). You are angry and your 'child' is afraid. Read the conversation several time expressing these feelings. Add a few words to finish the conversation.

3. Now change the moods and personalities of the characters. You — the parent — are timid. Your partner — the child — is demanding and insistent. Read the conversation several times expressing these changes. Add a few words to finish the conversation.

Activity 2

1. Here are some words and phrases. Their meanings depend on the order in which they are spoken, the way they are spoken and the speaker's expressions, gestures and stance.

money   maybe   perhaps   yes   no   OK   well don't know   really   when   what   did you/she /he/they...?   was it?   give me the...   pass me the... can I have the...?   can I go to...?   do you know what...?

2. With a partner select some of these words and phrases to make a conversation. Complete the unfinished phrases with your own choice of words. Decide:

Who you are. For example, parent and child, shopkeeper and customer, two friends of the same age, two strangers on a bus, an older and a younger child, and so on.
Where you are.
What each character wants.
The **mood** of each character. For example, angry, relieved, desperate, unconcerned, bored, interested, worried, amused.
The **personality** of each character. For example, timid, forceful, aggressive, submissive, shy, outgoing.

3. Practise the conversation expressing the moods and personalities of the characters.

4. Keep the same characters and conversation but change their moods and personalities, as you did in Activity 1. Practise the conversation.

5. Read the conversations from parts 3 and 4 to another pair or to the class. Tell them who and where your characters are. Ask them to describe their moods and personalities.

STOP! Keep your conversations. You will need them for the next section.

Stage Directions

The script of a play contains **stage directions.** They describe the setting and give directions to the actors. Stage directions are an essential part of any play.
To illustrate this point, imagine a married couple eating a meal. The husband complains about the quality of the food. The wife may ignore him, glare, laugh, burst into tears and so on. Her reaction may be very important for the development of the play. It will be given in the stage directions.

Activity 1

1. Write out your conversation from the previous activity twice, on two pieces of paper. Leave a gap of several lines at the top of the paper and a line space between each line of dialogue.

2. Write a brief description of the characters and setting at the top of the page. Add stage directions throughout the conversation indicating tone of voice, expressions, gestures. (See the example on the next page.)

3. Exchange your scripts with another pair. Ask them to act the scene following your directions. Was their performance as you imagined it?

4. If necessary, re-write your stage directions until the performance meets your requirements.

Example

Below is an extract from the film script for *A Private Function*. It describes the setting and gives directions to the actors. The film, a comedy, was made in 1984 and stars Maggie Smith and Michael Palin as Joyce and Gilbert Chivers. Gilbert is a chiropodist who lives in a small Yorkshire town. Joyce, his wife, longs for refinement and 'better things'. The film is set in 1947, two years after the Second World War, a time of hardship and austerity when luxuries, and even some essentials, were in very short supply.

A Private Function

INTERIOR, CHILVERS' DINING ROOM. NIGHT
JOYCE, GILBERT and MOTHER *are eating a sparse meal of luncheon meat, lettuce and one tomato. They eat in silence,* GILBERT *and* MOTHER *heartily,* JOYCE *daintily.*
GILBERT: I saw another verrruca today. Gone the wrong way again. They will hack at them with razor blades.
JOYCE: Don't bring feet to the table, Gilbert. And there's crumbs cascading on to this carpet.
GILBERT: You have to wait until they come to a head. Then it's a piece of cake.
(JOYCE *gives up any attempt to eat.*)
Still, Mrs Roach's ingrowing toenail seems to have turned the corner. Thanked me profusely. Gave me a macaroon.
JOYCE: *(Passionately)* A macaroon! A macaroon! We're better than this, Gilbert.
GILBERT: Better than what?
(JOYCE *sighs.*)
Are you not eating your Spam?

(MOTHER *is on to it like a rat, long before* GILBERT *reaches it.*)
Listen, Joyce. Once I'm into these premises on the Parade then it'll be different. They'll be rolling up in their cars.
We'll be going out to functions, having steak.
JOYCE: It's not just steak, Gilbert. Can't you see. It's status
MOTHER: Is there any?
JOYCE: What?
MOTHER: Taties?
JOYCE: It breaks your heart.

Activity 2

1. What are your impressions of Joyce and Mother judging from the stage directions?

2. Do you think the stage directions in the script of *A Private Function* are important? Give reasons for your answer.

3. With two other students, prepare the scene from *A Private Function*. Perform it for the class to illustrate your interpretation of the stage directions.

Activity 3

Below are the openings of three very different plays. Read the openings, aloud and with others in your class if possible. Where you can, follow the stage directions. Answer the questions which follow.

The Birthday Party

Act One

The living-room of a house in a seaside town. A door leading to the hall down left. Back door and small window up left. Kitchen hatch, centre back. Kitchen door up right. Table and chairs, centre.
PETEY *enters from the door on the left with a paper and sits at the table. He begins to read.* MEG'S *voice comes through the kitchen hatch.*

MEG. Is that you, Petey?

Pause.

Petey, is that you?

Pause.

Petey?
PETEY. What?
MEG. Is that you?
PETEY. Yes, it's me.
MEG. What? (*Her face appears at the hatch.*) Are you back?
PETEY. Yes.
MEG. I've got your cornflakes ready. (*She disappears and re-appears.*) Here's your cornflakes.

He rises and takes the plate from her, sits at the table, props up the paper and begins to eat. MEG *enters by the kitchen door.*

Are they nice?
PETEY. Very nice.
MEG. I though they'd be nice. (*She sits at the table.*) You got your paper?
PETEY. Yes.
MEG. Is it good?
PETEY. Not bad.
MEG. What does it say?
PETEY. Nothing much.

MEG. You read me out some nice bits yesterday.
PETEY. Yes, well, I haven't finished this one yet.
MEG. Will you tell me when you come to something good?
PETEY. Yes.

Pause

MEG. Have your been working hard this morning?
PETEY. No. Just stacked a few of the old chairs. Cleaned up a bit.
MEG. Is it nice out?
PETEY. Very nice.

Pause.

MEG. Is Stanley up yet?

Rosencrantz and Guildenstern Are Dead

ACT ONE

Two ELIZABETHANS *passing the time in a place without any visible character.*
They are well dressed — hats, cloaks, sticks and all.
Each of them has a large leather money bag.
GUILDENSTERN'S *bag is nearly empty.*
ROSENCRANTZ'S *bag is nearly full.*
The reason being: they are betting on the toss of a coin, in the following manner: GUILDENSTERN *(hereafter*

"GUIL") *takes a coin out of his bag, spins it, letting it fall.*
ROSENCRANTZ *(hereafter "ROS") studies it, announces it as "heads" (as it happens) and puts it into his own bag.*
Then they repeat the process.
They have apparently been doing this for some time.

  The run of "heads" is impossible, yet ROS betrays no surprise at all — he feels none. However, he is nice enough to feel a little embarrassed at taking so much money off his friend. Let that be his character note.

  GUIL *is well alive to the oddity of it. He is not worried about the money, but he is worried by the implications; aware but not going to panic about it — his character note.*

  GUIL *sits.* ROS *stands (he does the moving, retrieving coins).*

  GUIL *spins.* ROS *studies coin.*

ROS: Heads.
  (He picks it up and puts it in his bag. The process is repeated.)
  Heads.
  (Again.)
ROS: Heads.
  (Again.)
  Heads.
  (Again.)
  Heads.
GUIL *(flipping a coin):* There is an art to the building up of suspense.
ROS: Heads.
GUIL *(flipping another):* Though it can be done by luck alone.
ROS: Heads.
GUIL: If that's the word I'm after.
ROS *(raises the head at GUIL):* Seventy-six love.
  (GUIL gets up but has nowhere to go. He spins another coin over his shoulder without looking at it, his attention being directed at his environment or lack of it.)
  Heads.

The Tragedy of Macbeth

ACT 1

SCENE 1 — *(An open place.)*
Thunder and lightning. Enter three WITCHES.

1 *Witch.* When shall we three meet again?
  In thunder, lightning, or in rain?
2 *Witch.* When the hurlyburly's done, When the battle's lost and won.
3 *Witch.* That will be ere the set of sun.

1 *Witch.* Where the place?
2 *Witch.* Upon the heath.
3 *Witch.* There to meet with Macbeth.
1 *Witch.* I come, Graymalkin!
2 *Witch.* Paddock calls.
3 *Witch.* Anon! ·
All. Fair is foul, and foul is fair:
    Hover through the fog and filthy air.   *[Exit]*

Questions

1. Pick a stage direction from each of the openings. Briefly discuss how it contributes to the play. For example, how does it help to create an appropriate atmosphere or reflect a character's mood?

2. How does each opening capture, or fail to capture, the interest of the audience? Explain your answers.

Option

With a partner, or in a group of three, prepare one of the openings to perform for the rest of the class.

The three witches from the 1986 production of *Macbeth* at the Royal Shakespeare Theatre.

Plays in Outline

Successful plays are often translated into different media and re-told for different audiences. *Throne of Blood* is a Japanese film version of Shakespeare's *Macbeth* and *West Side Story* is a stage and film musical based on Shakespeare's play *Romeo and Juliet*. Whether on stage, film or television, drama has similar elements such as conflict, tension and crisis. The following activity will help you pick out some of these elements in a play.

Activity

1. For this activity you will need an outline or summary of the play you are reading. It is best to write one yourself.
The following may be helpful:
— a theatre programme which summarises the plot
— 'pass notes' on the play available from a library or bookshop
— the introduction to the play written by the editor.

2. Give a number to each stage in the plot.

3. Give each stage one or more of the labels shown. For example, if you think the opening scene of *Macbeth* creates suspense (Who is Macbeth? Why do the three witches want to meet him?) then you could write:

Macbeth
1. Act 1 Scene 1 : **Suspense**
The list below is not comprehensive. You will need to add more labels.

Labels
conflict
tension
suspense
comedy
crisis
resolution of conflict
climax/high point
turning point

Uses

A plot outline, appropriately labelled, has a number of uses. It allows you to see how a play develops, how it builds to a number of high points, changes direction and reaches a conclusion. It also provides a useful summary of the play.

Plays : Assignments

Writing

1. Choose a character who interests you from a play. Produce a file which includes an outline of the character's personality, interests, viewpoints on events, and attitudes towards others in the play.
OR
Write a guide to playing that character for a student who will take the part in a peformance of the play.

2. Choose a character who is accused or suspected of wrongdoing. Write a defence which argues that he or she did not do wrong or that there were good reasons for his or her actions.

3. Select a character who has a small part in a play. Write a scene, in the style of the play, in which the character plays a main role.

4. Does the play you have read have a prologue and an epilogue? A prologue is an introduction to a play spoken by a character not directly involved in the action. An epilogue is a conclusion, summarising the moral of the play, spoken by a character who has 'stepped outside' the play. Write a prologue and an epilogue if they are not included in the play you have read.

5. You are the director of a school production of a play. Choose one scene and write 'director's notes'. They should include reasons why you think the scene is important and how it relates to the play as a whole. You may also include stage directions, suggestions to the actors on how to play their parts and guidance on set design, costumes and lighting.

6. Choose a scene or episode from a play and re-write it with a particular audience in mind. You might choose to re-write part of a play by Shakespeare in modern English for a young audience.

7. Write a 'study-guide' for GCSE students on one aspect of a play, e.g. on a character, the author's message, background information on the time and place in which the play is set.

8. Collect some theatre programmes for plays. Study them, then write a programme for a play that you have read.

Speaking

1. Choose an incident in a play where more than one character could be blamed for a particular wrong-doing. Hold a trial for each of the suspects. Here are some of the roles you might play: the accused, prosecution lawyer, defence lawyer, judge, members of the jury.

2. Choose a character from a play. One person takes the role of the character, the other plays the part of an interviewer. Interview the character in order to discover his or her motives, attitudes towards events and relationships with other characters.

Role play, student's profile
(from page 100)
Y groups — her name is Lesley Rimmer

Unit 8 Skills

Aim: to help you to improve your writing.

Some ways to use this unit:

● work through from start to finish
● use it for reference to help you with activities in other units
● use it to plan, write and check each written assignment.

On the way: the following will help you to achieve your aim:

● an assessment checklist
● spelling — help yourself
● using a dictionary
● sentences
● punctuation
● summaries
● brainstorming
● organising ideas.

An Assessment Checklist

This unit begins with an example of a checklist for assessing written work. It can be used in a number of ways. To:

● assess your own work
● assess the work of others
● identify your strengths and weaknesses
● direct your attention to sections of this unit which will help to improve your work
● focus on points you must bear in mind when planning, drafting and writing

● understand some of the ways in which your work is marked and graded.

The checklist has been used to assess an essay entitled *The Family Snapshots*. It is a descriptive essay written in a lesson under supervised (controlled) conditions. The author was allowed to choose the title.

Read the essay three times, then read through the checklist. Note the different ways in which the essay has been assessed.

The family snapshots

The tastefully designed photograph album had a cover which depicted two small puppies with bows in their carefully groomed hair. Across the top of this elegant volume was written in fine script, 'Bargain Photo Album'. I opened the book and began to browse through it.

The first page had only one print on it which had been stuck in with a large amount of blu-tack. It depicted a family scene on one of our numerous holidays in Cornwall. A rather out of focus foreground and large, greasy thumb print in the top left corner typified the quality of the photographs throughout the album. This particular photograph did conjure up some memories as I studied it more closely. What then seemed a perfect holiday now looked decidedly dismal.

The sky in the photograph was of a dark, ominous colour which promised a heavy downpour. I remembered being there with the strong wind coming in from the sea making warm jumpers an absolute neccessity. Many a day was spent on the beach sheltering behind rocky outcrops waiting for the weather to change and eating the inevitable cornish pasties.

The sand which had seemed then to have been of a golden colour, just looked dull in the picture. wet and covered in seaweed the sand had then appeared to stretch away for a vast distance. small, sharp, shells dug into your bare feet as you ran down to the waters edge. Newspapers and plastic bottles were scattered about the beach. Destroyed sandcastles with their walls breached by wind and childrens' feet could be seen. I also remembered many of the people sat behind their indispensable windbreaks drinking hot coffee from thermos flasks.

Out to sea small fishing boats with peeling paintwork bobbed around as seagulls dived in search of scraps. This pleasant enough scene would be regularly disturbed by the appearance of a speed boat taking people on pleasure trips to see the picturesque coastline.

So it seemed that despite its poor composition the photograph did represent the sort of holiday we had. They had damp, windy weather with a severe shortage of things to do resulting in us posing for a supposidly beautiful picture to remember the holiday by. I then decided to close the album and put it back under the stairs with our other precious possesions.

Assessment Checklist

Example: The Family Snapshots

Item	Good	Fair	Poor	Comment	Examples
1. Spelling		✓		Simple words spelled correctly. Three, more difficult, words spelled incorrectly.	'dismall' should be spelled 'dismal'.
2. Words — variety and suitability	✓			Good range of appropriate adjectives. Used effectively to create atmosphere and mood.	'tastefully', 'ominous', 'indispensable', 'The sky ... a dark, ominous colour ...'
3. Punctuation		✓		Additional commas required in a number of sentences.	'The sand, which had seemed then to have been of a golden colour, just looked dull in the picture.' (paragraph 4).
4. Sentence Structure	✓			Written in clear, short/medium length sentences. Second half of sentences follows on from the first half.	'It depicted a family scene on one of our numerous holidays in Cornwall.' 'I remember being there with the strong wind coming in from the sea making warm jumpers an absolute necessity.'
5. Use of paragraphs/ sections	✓			Effective use of short, clear paragraphs. Each paragraph deals with a particular subject/topic.	Essay consists of six paragraphs. Paragraph 3 deals with the weather, paragraph 4 with the beach.

Item	Good	Fair	Poor	Comment	Examples
6. Organisation	✓			Essay clearly organised. Based around the theme of a photograph. Links between paragraphs. Each paragraph builds on the previous one to paint a picture.	Photograph specifically mentioned in five out of six paragraphs. Paragraph 2 ends with the holiday photograph appearing 'dismal'. Paragraph 3 goes on to describe the dismal weather.
7. Introduction and conclusion	✓			Effective introduction and conclusion — essay opened and closed.	Photograph album opened in the introduction and closed in the conclusion.
8. Realisation of aim	✓			Aim — to write a descriptive essay. Writer has succeeded. Reader left with a vivid picture of the beach, the weather and an overall impression of the holiday.	The 'dismal' holiday portrayed with scenes such as people sheltering behind windbreaks drinking hot coffee.
9. Content	✓			Appropriate and relevant. The writer aims to describe the photograph and the memories it evokes. The content of the essay relates to this aim.	Items on the beach such as newspapers, plastic bags and flattened sandcastles are used to create a desolate scene.
10. Interest	✓			The reader's interest is held as the essay builds and develops from one scene to the next. The writing has pace which maintains interest.	The essay moves from a photograph to the weather, to the beach, to the sea and back to the photograph.
11. Suitability for intended audience	✓			No audience specified but probably suitable for most teenage and adult readers.	Many people have had a holiday on British beaches and can relate to the feelings and scenes described in the essay.

Activity 1: do you agree?

Do you agree with the assessment of *The Family Snapshots?* Give reasons for your answer. In particular, discuss any points of disagreement.

Activity 2: group work.

1. Form a group of three to six students. Play the role of teachers on an assignment panel to judge written work for GCSE coursework in English.

2. Read the two pieces of work which follow.

3. Tell each other your first impressions — good, fair, poor? How far do you agree? What are your reasons for agreement or disagreement?

4. Analyse and assess each piece of writing using the checklist. Copy it out and fill it in as shown in the example above. You can add to the checklist if you feel that additional items and skills should be included.

5. As a group, decide on a grade for each piece of work. The grades at GCSE are A B C D E F G.

6. What advice would you give to each writer? Use the checklist you have completed to help answer this question.

A poem written over three days.

Cub Camp

I wish I'd brought my gloves and
scarf,
It's freezing waiting here.
Standing around in huddles,
Our legs bleached white and bare.
I hope the coach comes soon,
So we can be on our way,
And warm again, out of the rain.
Oh! what an awful day.
Why did I want to go to camp?
What made me want to go?
My friend says that it's dreadful,
And now I think I know,
Just what he means. The cold
baked beans
The army tents that leak.
I'm glad it's only for three days.

And not a flippin' week.
What's that? A diesel engine?
I feel I kind of dread,
It's my first night away from home,
And I'll miss my comfy bed.
But no time for that, the coach
is here,
I grab hold of my rucksack,
And remember what I'd forgotten,
My ruddy sleeping bag!
The coach is an old 'C' reg,
And it's really done some miles.
So has our driver, Eric. .
His head's as bald as all the tyres
The engine splutters suddenly,
The exhaust turns choking blue
It'll be a wonder if this thing,
Gets us a mile or two.
A brightly coloured border,
to the dirt engrained windscreen.
Is of gaudy peeling stickers from
Places this wreck has <u>never</u> seen.
Inside, the tasteless, itchy seats,
Are covered in grey ash.
And to say the least the
windows need
a very thoghrough wash.
Now the coach is off! The rain
And from behind a cloud, the sun
I smile at the funny side of it:
This camp thing could be fun.

T. Whiting

148

Article for a school magazine, written over one week.

CORONARY Heart Disease.

Stop! I know that the first thing that comes into your mind when heart disease is mentioned is 'turn the page'. Well, DON'T. You and many other people believe that it is a doctor's job to care for your health. Just because you are young and active is no reason to disregard heart care. Heart disease is one of the two major killers of modern times. Although it will be in adult life when it will affect you, now is the time something can be done about it.

What is Heart Disease?

The heart is split into two parts which are then split again: one half pumping oxygenated blood to the head and body, the other pumping blood that is deoxygenated from the head and body to the lungs. This is shown in the diagram.

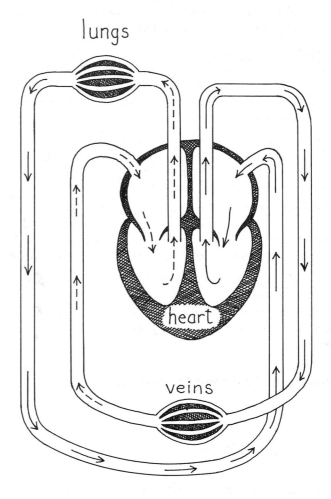

lungs

heart

veins

⟶ oxygenated blood

┄┄⟶ de-oxygenated blood

When fat is eaten some is used for energy, the remainder is stored. One of the storing places besides the stomach is the inside wall of these tubes leading to and from the heart. The correct name for 'these tubes' is Arteries from the heart, Veins to the heart. Some fats collect together

149

in a blob and travel around in the blood.

Due to the build up of fat or silting around the outside of the arteries they become thinner and thinner. When your arteries are in this state a blob of fat travelling in the blood could suddenly block up that tube so stopping the flow of blood.

What Causes Heart Disease?

The silting is caused by excess fat building up. If you eat a lot of junk food, such as chips from fast food shops, then more fat than the body needs will be taken so it will have to be stored. The intake of fat wouldn't be so bad if after you ate a fatty meal you had some exercise.

How & When does it Affect You?

Heart disease affects you now, as if you watch your health and diet you may never need worry about heart attacks. You may think or know that if you were to suffer a heart attack, providing a hospital was close by, modern medicine and skilled doctors can

patch you up. But it is far better not to run the risk of death.

The time of life when the disease and attacks occur noticable are over when you became over 40. Pains will appear in the upper chest and breath becomes difficult - signs of heart disease. 40% of the deaths between the ages of 40 and 60 are a result of coronary disorder. This is the seriousness of the problem and it is only you who can prevent it.

How to Prevent Heart Disease.

There are many ways to prevent heart attacks in adult life. It is never too late to start. Here is a list of a few ways to prevent heart attacks:

Eat more fruit and vegetables.
Jogging/Running.
Not smoking; or even walking to school - not using the bus.
It is so simple to reduce the risk of fatal heart attacks yet still so many people suffer from heart disease. I hope this article has made you think a little more about your health.

Activity 3: applying the checklist

1. Prepare and write an assignment from units 1-7.
OR
Select a piece of writing you have already completed from units 1-7 which will **not** be included in your coursework folder.

2. Give this to another group in exchange for a piece of writing from that group.

3. Each group now assesses the written work using the checklist and returns the writing, along with the assessment.

4. You now have an assessment of your work. Note the areas requiring improvement. Take each in turn and work through the appropriate section of this unit.

Spelling - Helping Yourself

You do not have to spell correctly to be a good writer — but it helps. Look at the letter below. It is an actual reply to an advertisement for a mechanical engineer.

> I have been reading your addvertisement in the popper and I hope you still have some Vacancies left I am applying for a Job but I haven't had any experience at it. So whould you write and let me know. my present work in the National Coal Board

The writer has made three spelling mistakes as well as other errors. He was not considered for the job, though he may well have been an excellent engineer.

Spelling matters.

Read the extracts below from newspaper articles.

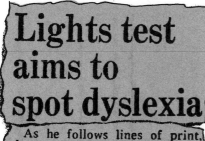

The girl who has lured Farrant away from midnight rituals in Highgate cemetery is 26-year-old Nancy O'Hoski, a sppepeech therapist from Grimsby

Hornsey Journal

Lights test aims to spot dyslexia

As he follows lines of print, the normal reader moves his eyes jump, stop to absorb one or eyqes jump, sop to absorb one or more words, then jump again. The fast reader will make shorter stops and fewer jumps, taking in more words more quickly than the slow reader.

The Sunday Times

What impression did the extracts make? In all probability you will remember the misprints rather than the content of the articles.

Think of your written work. If it is riddled with spelling mistakes, what impression will it create? Clearly you must do your best to spell correctly.

When you have finished a piece of written work:
— read it through carefully
— read aloud to prevent you from skimming
— look only for spelling mistakes — do not be distracted by other aspects of the writing
— in pencil, circle or underline possible spelling errors
— check the words in a dictionary
— correct any spelling mistakes.

Using the wrong word

A dictionary will not always help to prevent errors. Many common errors are not spelling mistakes as such, but rather the misuse of words. Small, everyday words, such as those below, are often misused. The list is followed by examples which show the corrrect usage.

Their there they're
to too two
your you're
were wear we're where
a lot (2 words)   **in front of** (3 words)
in fact (2 words)   **all right** (2 words)
quite quiet
lose loose

Examples

1. *Their* books are over *there*. *They're* going to put them on the shelf.

2. *Two* helpings of pudding are *too* much if you want *to* stay slim.

3. We *were* told to *wear* school uniform. However, *we're* allowed to put on trainers in the hall *where* we have P.E. lessons.

4. *A lot* of hopeful fans queued *in front of* the ticket office. *In fact,* there were two thousand in the queue, but it was *all right* because everyone got a ticket.

5. *Quite* a lot of people like peace and *quiet* when they are reading.

6. She kept her *loose* change in a purse so she wouldn't *lose* it.

Little words are misused more often than big words. Read through your work carefully and be sure to check words that seem simple and straightforward.

Speaking and spelling

Speech and writing differ in many ways. Writing is usually more formal and the audience more distant. This is one reason why we need standard spellings, so that people in different parts of the country can understand each other in writing.

The variety of ways we pronounce words in everyday speech can be a barrier to standard spelling. Here are some examples with the correct spelling in brackets.

standin (standing)   ave (have)
muvver (mother)   libary (library)
sutificate (certificate)

If you feel that your pronunciation may be causing spelling problems, be sure to check words in a dictionary.

Using a Dictionary

Most GCSE English courses allow you to use a dictionary both for coursework and examination. Get to know dictionaries and make them work for you. A good dictionary will tell you a word's pronunciation, meaning, spelling and origin (where it comes from).

Before using a dictionary, read the opening pages. They will explain the meaning of the various symbols and abbreviations used. For example, *n.* is an abbreviation of noun. Every noun listed in a dictionary is followed by *n.*

Looking up words

Words in a dictionary are listed alpahabetically. If you do not know the alphabet, learn it now. All the words beginning with 'a' are grouped together, followed by the words beginning with 'b' and so on. To find a word in the 'a' group look at the second letter. All words in this group are listed alphabetically in terms of the second letter. Thus 'above' comes before 'accept' because 'b' comes before 'c' in the alphabet. For words sharing the first two letters, look at the third letter. They are listed alphabetically in terms of the third letter. Thus 'ability' is listed before 'able' because 'i' comes before 'l' in the alphabet. The same applies to words sharing the first three letters — look at the fourth letter — and so on.

If you have problems finding words, complete the following exercise. List the words below in the order they appear in a dictionary. Check your order by looking them up in a dictionary.

brandish   bowl
bend   balcony
bald   burglar
bellow   brake
butane   border
borrow   baptism
beneath   brand

Checking spellings

● It can be difficult to find a word that you cannot spell. Take the word *chrysanthemum*. Try the most likely first four letters. If you tried *cris...*, don't give up. Try *chri...* as in the name Chris . If this does not work try *chry...* Now you should have no trouble finding the word.

● Some words begin with a silent letter, for example *knowledge* and *pneumonia*. Bear this possibility in mind when checking for spelling in a dictionary.

● Sometimes a word does not have a separate listing. Take the word *preferred*. It is the past tense of the verb *prefer* . To find how to spell it, read the entry for prefer which will usually contain the word *preferred*.

● Occasionally an alternative spelling is given, for example, *realize* and *realise*. In this case neither is incorrect and you must choose. However, it is advisable to ask your teacher as one version might be more generally used.

Pronunciation

A good dictionary will help you to pronounce words. It will show you which part of the word to stress or emphasise and what the word sounds like.

Emphasis

des'ert, *n.* barren, dry region.

The mark after the first syllable (des') shows which part of the word is emphasised. In this case the stress in on the first syllable. (*n.* tells you the word is a noun.)

desert', *v.* to leave; abandon; forsake.

The mark after the second syllable (desert') tells you that the emphasis is at the end of the word. (*v.* means the word is a verb.)

Question: In each case, how would you pronounce *desert?*

Sound

In many dictionaries the entries are followed by their phonetic spelling which tells you how the word sounds. In the first example below the **e** in **refuse** is pronounced as an **i**, the **u** is a long **u** which is written **ū**, and the **se** is pronounced as a **z**. Look in the front of your dictionary for a guide to phonetic pronunciation and the symbols used.

refuse, *ri-fūz', v.* to decline, to take or give.

refuse, *ref'ūs, n.* what is rejected as worthless, waste material.

Question: In each case, how would you pronounce *refuse?*

Origins

Some dictionaries will tell you the origin of words — where they come from. The origins of most words are lost in time, so this will only apply to a minority of entries. Two examples are given below. The first *(dial.)* means the word derives from a dialect — a local or regional way of speaking. The second derives from slang — informal and unconventional use of words.

bing, *bing, (dial.) n.* a heap or pile (especially of waste from a coal mine): a bin.

binge, *binj, n. (slang)* a spree.

Exercise: Find the origins of the following words.

    dopey   jeep
    nylon   uptight

Meanings

Possibly the most common use for a dictionary is to discover the meanings of words. Be sure to read the whole entry as many words have alternative meanings, as shown in the example below.

hŏ'tchpŏtch, *n.* **1.** Dish of many mixed ingredients, especially mutton broth with vegetables. **2.** jumble, confused mixture.

Alternative words

You are writing an essay and use the word **dismal** to describe a scene. You wish to repeat the description but you do not want to use the word **dismal** again. A dictionary will often provide one or more alternatives as shown below.

dismal, *adj.* causing or showing gloom, miserable, sombre, dreary.

If you frequently use a dictionary to find alternative words, you might find a **thesaurus** more useful. It contains lists of synonyms — words with the same or similar meanings.

Note

Dictionaries vary in size, quality and style. Buy yourself a good dictionary — ask your teacher's advice. Get to know it and learn how to use it.

Sentences

Writing without sentences can confuse. Read the following:

    when Carol got home she found a fire burning the dog lay in front of it she warmed her hands on the cooker was a pan of soup.

Confused? It is unlikely that the fire is burning the dog or that Carol warmed her hands on the cooker. Without sentences it takes time to work out the probable meaning. Here is the above passage written in sentences.

    When Carol got home, she found a fire burning. The dog lay in front of it. She warmed her hands. On the the cooker was a pan of soup.

Sometimes writers use **non-sentences** for effect. Read the following.

    Wind whipping around the tall buildings. Trees bending in the force of the gale. Snow gathered on their branches.

The first two 'sentences' are not sentences because they do not contain verbs — *whipping* and *bending* are

153

participles. You might find that the use of participles in the above passage adds pace and drama. However, as a general rule, the use of sentences is recommended for clarity and sense.

Varieties of sentence structure

Writing needs to be clear. This is particularly true of a set of instructions, like a recipe.

Example:
You will need two eggs, one pint of milk, half a pound of flour and a pinch of salt.
Break the eggs into a bowl.
Beat the eggs.
Add the milk and blend in.
Add the flour and beat.
Add salt and mix.

Short sentences give clarity. Precise instructions are provided, one at a time.

Short sentences may be clear, but they are not always effective. Imagine a descriptive essay written in sentences of six words or less.

> The sun shone. The sky was cloudless. The water sparkled. Boats bobbed in the harbour. Crews swabbed the decks. Seagulls swooped. The stench of fish was everywhere.

This passage reads like a list. It is abrupt and jerky. The meaning is clear but the writing does not flow. Longer sentences are needed to provide an effective description.

Long sentences have a variety of uses. They are often used to express complicated arguments.

Example: If the universe has no beginning and no end, then it could not have been created, therefore there is no creator.

Long sentences can reflect the tedium and slowness of an action or event.

Example: He sat exhausted in the oppressive heat of the summer's day, sweat trickling down his brow, palms clammy, his shirt sticking to his back, slowly twirling his pen in sticky fingers, unable to focus on his writing.

Longer sentences can also be used to build up to a high point in a story. Shorter sentences can create a fast pace.

Example: He glanced up the street, saw nobody, so he side-stepped a puddle and began his escape. He heard footsteps approaching. He stopped. He listened. He must get away. He ran.

Note: Descriptive essays, information leaflets and sets of instructions require different styles of writing. Make sure your sentence structure is appropriate.

Commas

● Commas break up or divide a sentence in order to make it easier to read and understand.
● They are used to separate items in a list.
Example: Pens, pencils, rulers, paper clips, etc.
● Commas are used before and after a phrase 'inserted' in the middle of a sentence. (The sentence

would still make sense if the phrase was removed.)

Example: The girl, a pupil at Park School, won first prize.

● Commas are used before and after words like *however* and *naturally*. Only one comma is needed if the word starts or ends a sentence.

Example: However, the pupil did not accept the prize.

● Commas are sometimes needed to avoid ambiguity — uncertainty about meaning.
The second sentence conveys the intended meaning.

Example: "Can you cook Mrs Smith?" asked the chef.
"Can you cook, Mrs Smith?" asked the chef.

The first sentence asks somebody whether they can cook Mrs Smith.
The second sentence asks Mrs Smith whether she is able to cook. Commas can make a difference.

Apostrophes

Apostrophes are used:

● To show missing letter/s. Place the apostrophe where letters have been left out.

Example:
I'll be home in ten minutes unless they've changed the times of the buses — I don't think the times have changed.
(I shall be home in ten minutes unless they have changed the times of the buses — I do not think the times have changed.)

● To show ownership or possession.

Example:
— child's toy (the toy of one child)
— ladies' dresses (clothes for or belonging to two or more ladies)
— men's clothes (clothes for or belonging to two or more men)
— newsagent's shop (the shop of one newsagent)

● Do not add apostrophes to words like hers, his, theirs, its, meaning belonging to her etc., as these words have possession built in. However, be careful with *its* and *it's*. *Its* means belonging to it, *it's* means it is.

Speech and Punctuation

In writing, **direct speech** is the term given to words which are spoken, for example in a conversation which is part of a story. Direct speech is indicated by quotation marks or inverted commas. They can be single or double inverted commas.

Example:
'I enjoyed my lunch,' he said.
(single inverted commas)
"I enjoyed my lunch," he said.
(double inverted commas)

Whether you use double or single inverted commas, be consistent — use one or the other. In the following example, double inverted commas have been used for direct speech.

Setting out direct speech

The following is a conversation taken from *The Hitch-hiker's Guide to the Galaxy* by Douglas Adams. Ford Prefect has arrived on Earth. He tries to convince Arthur Dent that the world will end in twelve minutes. They decide to have a last few pints. Ford's conversation with the barman is printed without punctuation and spacing in example 1. As you will see, it is difficult to follow.

Example 1

six pints of bitter said ford prefect to the barman and quickly please because the worlds about to end the barman didnt deserve this sort of treatment he was a dignified old man but he humoured his customers so the barman said yes sir nice weather for it and starting pulling pints he tried again with going to the match tonight no point replied ford looking out of the window foregone conclusion you reckon sir said the barman you think arsenal have no chance no said ford its just that the worlds about to end yes sir so you said muttered the barman and it would be a lucky escape for arsenal if it did

SIX PINTS OF BITTER

Example 2 shows the conversation correctly set out and punctuated. Notice how the inverted commas and the layout make it much easier to follow. There is a new paragraph each time the speaker changes.

Example 2

"Six pints of bitter," said Ford Prefect to the barman, "and quickly, please, because the world's about to end."

The barman didn't deserve this sort of treatment. He was a dignified old man, but he humoured his customers.

So the barman said, "Yes, sir. Nice weather for

it," and started pulling pints. He tried again with, "Going to the match tonight?"

"No point," replied Ford, looking out of the window.

"Foregone conclusion you reckon, sir? You think Arsenal have no chance?"

"No," said Ford, "it's just that the world's about to end."

"Yes, sir, so you said," muttered the barman, "and it would be a lucky escape for Arsenal if it did."

Summaries

A summary is an outline of the main points. The ability to summarise is an important skill. You may need to summarise the plot of a story or play, outline the main ideas in a poem or pick out the key facts in an article. Here are some guidelines to help you make a summary of written material.

1. Read the passage fairly quickly.

2. Jot down the main points in note form. These are your first impressions. They are important. Sometimes, when you read a passage again, you forget these impressions and get lost in detail. Your first reading can provide a clear overview.

3. Read the passage again, more slowly. Underline the main points in pencil and jot them down in note form.

4. Read your notes. You have probably repeated yourself. Write out the main points.

5. Put your points in order. You will often find that one point leads on to another.

6. Write the summary concisely — don't waste words.

GOT IT IN A NUTSHELL

Macbeth
William Shakespeare

Macbeth
Act 1 Summary

Writing concisely

A summary should be short and to the point. Do not use several words if one word will do.

Examples:
— He trimmed the tree, cutting away the dead and overgrown branches.
He pruned the tree.
— The car remained standing in the same position.
The car remained stationary.
— The speaker said that the heckler's comments had no bearing on the matter being discussed.
The speaker said that the heckler's comments were irrelevant.

The Campaign for Plain English argues for clear, simple and concise expression in official documents. You should follow their lead when writing a summary.

Example:
— The cessation of house construction, occasioned by the outbreak of international hostilities, continued for a period of five years.
Which simply means:
— Because of the war, no houses were built for five years.

In novels and plays, long-winded, verbose expression is sometimes used to show that a character is pompous and affected.

Example:
— I feel it incumbent upon myself to state without further hesitation that never yet in my natural existence have I perceived so great an affinity to any member of the oposite gender as to wish to engage on a course of friendship leading ultimately to matrimony.
Which simply means:
— I have to say it. I love you. I want to marry you.

Brainstorming

Where do I get my ideas for an assignment? They don't just come out of the blue. Or do they? You do not necessarily have to spend hours reading through books to discover ideas. Try sitting down and using your brain. Brainstorming means creating every single idea you can think of — however ridiculous some of those ideas might seem. Try to be creative, inventive, spontaneous. Set yourself a short time limit. Choose a topic. Jot down, in note form, each and every idea you can think of connected with a topic. The following example was written 'off the top of the head' in ten minutes.

Advertising.

To sell things. To make people want things.
To make people spend money they haven't got.
Would be happier without it.
Adverts on T.V., radio, in newspapers, magazines, on hoardings.
Creative — some entertaining T.V. ads.
Pop videos advertising singers and groups.
Could companies exist without adverts?
Could they sell their products?
Do ads inform, con, mislead?
Do they need controlling — Advertising Standards Authority.
Should some be banned — cigarette and alcohol ads?

Freedom of expression?
How do ads work?
Should political parties and
pressure groups be allowed to
advertise on T.V.?
Sexism in ads.
Would I like a career in
advertising?

The notes above are a jumble of ideas. However, they do provide a starting point. The next job is to decide which points (if any) will form the basis of your assignment and to organise and develop them.

Organising Ideas

● First, select the main theme/topic/question which will form the basis of your assignment.

Example:
Some advertisements should be banned.

● Next, think of the main points you will make.

Example:
Advertisements for cigarettes and alcoholic drinks should be banned.

● Outline the arguments for and against your main points.

Example:
FOR Cigarette smoking and the consumption of alcohol are harmful to health, therefore advertisements for these products should be banned.
AGAINST In a free society people should have the right to choose for themselves. Banning certain forms of advertising limits this right.

● Find evidence which relates to your argument — it may or may not support it.

Example:
Cigarette smoking has declined since cigarette advertising on television was banned.

● Question your findings.

Example:
Has the reduction in cigarette consumption actually been caused by the ban on T.V. advertising?

● Decide on the order in which you will make your points. Begin each stage in the argument with a new paragraph.

● Summarise your points and draw a conclusion. A conclusion weighs the evidence, assesses the arguments and reaches a decision — in this case whether certain forms of advertising should be banned.

Note
Careful planning is essential. It provides direction and a framework for a piece of work. There is no need to follow all the guidelines for planning and organisation outlined in this book. You may find that other approaches are more suitable. Whatever you do, be sure to plan your work.

Answers

Unit 1

Description of films, page 3.
The Colour of Money — A sequel to *The Hustler* which was about a pool player who played for money.
Platoon — An anti-war film set during the American invasion of Vietnam.
The Little Shop of Horrors — A story of a boy and girl and a man-eating plant.
Three Men and a Baby — A comedy about three confirmed bachelors who have to look after a baby.

Unit 2

Published ending to *The Specimen,* page 22.
... a tall bronze-skinned girl, simply dressed in white, her flowing black hair contrasting with the dress as it fell on her shoulders in curls and waves.

Stuart stood speechless, his eyes fixed for the first time in years on a beautiful girl, his mind in a whirl, his palms growing moist and cheeks reddening in embarrassment.

'It is only our specimen collector,' she said, smiling. 'Come,' she said, holding out a hand. 'Come and talk to me.'

Stuart stepped forward and reached for the warm, proffered hand. And as their fingers touched the lancing pain of the thin needle seared through his head.

Published ending to *The Conjurer's Revenge*, page 23.
... his watch, burnt his collar, smashed his spectacles, and danced on his hat. If he will give me the further permission to paint green stripes on his overcoat, or to tie his suspenders in a knot, I shall be delighted to entertain you. If not, the performance is at an end.'

And amid a glorious burst of music from the orchestra the curtain fell, and the audience dispersed, convinced that there are some tricks, at any rate, that are not done up the conjurer's sleeve.

Unit 4

Summary of articles which appeared under headlines, page 61.
Putting messages across without getting burned — Report on new, inexpensive electronic mail systems.
Russia poised to 'invade' Chunnel — Russian firms plan to bid for the £4.7 billion contracts for the Channel Tunnel.
Hot rock and the power it could deliver — Plans to generate electricity from hot, underground granite in Cornwall.

Rich drive out young — Rich outsiders buying homes in country villages.
Mountains of mystery — Report on EEC food mountains.
The Fabulous Forties — New clothes designs based on 1940s fashions.

Unit 5

Sequencing exercise for *Out, Out...*, page 89.

1	A
2	C
3	H
4	E
5	F
6	B
7	G
8	D

Completion exercise for *Innocence*, page 92.

he ever knew/soul/courage/loyalty/fat/feel disgusted/quietly

Unit 7

Selecting words and phrases for *Cider with Rosie,* page 134.
towered/tiger-skins/wicked green/chattered/monkeys/ giddy/I was alone/like a bully/nightmare/like shields

Acknowledgements

We are grateful to the following for permission to reproduce copyright material.

Associated Book Publishers — pp. 139 - 140, extract from *The Birthday Party* by Harold Pinter, Methuen, London.
Association for Consumer Research — pp. 46 - 49, article entitled 'No Smoking Please' from *Which?* March 1986.
Cambridge Nutrition Ltd — p. 36, advertisement.
Carcanet Press Ltd — p. 91, *The Important Man* by Jeffrey Wainwright.
Cheshire County Council — p. 113, leaflet entitled 'Finding Out'.
Collins Publishers — p. 122, front and back cover of *The Pigman* by Paul Zindel, Lions, an imprint of the Collins Group.
Daily Telegraph — p. 104, article entitled 'Maths Genius Ruth Scores Again'.
Faber and Faber Ltd — p. 91, *Limbo* from *Wintering Out* by Seamus Heaney; p. 94, *Tamer and Hawk* from *Fighting Terms* by Thom Gunn; pp. 127 - 128, extract and front cover from *Lord of the Flies* by William Golding; p. 139, extract from *A Private Function* by Alan Bennett; p. 140, extract and front cover from *Rosencrantz and Guildenstern Are Dead* by Tom Stoppard.
Guardian Newspapers Ltd — p. 15, article entitled 'Resurrection — or is it? — at Southfork'; p. 63, 'Young Guardian' page; p. 110, article entitled 'Ages of Responsibility'.
Guardian Newspapers Ltd and Richard Boston — pp. 42 - 43, article entitled 'When the Writing on Belshazzer's Wall is a Credit to Kilroy'.
Guardian Newspapers and Jaqueline Penrose — pp. 103 - 104, article entitled 'The Girl Who Always Says Yes'.
Her Majesty's Stationery Office — p. 105, bar charts; p. 108, table and bar chart; p. 117, table and bar chart. Reproduced with the permission of the Controller of Her Majesty's Stationery Office.
Hogarth Press — p. 134, extract from *Cider with Rosie* by Laurie Lee.
Julia MacRae Books — p. 126, extract from *The Nature of the Beast* ©1985 Janni Howker, published by Julia MacRae Books.
Oxfam — p. 35, advertisement.
Penguin Books Ltd — p. 123, front covers of two editions of *Cider with Rosie* by Laurie Lee.
W H Smith — p. 77, *Kick* by Louise Orr. Prizewinner in the 1985 W H Smith Young Writers' Competition, published in *Young Worlds* (Macmillan), the anthology of winning entries.
Today Newspapers Ltd — p. 62, article entitled 'Nice Ad, Shame about the Product'.

War on Want — pp. 114 - 115, leaflet entitled 'Living on the Edge of the Desert'.

Every effort has been made to locate the copyright owners of material quoted in the text. Any omissions brought to our attention are regretted and will be credited in subsequent printings.

We are grateful to the following for permission to reproduce photographs and artwork.

Allen, Andrew, p. 78 (top left, top right)
Associated Press, pp. 32, 34, 55 (2), 58 (right)
David Peters Photography, p. 60 (bottom left)
Granada T.V., pp. 57, 59
Greensmith, Bill, p. 79 (right)
Hamer, Ingrid, p. 78 (bottom left), p. 111 (3)
Independent Television News, pp. 58 (left), 65
Joe Cocks Studio, p. 141
John Craven's Newsround, p. 56
Ladybird Books, pp. 102 - 103. Reproduced from a former edition of *We Like to Help*, published by Ladybird Books Limited, Loughborough, with the permission of the publishers.
Lorimar - Telepictures, p. 15
Mary Evans Picture Library, pp. 75 (left), 110
Merit Toys and Games, p. 104
Norwyn Photographics, p. 78 (bottom right)
Photo Source, pp. 31, 40, 44, 60 (top left)
Rex Features, pp. 43, 60 (top right), 67

The author and publisher are particularly grateful to the many students who granted permission for the reproduction of their work. They would also like to thank Colin Eastwood for supplying the anecdote on page 2 and Bob Attenburg for the artwork on page 19.

Scottish Islands

Arran stands geography on its head by coughing up mountains off the Ayrshire coast. Islay seems to breed whiskies of pungent distinction on every other burn. Lismore paves its roadsides with orchids. Tiree ought to be under water. Rum disburses the largesse of sea eagles all across the western seaboard. Skye has succoured two great benchmarks of all Gaeldom – the Cuillin and the late Sorley MacLean. Barra has a beach for an airport. St Kilda shrugs at the rest of the world and makes home-brewed storms. Harris is the body of an island with the bones showing. Shapinsay in the midst of Orkney is as many shades of green as Ireland. Yell in the midst of Shetland is the colour of peatbogs and otters. Iona is blessed.

No Scottish island is like any other, and in the fractured land-and-sea-scapes of the west and north coasts with their fast-changing weathers and tapsalteerie seasons, no island is even like itself for very long. The volcanic runts of the Bass Rock in the Firth of Forth and Ailsa Craig in the Firth of Clyde stand within the force-fields of Edinburgh and Glasgow. There are a hundred seaward miles between St Kilda and the westmost point of mainland Scotland at

THE SOUND OF IONA at dawn. The unmistakeable silhouette of Iona Abbey prominent behind the village.

IONA from the air. (opposite) Looking north, showing both the barren and fertile aspects of its landscape.

*THE SLEAT
PENINSULA
in the south of Skye.
A blue day of long sea
views towards Eigg
and Rum.*

Ardnamurchan. No Shetland island thinks of itself as Scottish at all, but inclines more naturally the way it has always done, towards the Norwegian coast, which is closer.

They have in common these three things: exquisite light, fickle weather which falls short of anything remotely identifiable as climate, and a history more chequered by cruelties than glories. If you insist on a quick summary, try a verse of American poet Richard Hugo's *A Map of Skye*, from his tellingly titled collection, *The Right Madness On Skye*:

> We'll be confined and free. Roads end fast
> and water leads slow ways to open water.
> The harsh names on this map are Nordic,
> the soft words Gaelic. We can love there well
> grateful what is cruel ran out.
> Even ruins will be civil, moss on ruins,
> anger drained from ghost.
> The only irritants, a soft longing for mist to clear
> and a nagging feeling more should happen.

Arran's mountains are further south than Berwick, which is perhaps why you don't expect mountains there, a Highland outpost cheek by jowl with the green fertility of unmistakeably Lowland Ayrshire. Strange things happen in the geography of south-west Scotland. There are red deer and golden eagles in the Galloway hills, and that long, mysterious arm of land which spares Arran the worst of the Atlantic weather is Kintyre, and unashamedly Highland, and so Celtic it's almost Irish. So Arran is its own world caught between Scotland's Highlands and Lowlands, and not obviously a part of either of them, for its most conspicuous feature is not its mountain profile but its independence.

Proximity to Glasgow is a mixed blessing. It will never starve, but don't go repeating the words of one Glaswegian within earshot of the natives: 'Arran's Glasgow's Skye', he said, and only lived to tell the tale because he was already on the boat heading back to the mainland. Neither Arran nor Skye would much care for the sentiment, but if you would begin your island odyssey at its southmost point, Arran is startlingly Hebridean.

Arran's mountains are encamped in the north-east of the island, tight swirls of curving and

HOUSES OF SKYE
Portree harbour (above)
on a still November
morning and a croft
house at Boreraig (below)
in the north-west of Skye.

ARRAN

The peaks clustered around Glen Sannox, Cioch na h-Oighe (left), Suidhe Fhearghas (right), Ceum na Caillich and Cir Mhór beyond.

occasionally unnervingly narrow ridges, exhilarating highways pinned to the island by the magical centrepiece of Cir Mhór. These airy places not only spreadeagle the island at your feet, they also give you glimpses of island worlds beyond. You are high enough on such as Cir Mhór or Goat Fell to see beyond the drawn curtain of Kintyre. Your reward is Atlantic distance, the mountains of Jura and Mull, signposts on the journey.

Arran establishes three characteristics of the island journey. One is that if there are mountains they are herded together. The second is that if there is settlement it is on the coast. The third is that the map will bedevil you with the written Gaelic tongue. What are you to make of *Bealach an Fhir-bhogha* or *Cioch na h-Oighe*? Heed the advice of Argyll writer Marion Campbell: 'Don't let the Gaelic words frighten you; they are not as difficult as they are made to look by a standard spelling devised by bygone pedants, mostly non-Gaels.'

Once you reach Orkney and Shetland, of course, there is no Gaelic at all, and never was. You can relax sure in the knowledge that all you have to worry about is Old Norse corrupted by Scots.

That does not mean, however, that there is no Norse among the Gaelic names. Island names ending in *-a* or *-ay* are usually Viking hangovers. There is a clutch of them on the far side of the Kintyre peninsula – Gigha, Islay, Jura and Colonsay. But be careful, too, whose advice you listen to, otherwise you will be caught out committing a cardinal sin. One island book, whose author had better remain anonymous, in case he ever wants to come back, pronounces that 'Gigha rhymes with pier'. Not in any of the tongues of Scotland it doesn't. Give it a hard 'G' and the end of 'Korea' with the hint of a rough 'h' on the end.

To most travellers, Gigha is a low-lying sideshow seen from the Islay ferry. It deserves better. Its name translates as 'God's Island' and whether God lays claim to it or not, it is a divine place. Gigha's beauties are soft and subtle which is rare in Atlantic islands, its secrets well tended. You cannot unravel them all in a day trip. You must give it time. It is the first principle of island-going, and it does not become less relevant just because the island is small.

Gigha has always seemed to me to be the perfect island. Four miles long, a mile wide, overlooked by its own small and singular summit (with views which unravel the geography of the southmost Hebrides better than any map), lush,

GIGHA
Agriculture moves at its own pace (above) and a wild corner above East Tarbert Bay (below).

THE PAPS OF JURA
and lower hills of Islay
from Oronsay.

fertile enough to sustain good small farms and the astonishing Achmore gardens, temperate enough to grow palm trees. And yet Gigha seems to have had almost as many owners as wet winters in recent years, neither of which is good for the health of the islanders. Here is another resurfacing theme – the way islands change hands, often on a whim, sometimes for financial expediency. A simple thought slips into place as you sit on the lowly summit of Gigha contemplating the island worlds which lie beyond: the islands and the islanders deserve better.

PORTNAHAVEN
in the west of Islay.

Islay and Jura look vast from Gigha, Jura heaped high and as unmistakable at such close quarters as it is from the summit of Ben

Lomond, worlds away; Islay as always its own dark enigma, tilting towards Ireland.

There are those who will tell you that the best thing about Islay is the view of Jura. It is a cynic's view, or a postcard-maker's, and if it is fair to say that Islay's is not the most breath-catching of landscapes, it is also fair to say that the island is as abundantly charmed as it is bereft of mountains. The long, slow miles of its Atlantic coasts and low hills,

its repertoire of moorland lochs, its goose hordes, its isolated and indiscreet population of choughs (rare scarlet-billed crows which rhyme with puffs as the Gigha writer would have it), its famously hospitable tribe of islanders, its ancient stone souvenirs (crosses, footprints, arrow-makers' flints) of those eras of history when the Lordship of the Isles was its own dynasty in charge of its own destiny and feared by neighbouring kings – all these have been swilled in tumblers shaped by human history and nature and an ocean's winds, swilled into that peaty distillation which sets Islay apart. Oh, and then there is the whisky.

The malt whiskies of Islay have produced more salivating prose than almost any other aspect of any other island anywhere. Even to pronounce their roll call is to eulogise. They are, to be sure, an acquired taste. But having acquired it (diligent research is the only way) they are as diverse as Islay herself, and as delectable as they are mispronounceable. They should, too, reflect the wealth they generate in the island's communities, but there is no opulence here. Islay's many charms are the gifts of nature, not the whisky industry. Richard

'ISLAY's many charms are the gifts of nature...' *Looking south across Lossit Bay, on the Atlantic shore of the Rinns of Islay.*

COLL

The striking geometric shapes of Breachacha Castle grow out of the machair.

Hugo's sentiment crops up again:

'....a nagging feeling more should happen.'

Jura's principal relationship with the world is by way of two ferries, one on to Islay, the other one which connects Islay to the mainland. So eventually your Islay explorations will wash up at Port Askaig where Jura's famed skyline obliterates the rest of the world. Jura is magnificently wild, and absolutely uncompromising. It is many people's idea of the ultimate island wilderness, scant with the trappings of civilisation (one distillery, one village, one hotel, half a road, unforgettable mountains, eerie caves, the proximity of the ocean phenomenon which is Corryvreckan's roaring whirlpool, deer and eagles, emptiness). Writers are lured too, for George Orwell lived here and lesser mortals are forever hoping that something of the great man will rub off, only to find that Jura's sparseness could sustain Orwell, but most of them have no stomach for it.

And that sparseness, even that wilderness, is harsher than it should be, for those who own the place have more interest in the philosophies of 1884 than 1984, such is the predominance of that

most euphemistic of all island land uses – 'sporting estate'. Deer and fishing keep the island landscape raw and naked, a magnificently disturbing piece of Victoriana, for it is in the Victorian era that such practice is rooted.

Islands like Jura should be able to sustain many more people than they do, than they did, but a vigorous human population is not compatible with the long-standing preference for red deer over-population. That 'nagging feeling more should happen' is at least partly due to a very specific kind of land ownership. But on Jura, too, there is an alchemy in the air, a thing of nature, a quality of wildness which no amount of human interference can diminish.

If you would sense the essence of the alchemy at work among islands you could do worse than dwell on what it is in the Jura air which is different from the Islay air, and I don't mean distilleries.

Then cast off and head-butt the waves that lie between you and such sea-level, ocean-going outliers as Colonsay, Coll and Tiree, with hardly a contour line among them.

Oronsay, Colonsay's Siamese twin island (joined at the sandbar, a strictly low-tide relationship) is where – they say – Columba first paused in search of his missionary destination. Alas for Oronsay and Colonsay's tourist/pilgrim trade, it was a good day and he could still see

TIREE
A typical island profile from Gunna Sound.

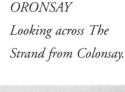

ORONSAY
Looking across The Strand from Colonsay.

STAFFA
*The astounding natural
architecture around
Fingal's Cave.*

IONA *(opposite)
Skyscape as compelling as
landscape.*

THE TRESHNISH
ISLES
Bac Beag and Bac Mór.

the Irish coast, so he sailed on until it was sunk below his horizon, and washed up on Iona. It's not quite the same, trying to build up a pilgrimage business to the island where Columba might have set up his abbey, if only…

What you learn, however fleetingly you alight on such low-lying islands, is what it feels like to live perpetually in the thrall of the ocean. Stay longer and you learn the psychology of winds, and how you match up to that confrontation is as likely as anything to determine how long you will stay. It is no wonder that the island humour takes a bit of tuning in to. Humour born of the extremes of adversity is often elusive to stranger's ears.

Then, a day dawns when the sky lifts, the wind withers, the sea flattens, and if you have stayed long enough to see it dawn, you know in your heart that God lives not on Gigha but Coll, or Tiree maybe. There again, if these really are God's islands, why does he deave the ears of the islanders with the most irritating bird voice on the planet, the one so beloved by so many ornithologists who don't live within earshot of the corncrake?

TOBERMORY, MULL
The perfect island
capital, a sheltered
harbour, a beautiful
setting, a distillery at the
end of the street.

Inshore lies Mull, its great bulk and mountainous profile looking more mainland than island from Tiree. But from Oban, which is where most people clap eyes on Mull for the first time, it looks sensational, and unmistakably island, a blue and mountainous distance. For such a large island, Mull is quiescent.

Outwith the two months of high summer tourist domination of the place (lousy weather, luftwaffes of midges and all that greenness – why do they do it?) Mull's population of around 3000 is all but invisible. Even Tobermory (the perfect island capital – a beautiful setting, a sheltered anchorage and a distillery at the end of the street) which makes such a show of summer finery, battens down and with-draws below decks for half the year.

It was not always thus. Mull's population in 1821 was more than ten thousand, but then the Highland Clearances began to bite deep. Tobermory became a transit camp full of refugees with the smell of the smoke of their burned-out homes still on their clothes. From there they dispersed to Glasgow, America, Canada, New Zealand, and the perversely imposed culture of sheep moved in.

All across Mull, you will find ruined souvenirs of the days of the ten thousand. All across the islands, the Highland Clearances of the 19th century drove people from the fertile valleys and replaced them with sheep. Roofless ruins, standing and fallen walls, and the patterns of their old fields – these are the headstones which remember lives once lived closer to the land.

Out on the headland of Treshnish, with the hulls of Staffa, Tiree

and Coll low in the west, and signposted by the tall and hapless ruin
of Reudle schoolhouse alone on its moorland plinth, a path crosses
the watershed and descends to a sea-facing township whose name
translates as the Hollow of the Dark Grazings. There, the shame of
what was done all over the islands – and mainland Highlands – of
Scotland in the name of sheep (and the subjugation once and for all
of the troublesome natives by the uncomprehending London
Government) still emits a potency to make you weep.

But nature thrives on Mull. There are few places where it is easier
to see both our native species of eagle – the golden one and the
happily reintroduced white-tailed sea eagle – and it is the only place
where, on a certain winter-quiet shoreline road of the island west, I
have followed an otter in my car for 50 yards at 15 miles an hour.

If it is the landscapes of islands you crave, Mull has them all. And
on Ben More and its mountain acolytes (including the captivating Dun
da Gaoithe, Hill of the Two Winds) there are summits where the views
can pin you to the cairn for hours. Try them in early spring with a
topcoat of new snow and the threnody of golden plover for company.

MULL
Ben More seen across
Loch Scridain – summit
views can pin you to the
cairn for hours.

RUM
The best of all island profiles? Snow on the Rum Cuillin adds to the distinction.

Mull is also the highway to Iona. The pilgrim business was never brisker. But if you have anything in mind other than a whistlestop visit to the Abbey and the tea-room, anything more symbolic and profound, make your pilgrimage in the quiet months. Iona still harbours many tranquilities, still wears its aura of deep peace. But the traipsing of summer feet smothers it. Go quietly in the darker days of winter, the vivid days of autumn, the vigorous days of spring, and Iona still has powers to grant all your pilgrimage might ask of it.

In the north, the ocean sprouts mountains. Is there a better island profile in the Hebrides than Rum? Rum is the biggest of the Small Isles, the collective name for Rum, Eigg, Canna and Muck, though why they should have a collective name at all, given their diverse natures and histories, is a mystery. Rum is a national nature reserve, owned by Scottish Natural Heritage and populated exclusively by its employees. Its small, ridgey and Norse-tongued mountains are tricky in bad weather, which is often, and they are home to a high-level colony of shearwaters. Rum is also the heart of the sea eagle reintroduction programme, an ambitious and far-sighted venture which

is beginning to repay patient endeavour. There are, of course, sheep farmers who disagree. Rum's other claim to fame is Kinloch Castle, an astounding treasure trove, an architectural imposter, over-the-top and larger than life. No-one who sees it is indifferent to it. The fact that it exists where it does at all – that is its true achievement.

Eigg, should you catch it in the right mood, is exquisite. Its singular summit, the Sgurr, the best little rock in the islands, is unforgettable in any conditions. There is many a Munro (a mountain which is 3000 ft or higher) for which the same cannot be said. But in recent years, the islanders of Eigg have taken exception to what they see as unsympathetic lairds. Now they are seeking a brave new path to the future, a co-operative land ownership wedding crofting and conservation together. If it can be shown to work here, islanders and island-lovers should rejoice, and thoughtless lairds tremble!

Muck is better served. It has a live-in laird who works as hard as anyone at keeping the community afloat. It is a terse little island, low to the waves and tormented at times by the wind. What you see is what you get with an island like this. Nothing is hidden other than the casual stoicism of the islanders. On the days when the Rum mountains

CANNA
From Sanday at dawn.

EIGG
The Sgurr, the best little rock in the islands.

RAASAY

A croft at Balmeanach in summer greenery, with Ben Tianavaig on Skye and the entrance to Portree Bay across the Sound of Raasay.

SKYE (opposite)

The classic Skye-scape of the Cuillin seen across the pebbled beach at Elgol.

flaunt their alpine best with spring sun on new snow, Muck is marvellous. The few visitors who stay for longer than the brief forays of steamer-borne tourism usually know exactly what they are letting themselves in for, and, usually, they have been before. What was Richard Hugo's opening line?

'We'll be confined and free...'

Canna recently passed from the hands of its long-standing and benevolent owner, the late John Lorne Campbell, to the National Trust for Scotland. Canna leans towards a 600 ft high clifftop, and its hilltop has long been known for its capacity to make nonsense of a compass bearing. Martin Martin, who was among the earliest of Hebridean chroniclers, wrote in his 1703 book, *A Description of the Western Isles of Scotland*:

There is a hill in the north end which disorders the needle in the compass. I laid the compass on the stony ground near it, and the needle went often round with great swiftness, and instead of settling to the North as usual, it settled here due East.

BARRA
On such a day, Kisimul
Castle in Castle Bay has
a vaguely Mediterranean
feel.

The island also owns the curious legend that sailors hereabouts would refrain from calling the island by its real name. If they did, storms would confound their journey and prevent them reaching their destination. So they called it Tarsin instead, and travelled safely. You have been warned.

All the Small Isles, even lofty Rum, defer to the supreme island presence in the north. Rum calls its mountains Cuillin, but the real Cuillin, the great gabbro horseshoe which forms one of the world's most famous mountain skylines, bear down hugely on the Small Isles and the ocean-going pancake of Soay. They signify Skye.

Skye is many islands, many glories, many subtleties, many magics,

COMMON SEALS
A familiar sight to island
travellers.

many legends. It is a lifetime's island, not a day-tripper's. It does things with sunsets which have to be seen to be believed. And here is made Talisker, golden eagle among whiskies. Against all that it is willing host to virulent strains of midge and rain, and it has recently acquired an expensive bridge. If you find the bridge as unacceptable in this of all landscapes as I do, I cannot recommend too highly the

20

alternative of the ferry crossing from Glenelg to Kylerhea. But as for Skye, she will be away with your heart, and you will forgive her everything!

And there, wedged between Skye and Applecross (which is no bad place to be wedged) lies Raasay, wooded and green in the south, rocky and bare as Assynt in the north. There are those who hold Raasay the fairest acres in all Gaeldom. They get no argument from me.

Every island addict has had nightmare crossings of the Minch, the smaller the boat, the bigger the nightmare. The St Kildans used to row it, and 40 miles of ocean too, to pay their dues to their Skye-based landlords, then row home again. Most of us, lesser mortals that we are, go by ferry to the Western Isles, those enigmatic shapes on Skye's skyline, shimmering weirdly in summer mirages. Inner Hebrideans and Northern Highlanders call it all, with a certain indifference born of the lack of any necessity to go there, 'the Long Island'. It is, of course, many islands. Barra and Vatersay are Catholic strongholds; Eriskay, which made a passable reputation as the place

MINGULAY
seen from Berneray in the
far south of the Outer
Hebrides. Mingulay is
long abandoned;
a century ago its
population was 150.

SOUTH UIST: Dawn over Loch Maddy rewards the early riser with a flat calm.

SOUTH UIST: Eochar, rose-tinted at dusk, and Hecla, shyly mist-clad, seen from Liniclate, Benbecula.

where Bonnie Prince Charlie first landed in Scotland until *Whisky Galore* made it really famous; South Uist, where Flora MacDonald was born, where green hills stand above the Minch, and Loch Druidibeg and its neighbouring machairs put the sound and the scent and the spectacle of birds and flowers against suns which dip into the sea beyond St Kilda. Benbecula (why 'Ben' anything on an island so devoid of bens?) with possibly the best beach anywhere; North Uist (more best beaches); Berneray (absolutely the best beach anywhere, apart from possibly Benbecula); Harris where all is suddenly stern and mountainous and Clisham leaps at the sky from the sea and Loch Seaforth winds its way into your heart, and the church at Rodel is a tranquil little marvel, and you gasp at the nature of the land from which human toil has fashioned sustenance and hospitality; and Lewis, a smother of moors and moorland lochs, the astonishing lost speech of the Calanais stones, the startling trees in the midst of Stornoway which is full of surprises itself – its size, its young men who while away the evenings circumnavigating the streets in their cars hooting, hooting, hooting. A long paragraph for a

LOCH DRUIDIBEG,
South Uist.
Haunt of teeming
wildfowl, with Boreray,
St Kilda, just visible on
the left of the horizon.

ISLAND SUMMER
Wild flowers transform
the machair in July.

LEWIS
Loch Achmore and the
distant hills of Harris.

HARRIS (opposite)
Tràigh Seilebost and the
Harris Hills.

CALANAIS, Lewis.
Bewildering and
charismatic standing
stones.

Long Island, an impossible compacting of a chain of island worlds, each link in the chain 'confined and free'. And utterly, utterly different. Time. You need time. Time to adjust to the pace of life lived no less fully than yours. Just differently.

The Pentland Firth is to Orkney what the Minch is to the Western Isles, only more so. Here the Atlantic and the North Sea collide and joust and make mincemeat of mariners daring to travel their waters. The *St Ola* is your passport across, craftily riding the tumultuous waves, gazing into the rocky navel of the Old Man of Hoy, curving into Stromness (calm, couthy little stone town) where the islanders welcome their prodigal firth-plier home.

Orkney is green and stone, a compact scattering of islands much cultivated on confident bedrock which splits wondrously into any thickness you care to use – standing-stone parliaments, tombstone wafers, roof tiles. Kirkwall drops a medieval cathedral into the mix, a red sand-stone wonder, and Highland Park malt whisky, a golden wonder, and (a real island rarity), its own brewery. With regard to the brewery, beware the one they call Skullsplitter.

ROUSAY: The green fertility and stone-flagged Orkney roofs, with Egilsay across the sound.

ORKNEY: The Old Man of Hoy, famed rock stack well known to regulars on the ferry St Ola.

The short sail to Shapinsay as Orkney begins to unwrap itself from a morning mist puts in your mind a wing-flexing butterfly shaking off its chrysalis. From the low island spine, all Orkney unfurls, a scatter of jigsaw pieces which don't fit anything other than their own ragged-edged niche in their own sundered sea. A lifetime devoted to the prising of these islands' secrets would be well spent. One such lifetime was George Mackay Brown's. He lived where he was born in Stromness. Orkney sustained and succoured his writing life and the literature of our islands is uniquely graced as a result. He died in the spring of 1996. He wore his Orkney lineage proudly and his genius lightly.

FAIR ISLE
Perched between Orkney and Shetland and famed for its birdlife and stack-encrusted coast.

PUFFIN
Irresistible bird-clown of the islands.

Shapinsay is the one which looks like a map of Australia gone green. On Shapinsay, they will tell you it's the other way round: Australia is the one which looks like Shapinsay. Shapinsay from Shapinsay is the centre of the universe and Australia just another island over the horizon like Fair Isle.

Fair Isle is halfway to Shetland (or if you are a Shetlander, halfway to Orkney), but it's a long halfway. If there is a windier place on the

planet than Fair Isle, I have not met it. There is a kindly honesty here which pervades the land as it pervades the people. Like Muck, what you see is what you get. There is a democratic island council, a presumption against holiday homes, and a standing invitation to would-be residents to spend a winter here first, before they make up their minds. The bird-life, which is what lures 99 per cent of Fair Isle's visitors, is miraculous.

Shetland's isolation unifies the archipelago in common cause. The ferry from Aberdeen takes 14 hours, and its destination is a different country in all but name. Shetland is about as Scottish as the Isle of Wight, and about as far from Edinburgh. In its heart of hearts, Shetland remains Norse. The thing you relish most is the difference: the wide-vowelled voices which fall trickily on untuned ears, the incursion of voes deep into the land, the phenomenon of shores smashed and reordered by countless storms into tenuous, impermanent architecture (stacks topple, arches collapse, cliffs splinter and make new stacks...).

Shetland crowds my mind with memories: storms on the tortured headland of Eshaness, the spring miracle of the terns' arrival, Foula in a heatwave, Weisdale in spring snow, Muckle Flugga

SHETLAND
The tombolo sandbar,
St Ninians Isle (above),
Foula cliffs (opposite), &
Jarlshof's multi-storeyed
civilisations (below).

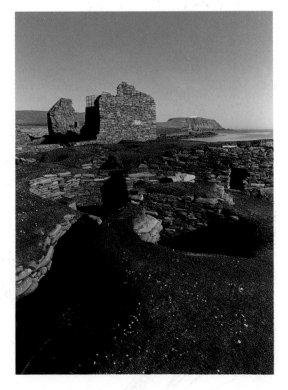

ST KILDA
The 564 ft Stac Lee, seen
from Boreray, dwarfs the
brigantine Jean de la Lune.

SOAY, ST KILDA
(opposite) in shadow, with
the low evening sunlight
drenching Hirta's western
cliffs.

becalmed, Yell in every imaginable shade of light and weather and some wholly unimaginable, a place of otters and fiddle virtuosi and red-throated divers and slow peaty burns, Lerwick in a clinging haar, Papa Stour drenched in flowers, the barely credible survival of Mousa's broch, mist adrift among the tiered civilisations of Jarlshof. Just to write these down is to remind myself that it is too long since I was last there, but then that is the perpetual affliction among the island-addicted.

I have left St Kilda until last. I once spent two weeks camping alone there, two weeks which changed my life. St Kilda, 40 miles west of Harris, was evacuated in 1930. In the hearths of the cottages (a single curving village 'street') the islanders have placed stones commemorating dates when they left and when they returned for one more look round.

I have made much, in this short account, of the differences among our islands. St Kilda is island landscape wrought in magnificent differences and in just as magnificent isolation. For these reasons, for the nature of my solitary sojourn, and for the stones in the hearth which made me feel disturbingly intrusive, St Kilda is the one shore to which I will perhaps not return. My endless waking dreams are enough, for the time being at least. But if the right time and tide coincide again, who knows?

BEN MORE and LOCH TUATH, Isle of Mull.

KILORAN BAY, Colonsay, at sunset.

First published in Great Britain in 1997 by
Lomond Books, 36 West Shore Road, Granton, Edinburgh, EH5 1QD

A CIP catalogue record for this book is available from the British Library
ISBN 0 947782 91 5

Printed in Hong Kong

Front cover photograph: LUSKENTYRE & SOUND OF TARANSAY, Harris   Back cover photograph: LYRA SKERRY & FOGLA SKERRY, Shetland